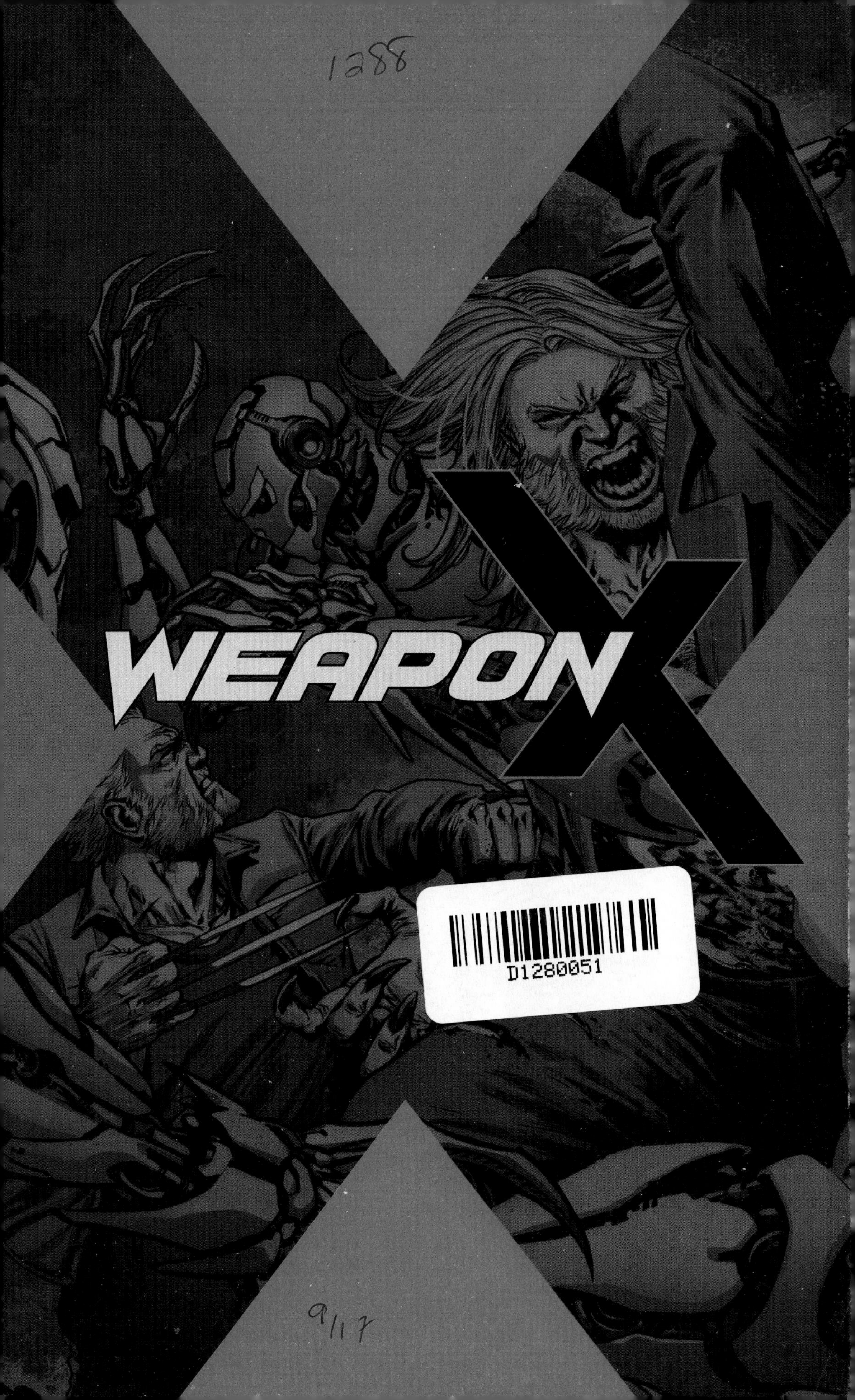
WEAPON X

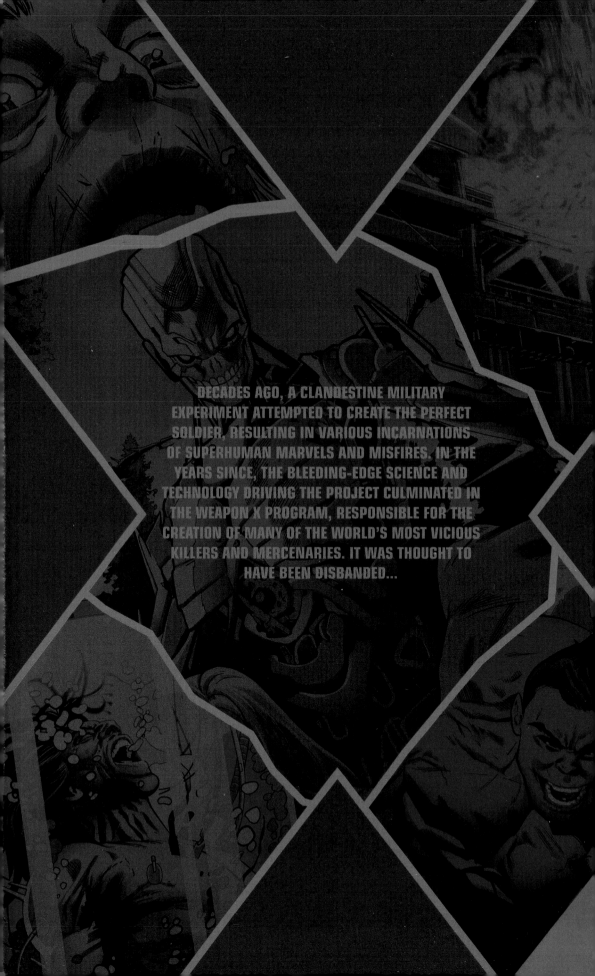

DECADES AGO, A CLANDESTINE MILITARY
EXPERIMENT ATTEMPTED TO CREATE THE PERFECT
SOLDIER, RESULTING IN VARIOUS INCARNATIONS
OF SUPERHUMAN MARVELS AND MISFIRES. IN THE
YEARS SINCE, THE BLEEDING-EDGE SCIENCE AND
TECHNOLOGY DRIVING THE PROJECT CULMINATED IN
THE WEAPON X PROGRAM, RESPONSIBLE FOR THE
CREATION OF MANY OF THE WORLD'S MOST VICIOUS
KILLERS AND MERCENARIES. IT WAS THOUGHT TO
HAVE BEEN DISBANDED...

WEAPON X

WEAPONS OF MUTANT DESTRUCTION PRELUDE

Writer/**GREG PAK**

WEAPON X #1-4

Pencilers/**GREG LAND**
with **IBRAIM ROBERSON** (#2-3)
Inkers/**JAY LEISTEN**
with **IBRAIM ROBERSON** (#2-3)
Colorist/**FRANK D'ARMATA**
Letterer/**VC's JOE CARAMAGNA**
Cover Art/**GREG LAND, JAY LEISTEN
& FRANK D'ARMATA**

THE TOTALLY AWESOME HULK #19

Artist/**ROBERT GILL**
Color Artist/**NOLAN WOODARD**
Letterer/**VC's CORY PETIT**
Cover Art/**STONEHOUSE**

Assistant Editor/**CHRIS ROBINSON**
Editor/**MARK PANICCIA**

Collection Editor/**JENNIFER GRÜNWALD** · Assistant Editor/**CAITLIN O'CONNELL**
Associate Managing Editor/**KATERI WOODY** · Editor, Special Projects/**MARK D. BEAZLEY**
VP Production & Special Projects/**JEFF YOUNGQUIST** · SVP Print, Sales & Marketing/**DAVID GABRIEL**
Book Designer/**JAY BOWEN**

Editor in Chief/**AXEL ALONSO** · Chief Creative Officer/**JOE QUESADA**
President/**DAN BUCKLEY** · Executive Producer/**ALAN FINE**

WEAPON X VOL. 1: WEAPONS OF MUTANT DESTRUCTION PRELUDE. Contains material originally published in magazine form as WEAPON X #1-4 and THE TOTALLY AWESOME HULK #19. First printing 2017. ISBN# 978-1-302-90734-1. Published by MARVEL WORLDWIDE, INC., a subsidiary of MARVEL ENTERTAINMENT, LLC. OFFICE OF PUBLICATION: 135 West 50th Street, New York, NY 10020. Copyright © 2017 MARVEL No similarity between any of the names, characters, persons, and/or institutions in this magazine with those of any living or dead person or institution is intended, and any such similarity which may exist is purely coincidental. **Printed in Canada.** DAN BUCKLEY, President, Marvel Entertainment; JOE QUESADA, Chief Creative Officer; TOM BREVOORT, SVP of Publishing; DAVID BOGART, SVP of Business Affairs & Operations, Publishing & Partnership; C.B. CEBULSKI, VP of Brand Management & Development, Asia; DAVID GABRIEL, SVP of Sales & Marketing, Publishing; JEFF YOUNGQUIST, VP of Production & Special Projects; DAN CARR, Executive Director of Publishing Technology; ALEX MORALES, Director of Publishing Operations; SUSAN CRESPI, Production Manager; STAN LEE, Chairman Emeritus. For information regarding advertising in Marvel Comics or on Marvel.com, please contact Vit DeBellis, Integrated Sales Manager, at vdebellis@marvel.com. For Marvel subscription inquiries, please call 888-511-5480. **Manufactured between 6/30/2017 and 8/1/2017 by SOLISCO PRINTERS, SCOTT, QC, CANADA.**

10 9 8 7 6 5 4 3 2 1

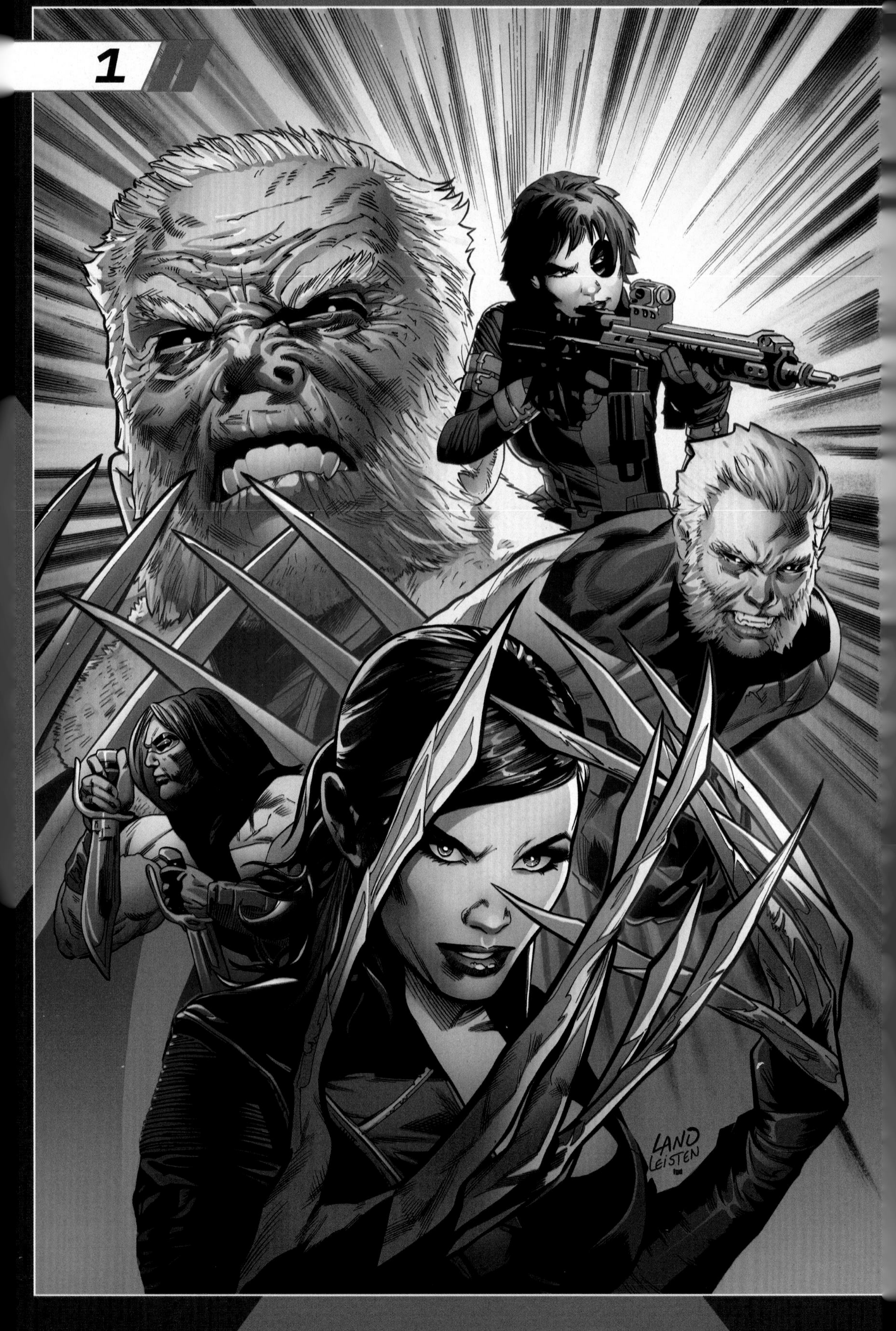
1
LAND
LEISTEN

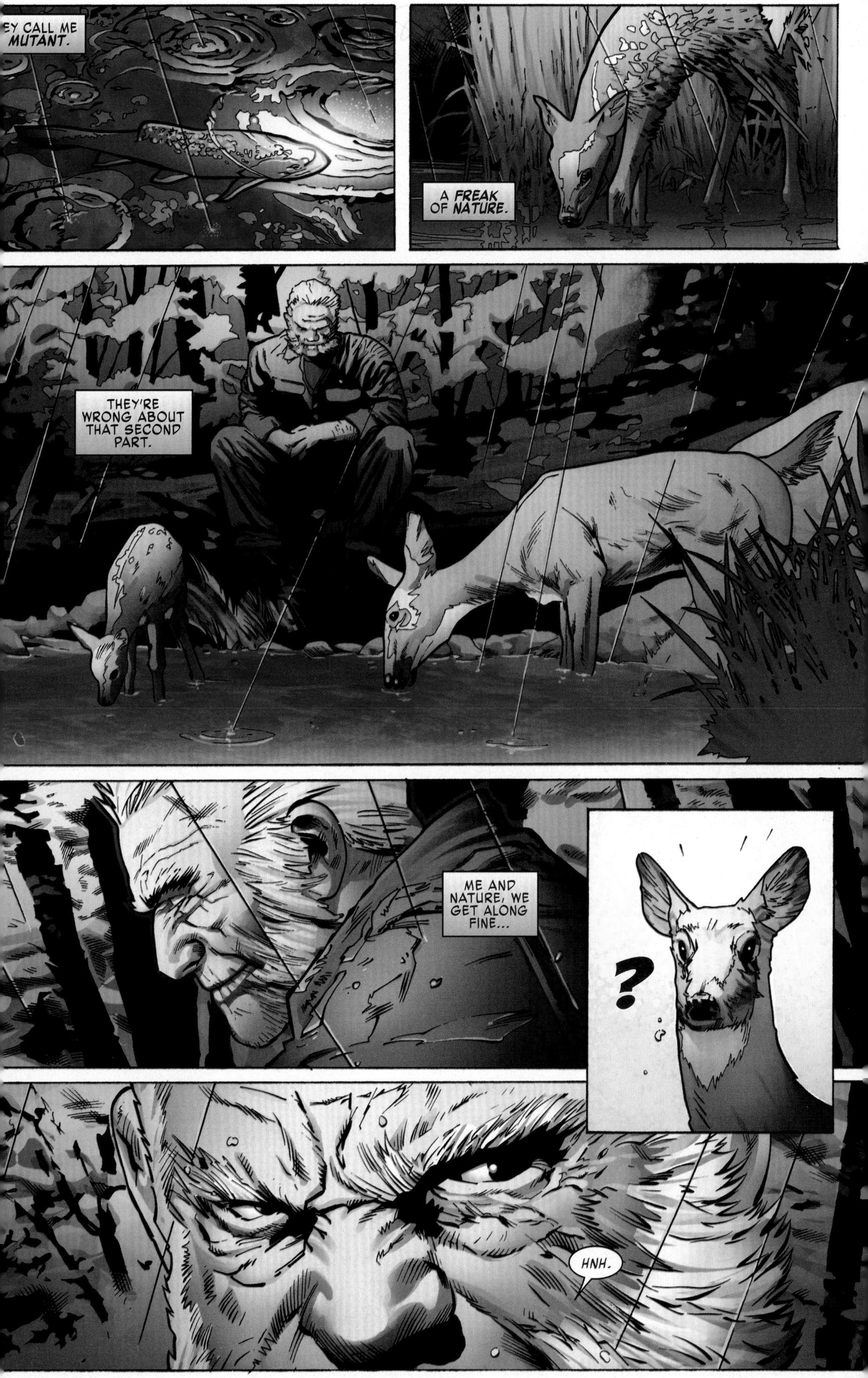
EY CALL ME MUTANT.
A FREAK OF NATURE.
THEY'RE WRONG ABOUT THAT SECOND PART.
ME AND NATURE, WE GET ALONG FINE...
?
HNH.

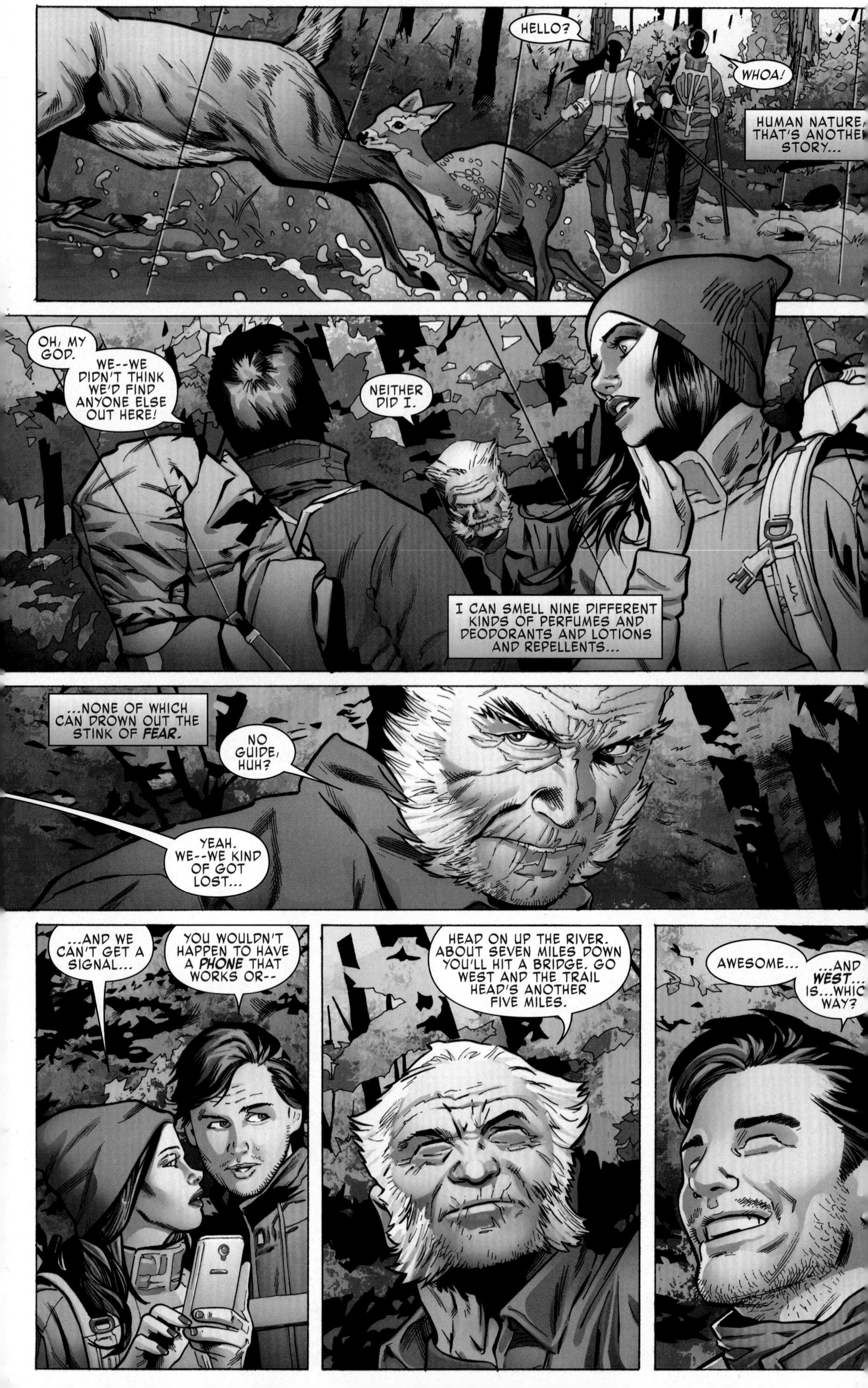
HELLO?
WHOA!
HUMAN NATURE, THAT'S ANOTHE STORY...
OH, MY GOD.
WE--WE DIDN'T THINK WE'D FIND ANYONE ELSE OUT HERE!
NEITHER DID I.
I CAN SMELL NINE DIFFERENT KINDS OF PERFUMES AND DEODORANTS AND LOTIONS AND REPELLENTS...
...NONE OF WHICH CAN DROWN OUT THE STINK OF FEAR.
NO GUIDE, HUH?
YEAH. WE--WE KIND OF GOT LOST...
...AND WE CAN'T GET A SIGNAL...
YOU WOULDN'T HAPPEN TO HAVE A PHONE THAT WORKS OR--
HEAD ON UP THE RIVER. ABOUT SEVEN MILES DOWN YOU'LL HIT A BRIDGE. GO WEST AND THE TRAIL HEAD'S ANOTHER FIVE MILES.
AWESOME...
...AND WEST... IS...WHIC WAY?

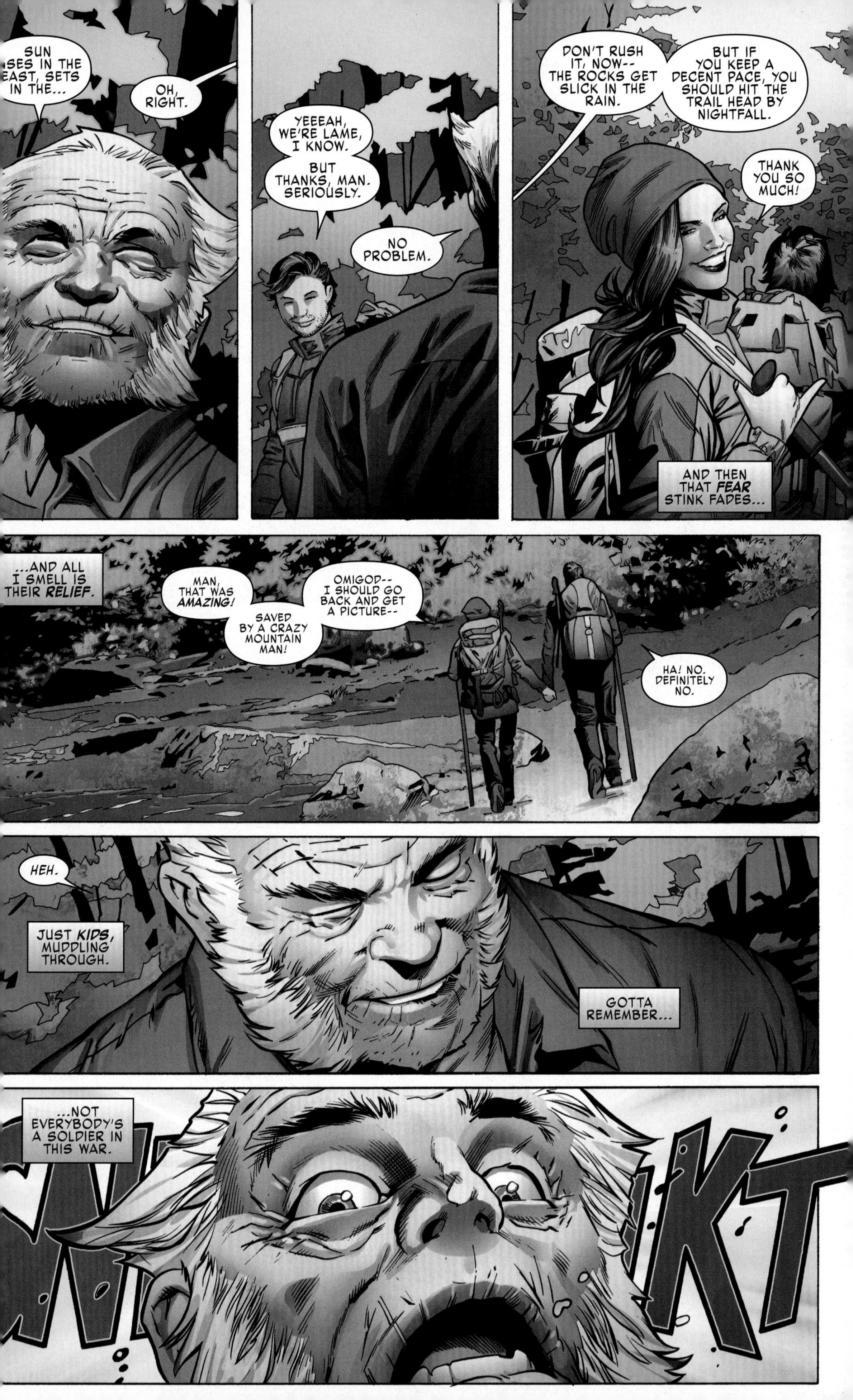
SUN ...SES IN THE EAST, SETS IN THE...
OH, RIGHT.
YEEEAH, WE'RE LAME, I KNOW.
BUT THANKS, MAN. SERIOUSLY.
NO PROBLEM.
DON'T RUSH IT, NOW-- THE ROCKS GET SLICK IN THE RAIN.
BUT IF YOU KEEP A DECENT PACE, YOU SHOULD HIT THE TRAIL HEAD BY NIGHTFALL.
THANK YOU SO MUCH!
AND THEN THAT FEAR STINK FADES...
...AND ALL I SMELL IS THEIR RELIEF.
MAN, THAT WAS AMAZING!
SAVED BY A CRAZY MOUNTAIN MAN!
OMIGOD-- I SHOULD GO BACK AND GET A PICTURE--
HA! NO. DEFINITELY NO.
HEH.
JUST KIDS, MUDDLING THROUGH.
GOTTA REMEMBER...
...NOT EVERYBODY'S A SOLDIER IN THIS WAR.

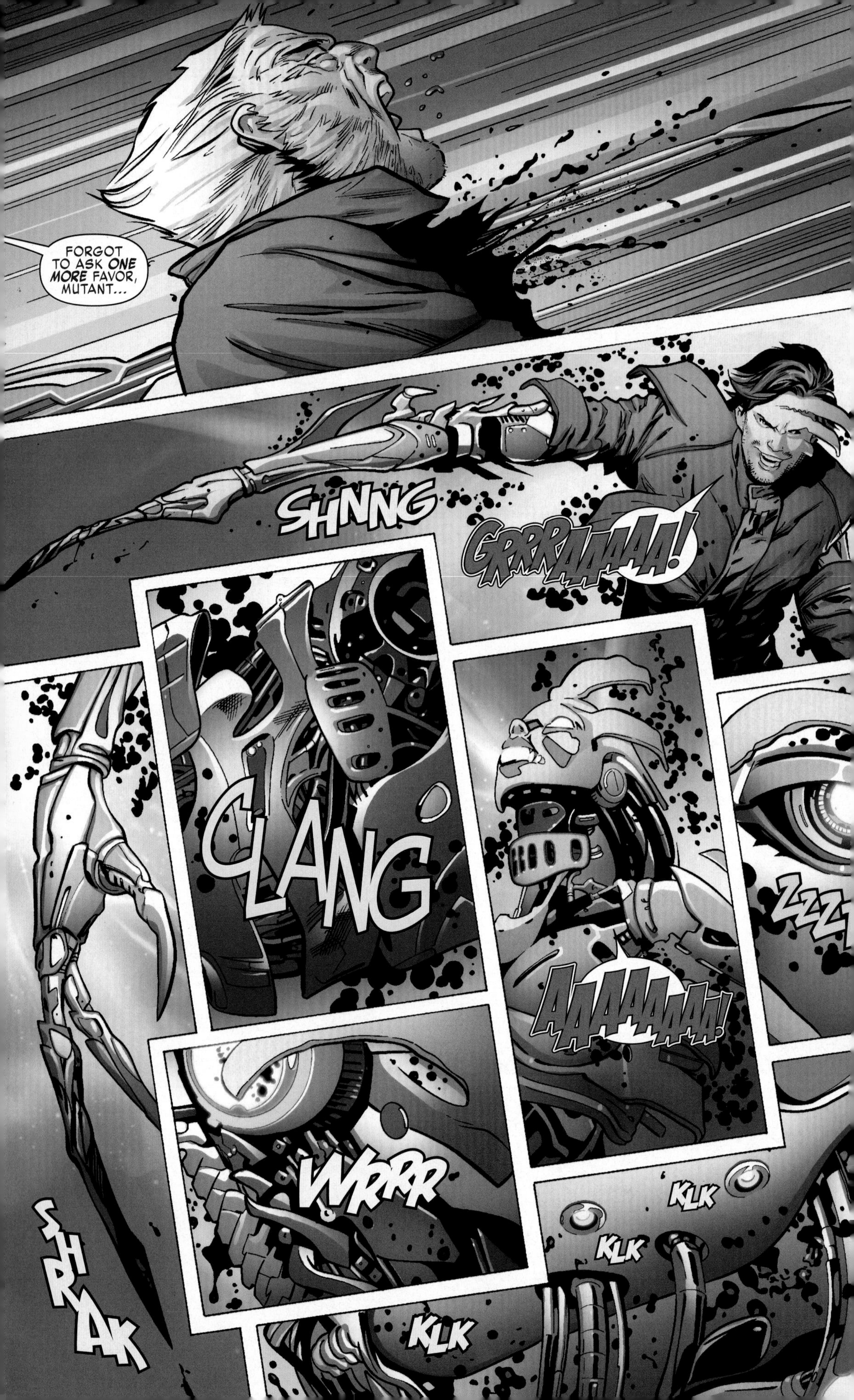

FORGOT TO ASK **ONE MORE** FAVOR, MUTANT...
SHNNG
GRRRAAAAAA!
CLANG
AAAAAAAA!
ZZZT
WRRR
SHRAK
KLK
KLK
KLK

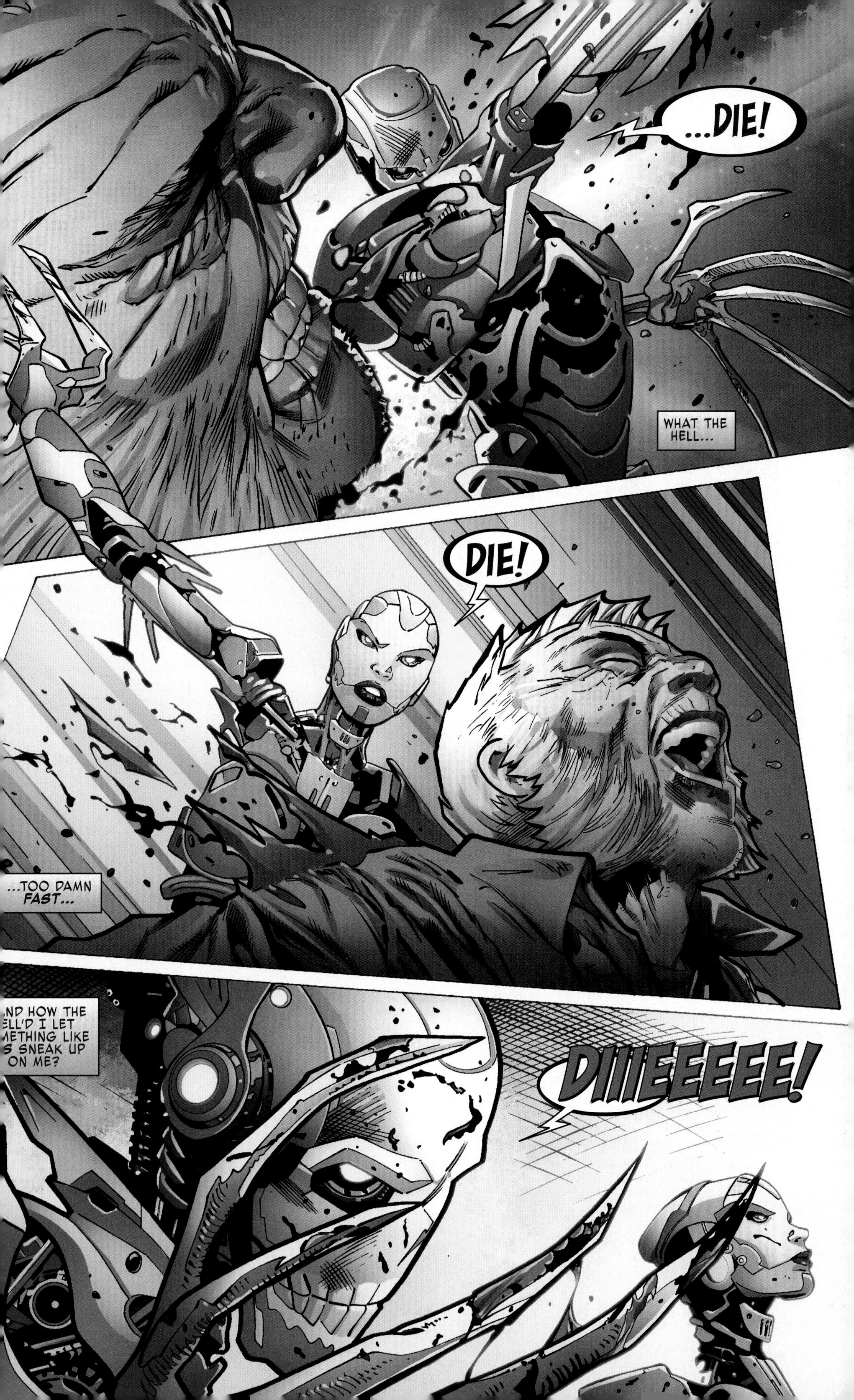
...DIE!
WHAT THE HELL...
DIE!
...TOO DAMN *FAST*...
ND HOW THE ELL'D I LET METHING LIKE S SNEAK UP ON ME?
DIIIEEEEEE!

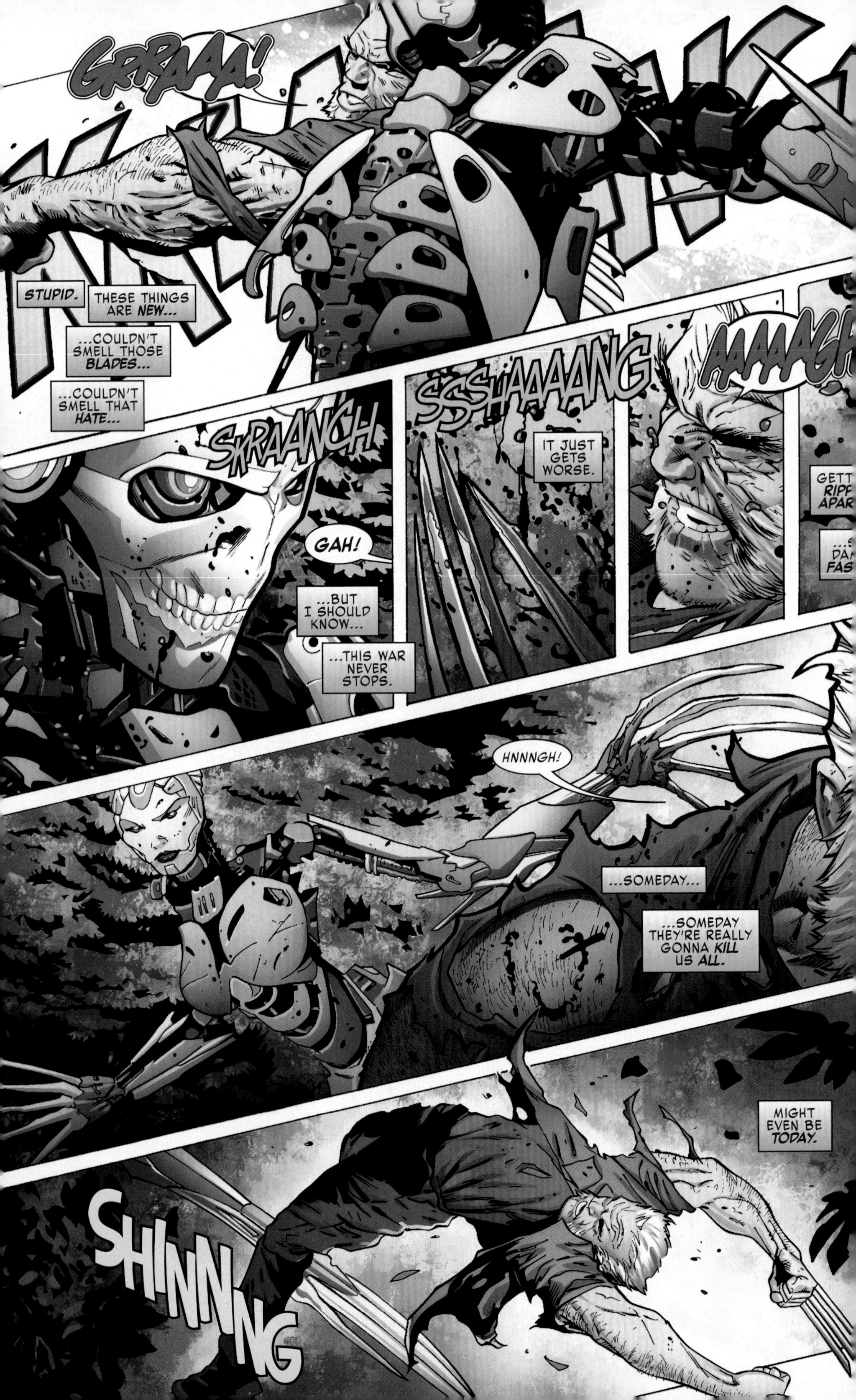
GRRAAA!
STUPID.
THESE THINGS ARE NEW...
...COULDN'T SMELL THOSE BLADES...
...COULDN'T SMELL THAT HATE...
SKRAANCH
GAH!
...BUT I SHOULD KNOW...
...THIS WAR NEVER STOPS.
SSSHAAAANG
IT JUST GETS WORSE.
HNNNGH!
...SOMEDAY...
...SOMEDAY THEY'RE REALLY GONNA KILL US ALL.
MIGHT EVEN BE TODAY.
SHINNNG

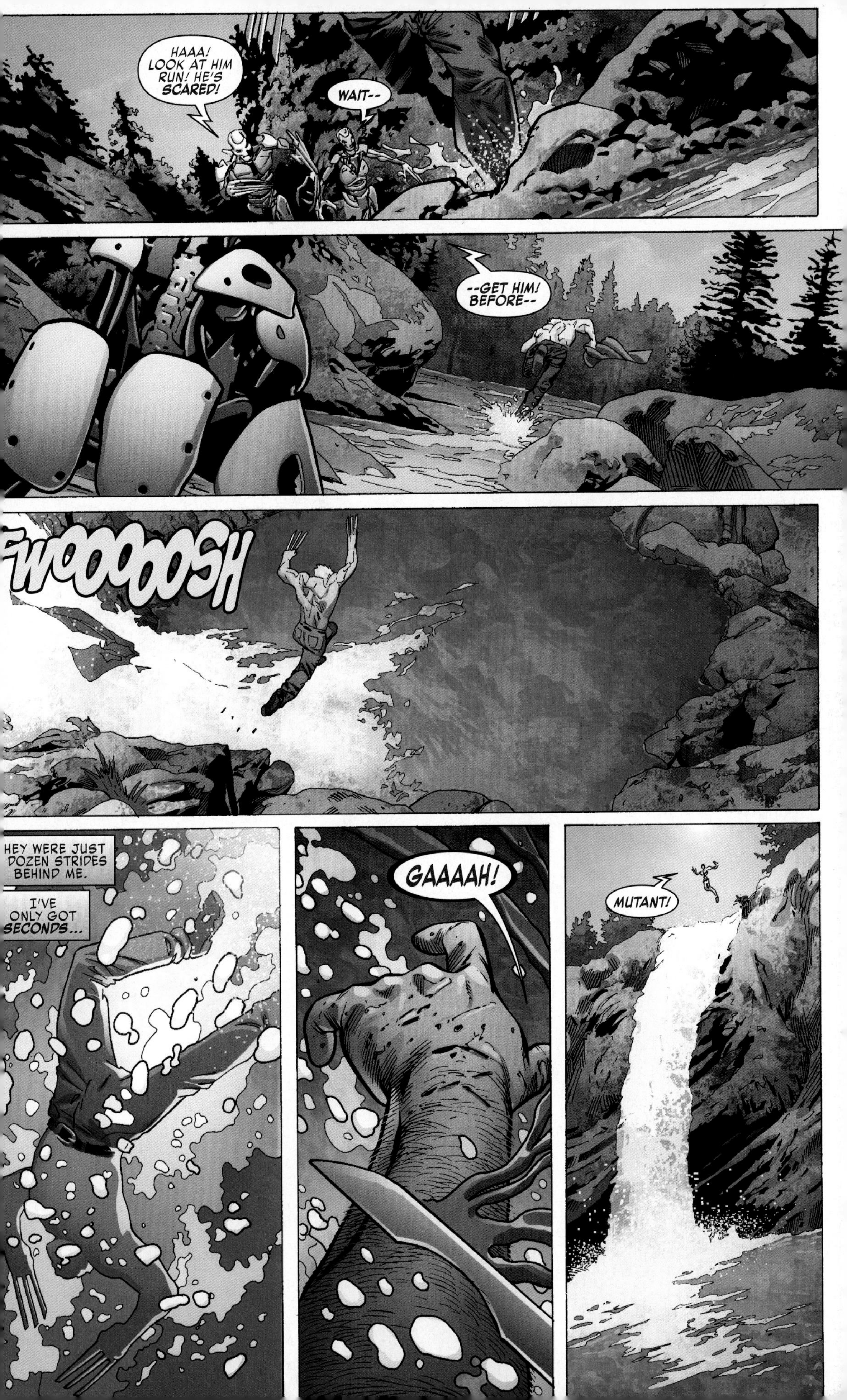
HAAA! LOOK AT HIM RUN! HE'S SCARED!
WAIT--
--GET HIM! BEFORE--
FWOOOOOSH
HEY WERE JUST DOZEN STRIDES BEHIND ME.
I'VE ONLY GOT SECONDS...
GAAAAH!
MUTANT!

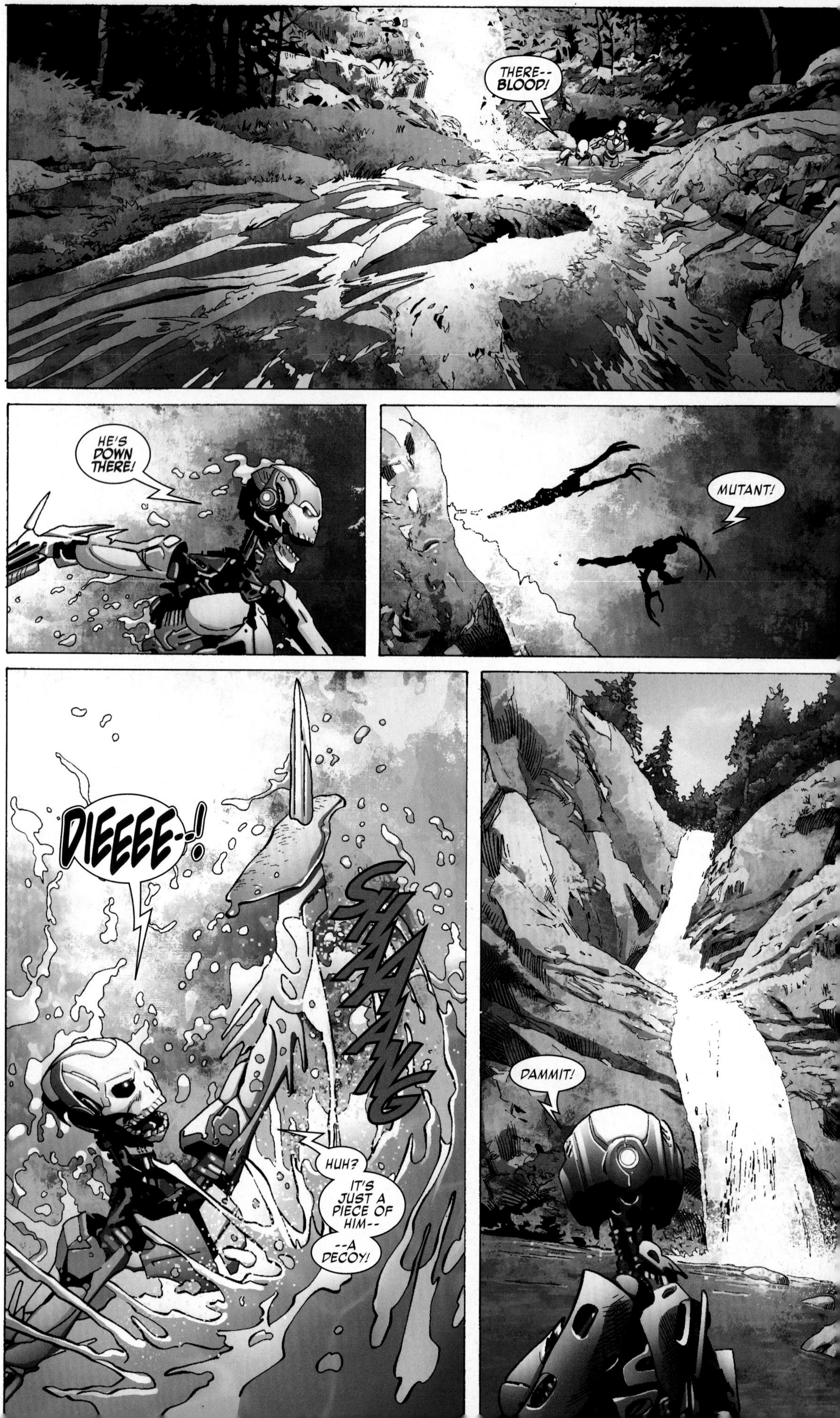
THERE--
BLOOD!
HE'S DOWN THERE!
MUTANT!
DIEEEE--!
SHAAANG
HUH?
IT'S JUST A PIECE OF HIM--
--A DECOY!
DAMMIT!

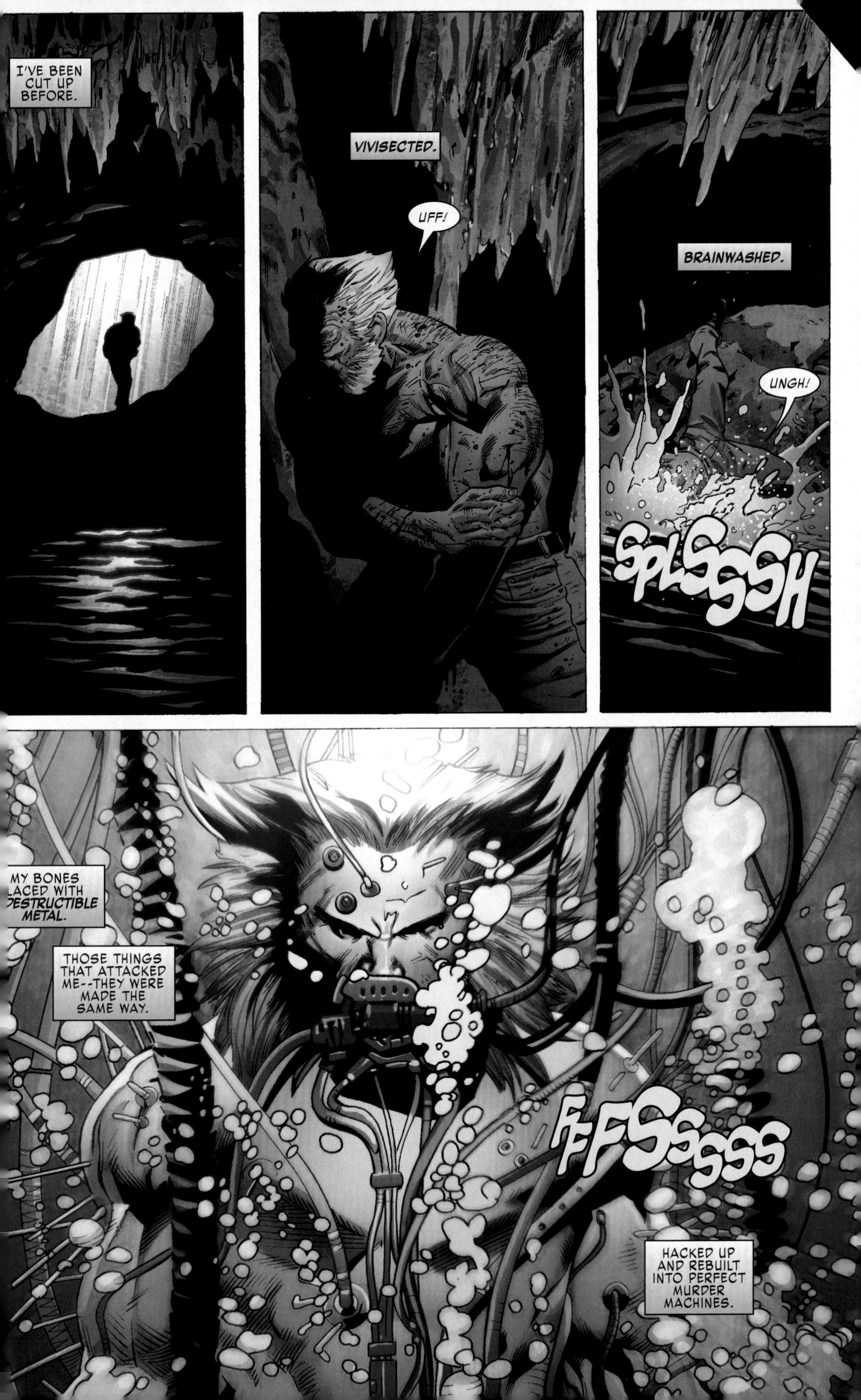

I'VE BEEN CUT UP BEFORE.
VIVISECTED.
UFF!
BRAINWASHED.
UNGH!
SPLSSSH
MY BONES LACED WITH DESTRUCTIBLE METAL.
THOSE THINGS THAT ATTACKED ME--THEY WERE MADE THE SAME WAY.
FFFSSSSS
HACKED UP AND REBUILT INTO PERFECT MURDER MACHINES.

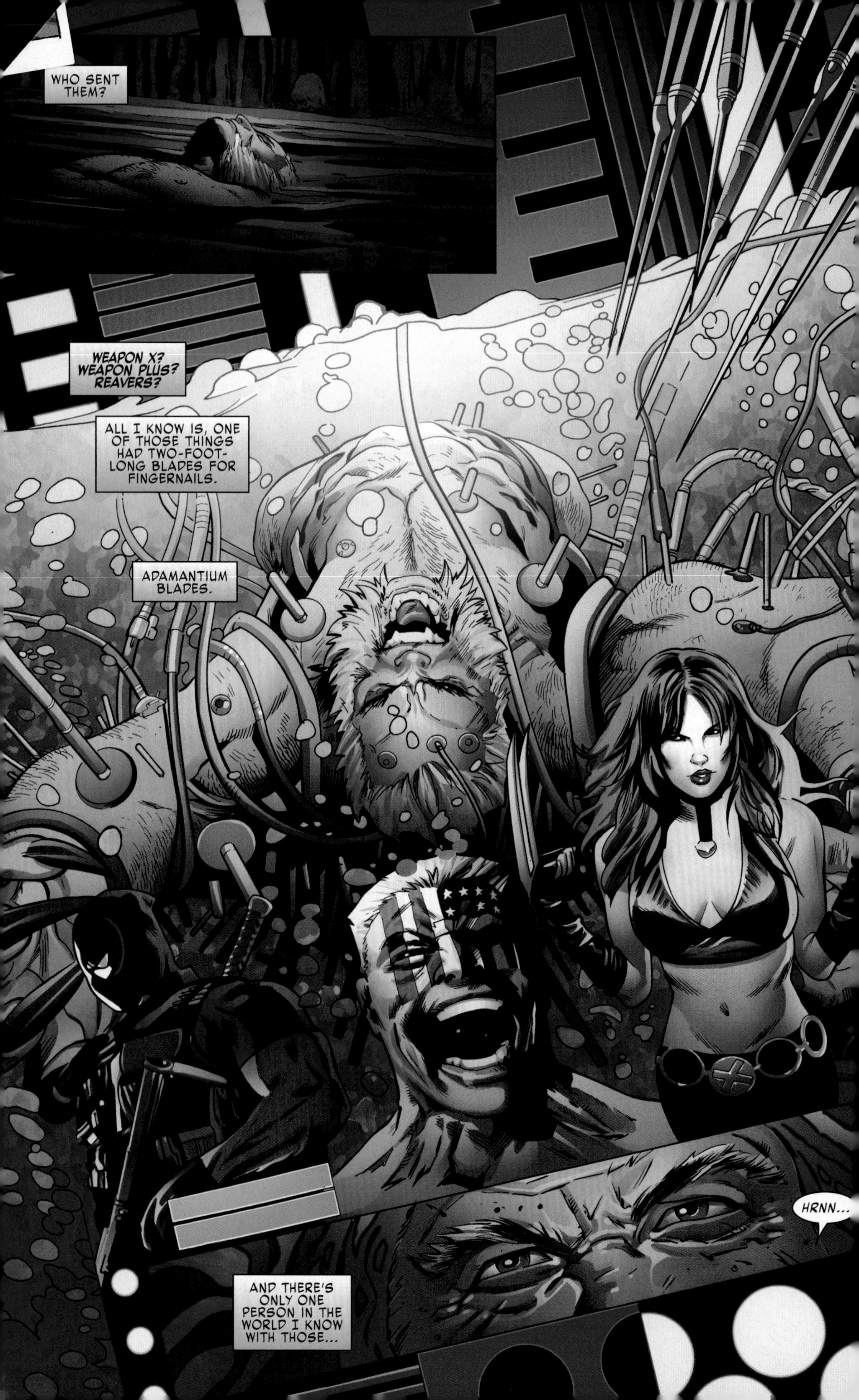
WHO SENT THEM?
WEAPON X? WEAPON PLUS? REAVERS?
ALL I KNOW IS, ONE OF THOSE THINGS HAD TWO-FOOT-LONG BLADES FOR FINGERNAILS.
ADAMANTIUM BLADES.
HRNN...
AND THERE'S ONLY ONE PERSON IN THE WORLD I KNOW WITH THOSE...

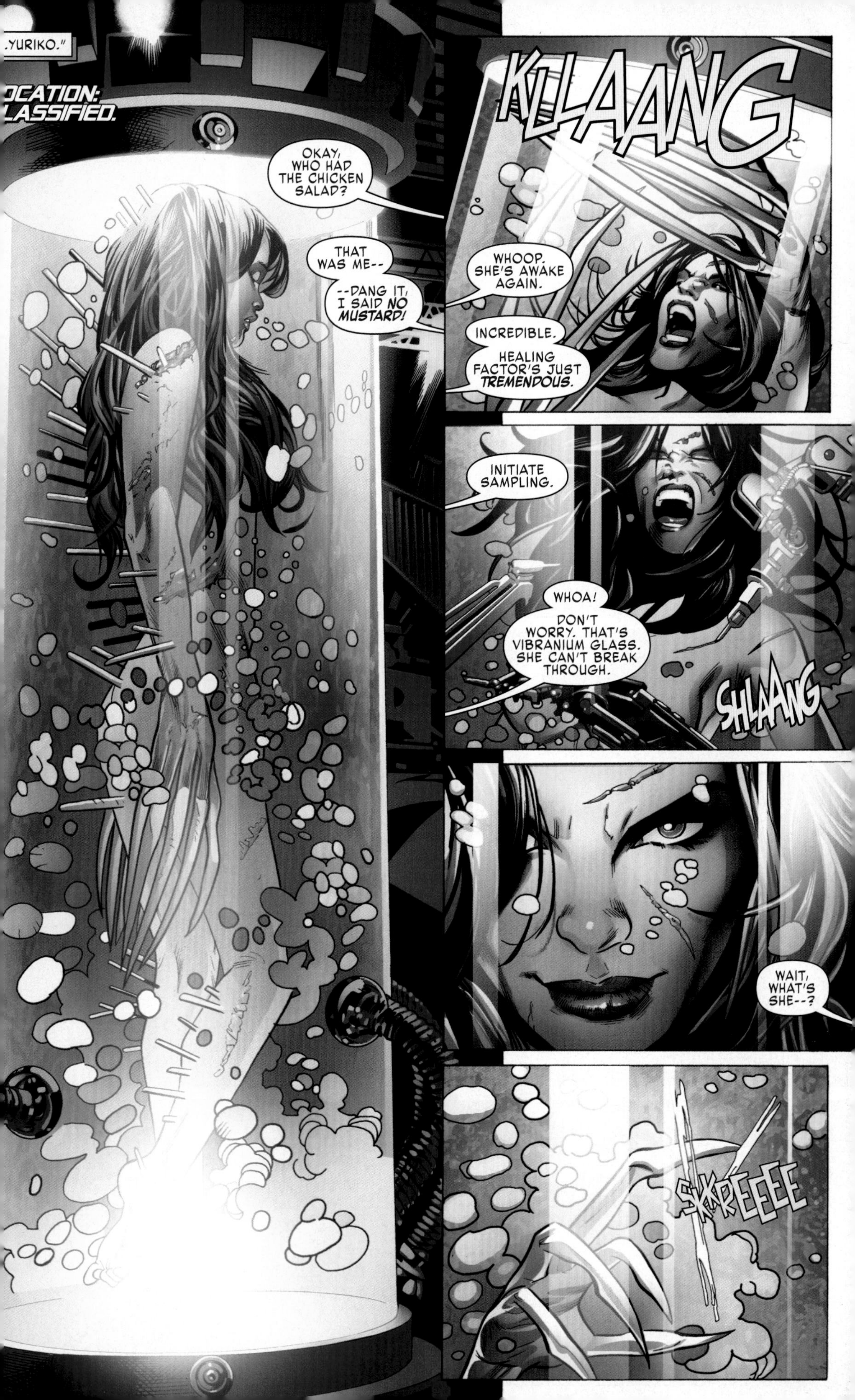
.YURIKO."
OCATION: LASSIFIED.
OKAY, WHO HAD THE CHICKEN SALAD?
THAT WAS ME--
--DANG IT, I SAID NO MUSTARD!
KLLAANG
WHOOP. SHE'S AWAKE AGAIN.
INCREDIBLE.
HEALING FACTOR'S JUST TREMENDOUS.
INITIATE SAMPLING.
WHOA!
DON'T WORRY. THAT'S VIBRANIUM GLASS. SHE CAN'T BREAK THROUGH.
SHLAANG
WAIT, WHAT'S SHE--?
SKREEEE

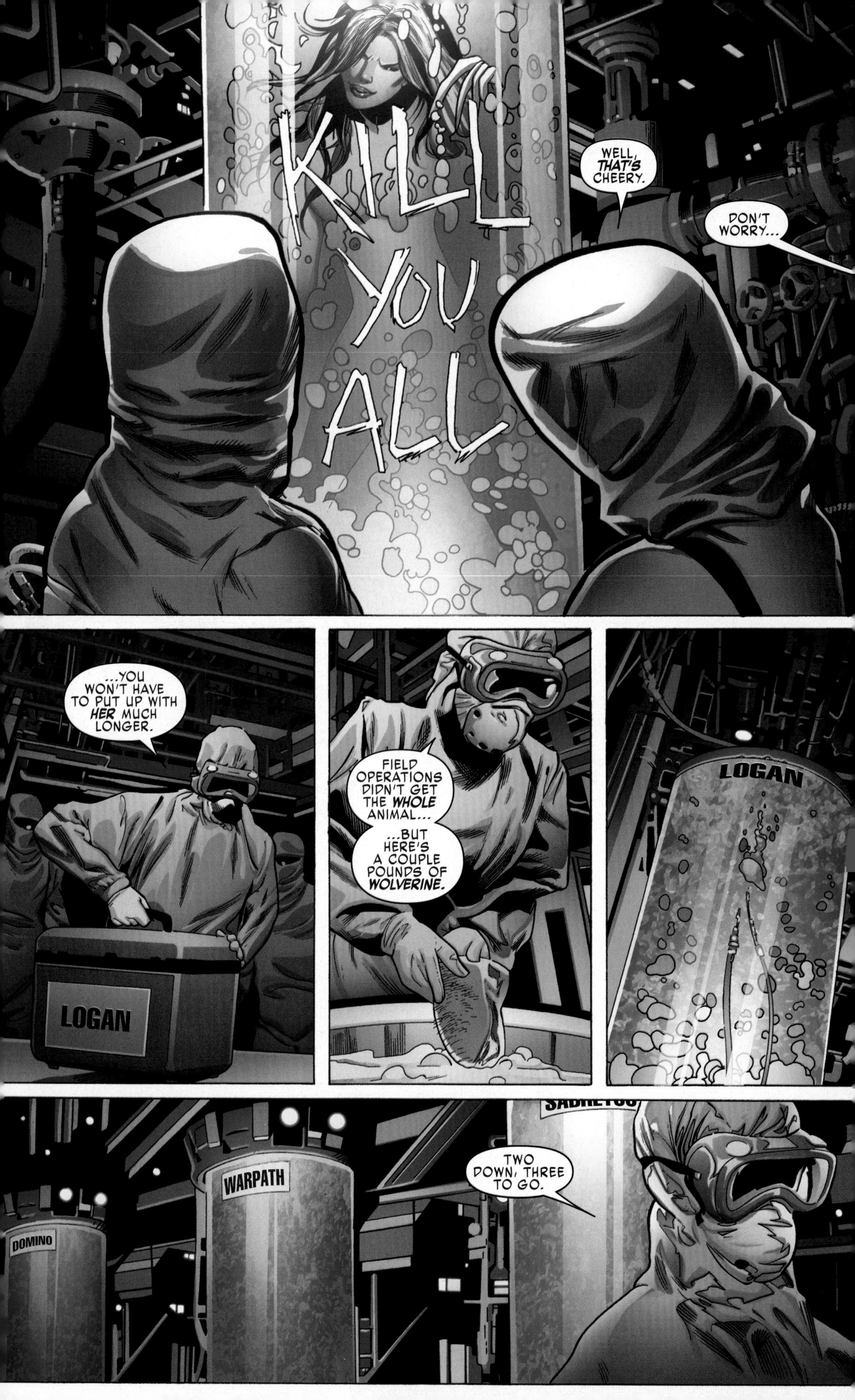

KILL YOU ALL
WELL, THAT'S CHEERY.
DON'T WORRY...
...YOU WON'T HAVE TO PUT UP WITH HER MUCH LONGER.
LOGAN
FIELD OPERATIONS DIDN'T GET THE WHOLE ANIMAL...
...BUT HERE'S A COUPLE POUNDS OF WOLVERINE.
LOGAN
DOMINO
WARPATH
TWO DOWN, THREE TO GO.

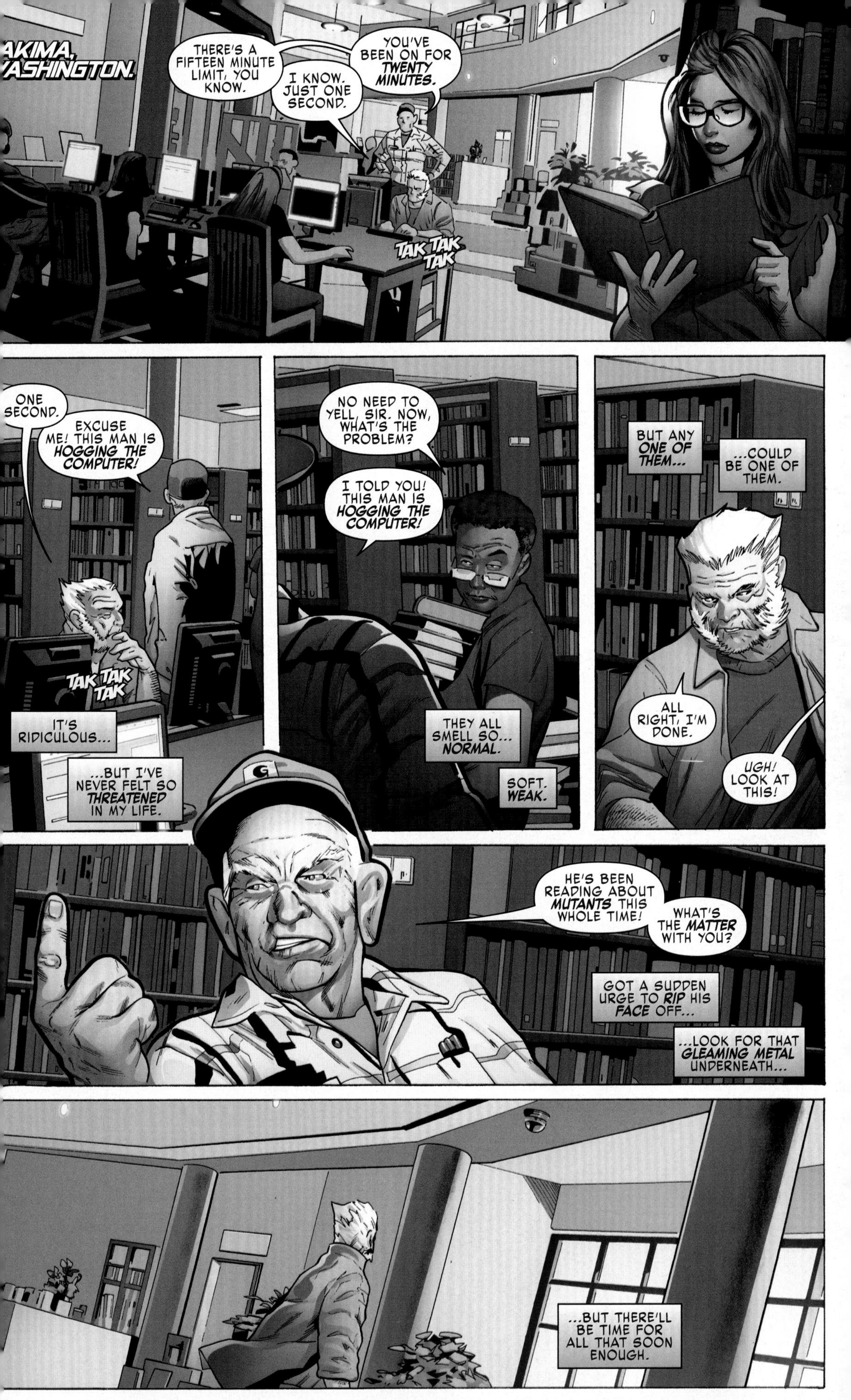

AKIMA, WASHINGTON.
THERE'S A FIFTEEN MINUTE LIMIT, YOU KNOW.
YOU'VE BEEN ON FOR TWENTY MINUTES.
I KNOW. JUST ONE SECOND.
TAK TAK TAK
ONE SECOND.
EXCUSE ME! THIS MAN IS HOGGING THE COMPUTER!
TAK TAK TAK
IT'S RIDICULOUS...
...BUT I'VE NEVER FELT SO THREATENED IN MY LIFE.
NO NEED TO YELL, SIR. NOW, WHAT'S THE PROBLEM?
I TOLD YOU! THIS MAN IS HOGGING THE COMPUTER!
THEY ALL SMELL SO... NORMAL.
SOFT. WEAK.
BUT ANY ONE OF THEM...
...COULD BE ONE OF THEM.
ALL RIGHT, I'M DONE.
UGH! LOOK AT THIS!
HE'S BEEN READING ABOUT MUTANTS THIS WHOLE TIME!
WHAT'S THE MATTER WITH YOU?
GOT A SUDDEN URGE TO RIP HIS FACE OFF...
...LOOK FOR THAT GLEAMING METAL UNDERNEATH...
...BUT THERE'LL BE TIME FOR ALL THAT SOON ENOUGH.

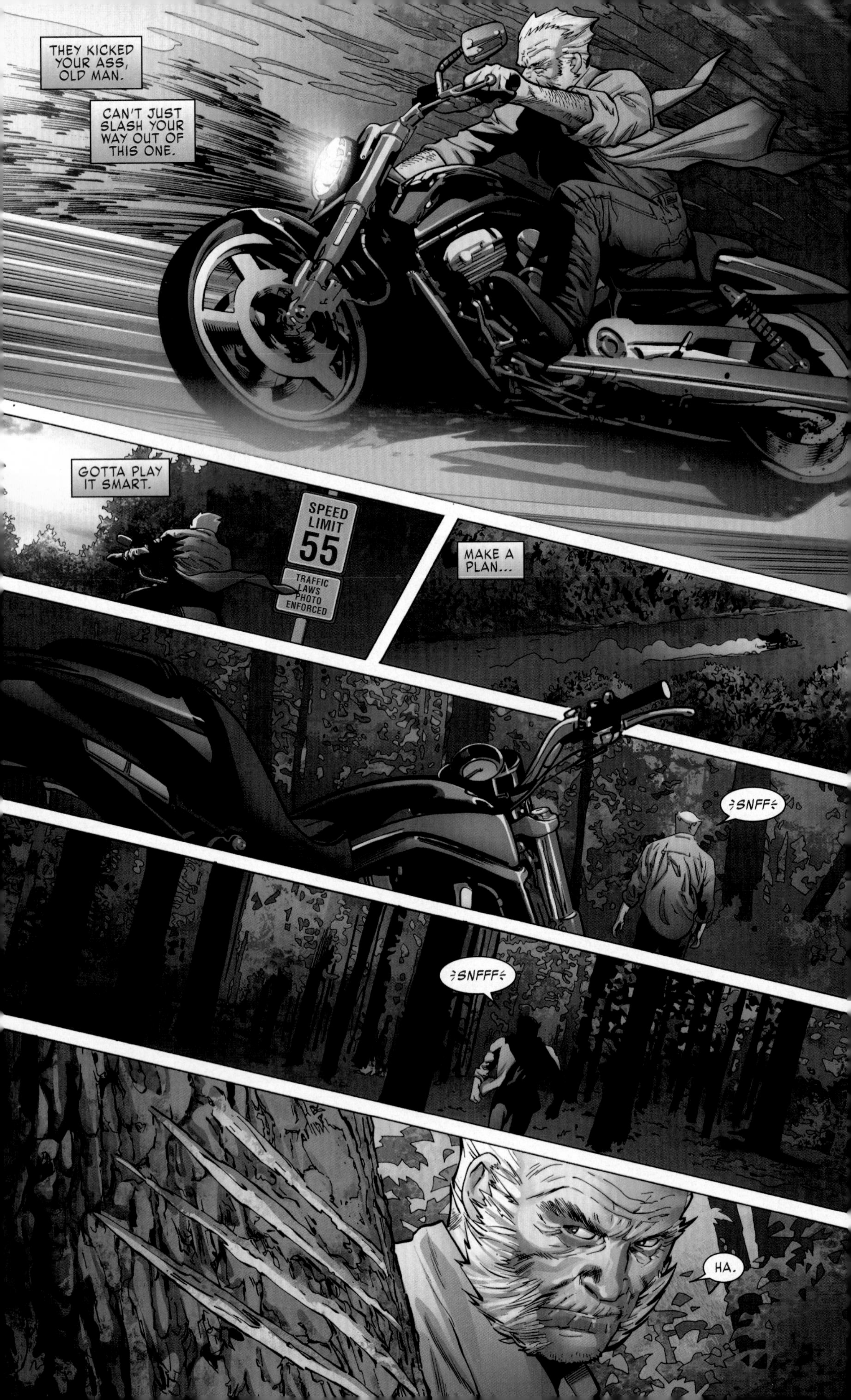
THEY KICKED YOUR ASS, OLD MAN.
CAN'T JUST SLASH YOUR WAY OUT OF THIS ONE.
GOTTA PLAY IT SMART.
SPEED LIMIT 55
TRAFFIC LAWS PHOTO ENFORCED
MAKE A PLAN...
SNFF
SNFFF
HA.

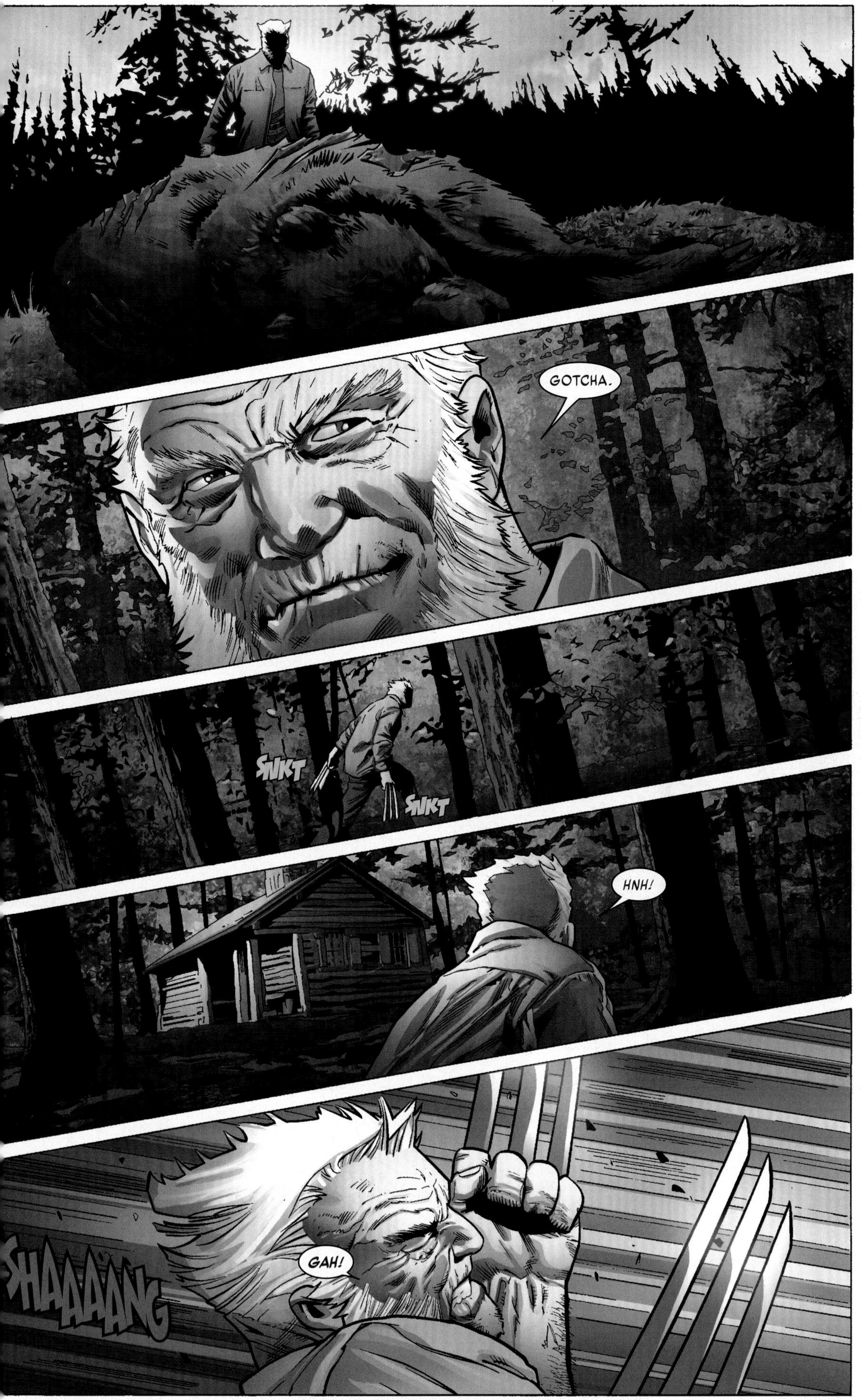
GOTCHA.
SNIKT
SNIKT
HNH!
SHAAAANG
GAH!

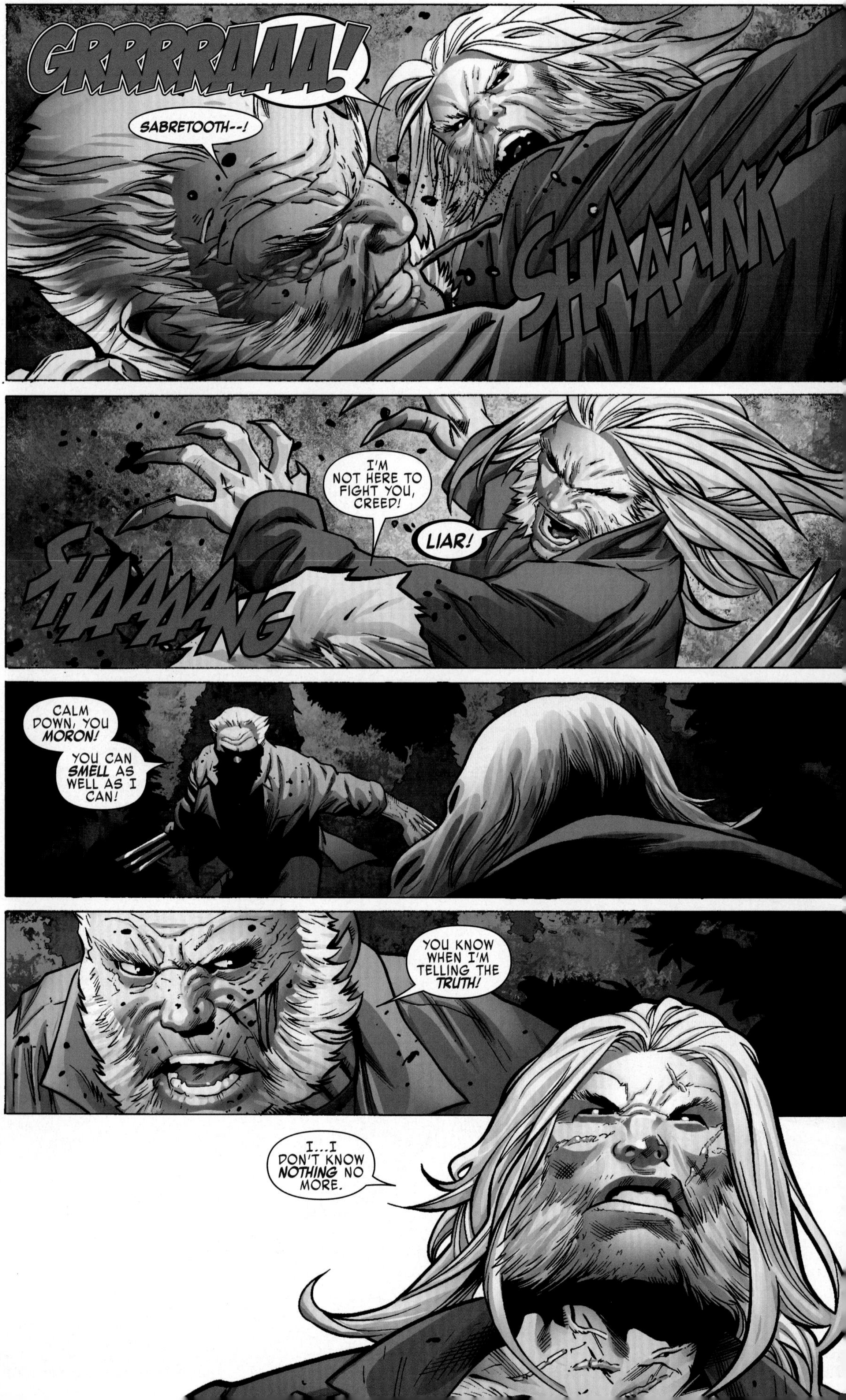
GRRRRAAAA!
SABRETOOTH--!
SHAAAKK
I'M NOT HERE TO FIGHT YOU, CREED!
LIAR!
SHAAAANG
CALM DOWN, YOU MORON!
YOU CAN SMELL AS WELL AS I CAN!
YOU KNOW WHEN I'M TELLING THE TRUTH!
I...I DON'T KNOW NOTHING NO MORE.

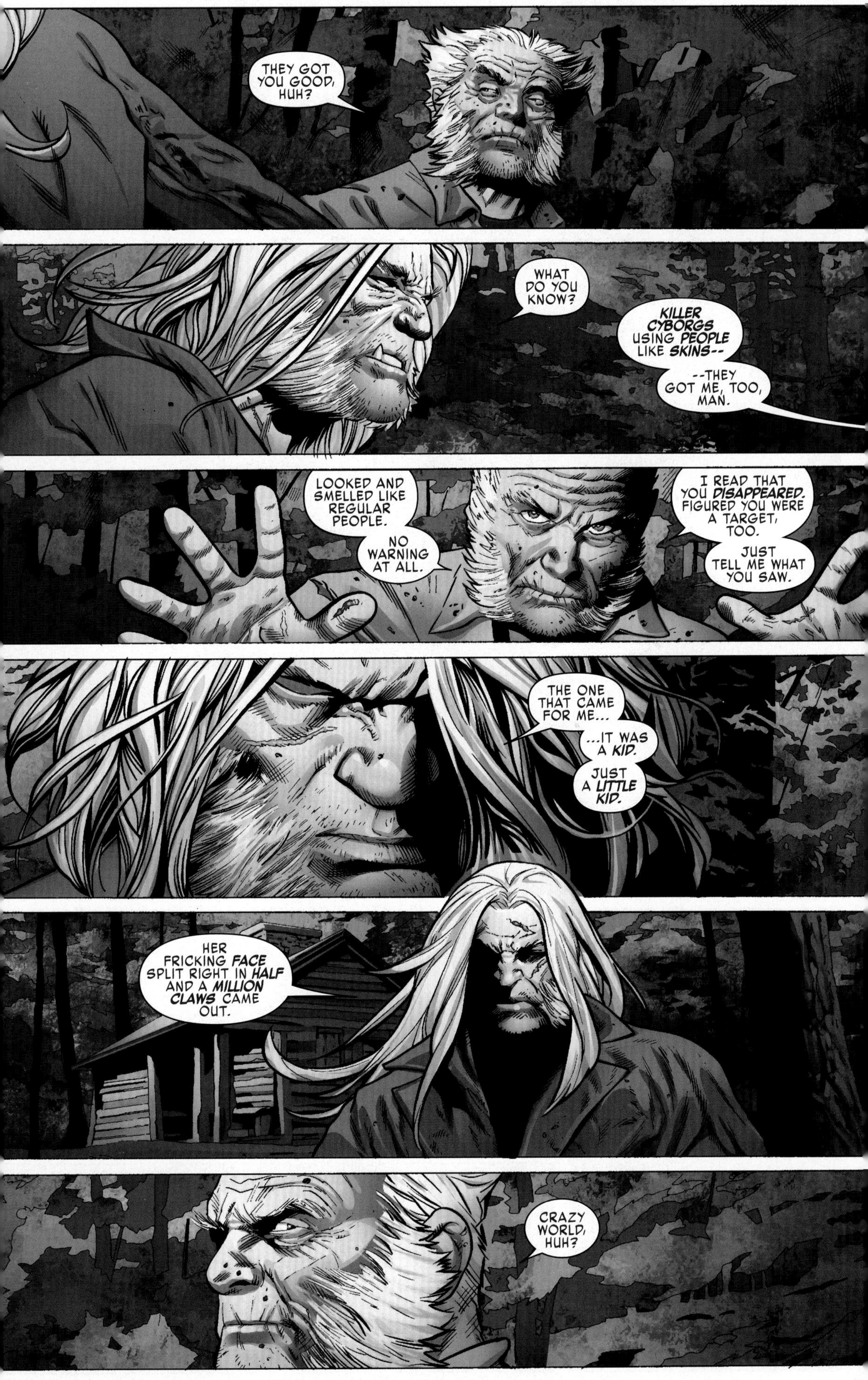
THEY GOT YOU GOOD, HUH?
WHAT DO YOU KNOW?
KILLER CYBORGS USING PEOPLE LIKE SKINS--
--THEY GOT ME, TOO, MAN.
LOOKED AND SMELLED LIKE REGULAR PEOPLE.
NO WARNING AT ALL.
I READ THAT YOU DISAPPEARED. FIGURED YOU WERE A TARGET, TOO.
JUST TELL ME WHAT YOU SAW.
THE ONE THAT CAME FOR ME...
...IT WAS A KID.
JUST A LITTLE KID.
HER FRICKING FACE SPLIT RIGHT IN HALF AND A MILLION CLAWS CAME OUT.
CRAZY WORLD, HUH?

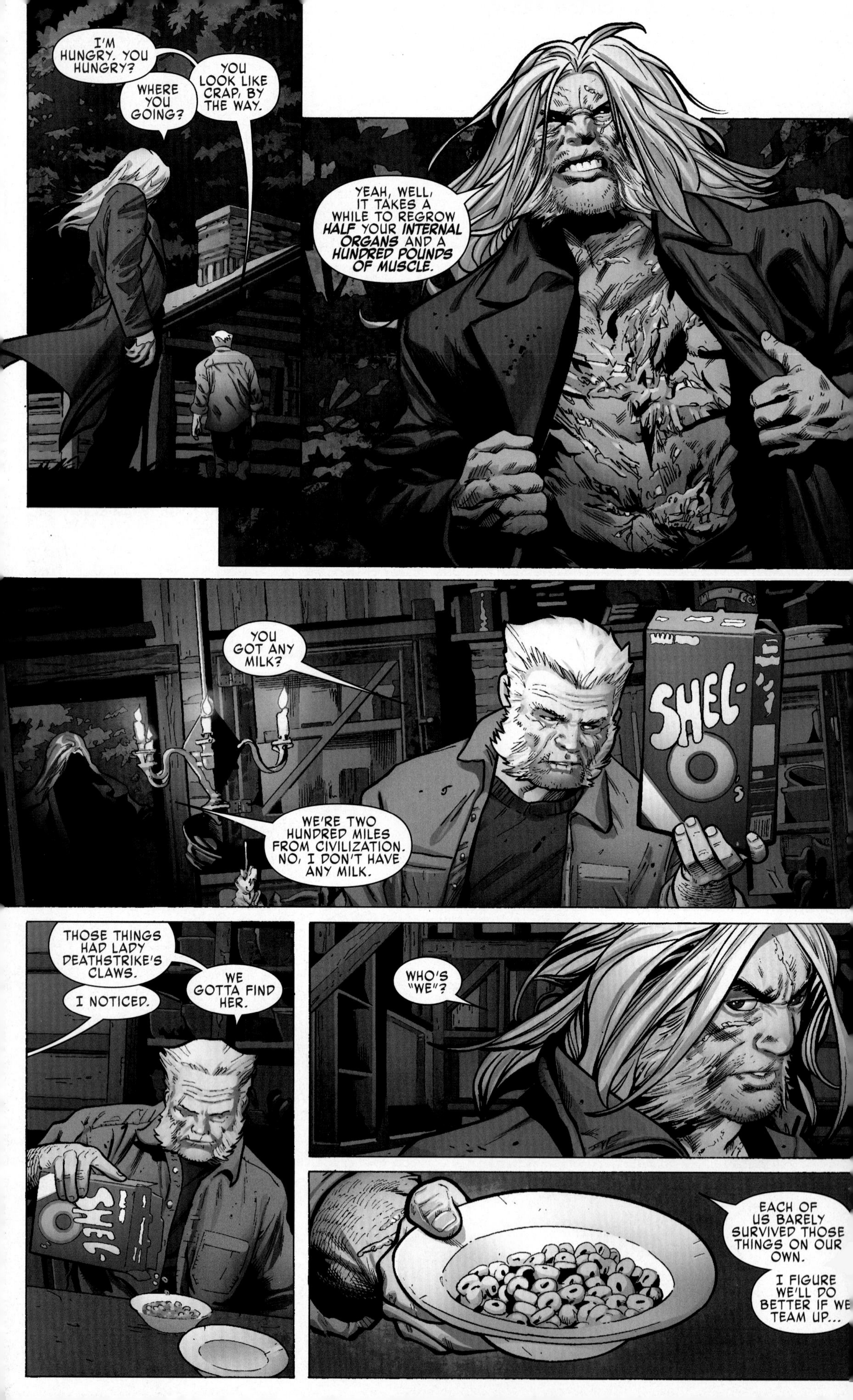
I'M HUNGRY. YOU HUNGRY?
WHERE YOU GOING?
YOU LOOK LIKE CRAP, BY THE WAY.
YEAH, WELL, IT TAKES A WHILE TO REGROW *HALF* YOUR *INTERNAL ORGANS* AND A *HUNDRED POUNDS OF MUSCLE.*
YOU GOT ANY MILK?
SHEL-O'S
WE'RE TWO HUNDRED MILES FROM CIVILIZATION. NO, I DON'T HAVE ANY MILK.
THOSE THINGS HAD LADY DEATHSTRIKE'S CLAWS.
I NOTICED.
WE GOTTA FIND HER.
WHO'S "WE"?
EACH OF US BARELY SURVIVED THOSE THINGS ON OUR OWN.
I FIGURE WE'LL DO BETTER IF WE TEAM UP...

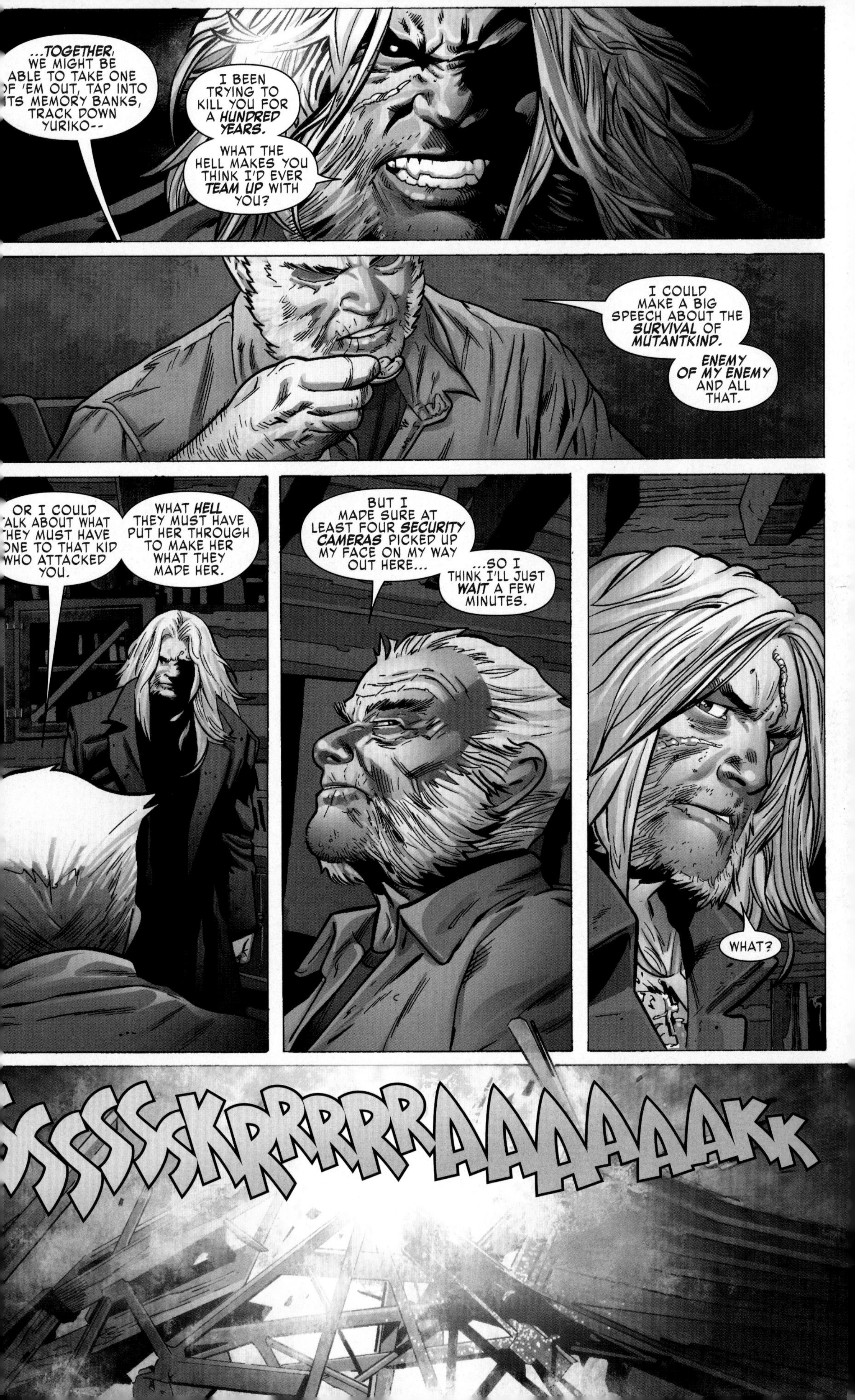
...TOGETHER, WE MIGHT BE ABLE TO TAKE ONE OF 'EM OUT, TAP INTO ITS MEMORY BANKS, TRACK DOWN YURIKO--
I BEEN TRYING TO KILL YOU FOR A HUNDRED YEARS.
WHAT THE HELL MAKES YOU THINK I'D EVER TEAM UP WITH YOU?
I COULD MAKE A BIG SPEECH ABOUT THE SURVIVAL OF MUTANTKIND.
ENEMY OF MY ENEMY AND ALL THAT.
OR I COULD TALK ABOUT WHAT THEY MUST HAVE DONE TO THAT KID WHO ATTACKED YOU.
WHAT HELL THEY MUST HAVE PUT HER THROUGH TO MAKE HER WHAT THEY MADE HER.
BUT I MADE SURE AT LEAST FOUR SECURITY CAMERAS PICKED UP MY FACE ON MY WAY OUT HERE...
...SO I THINK I'LL JUST WAIT A FEW MINUTES.
WHAT?
SSSSSKRRRRRAAAAAAKK

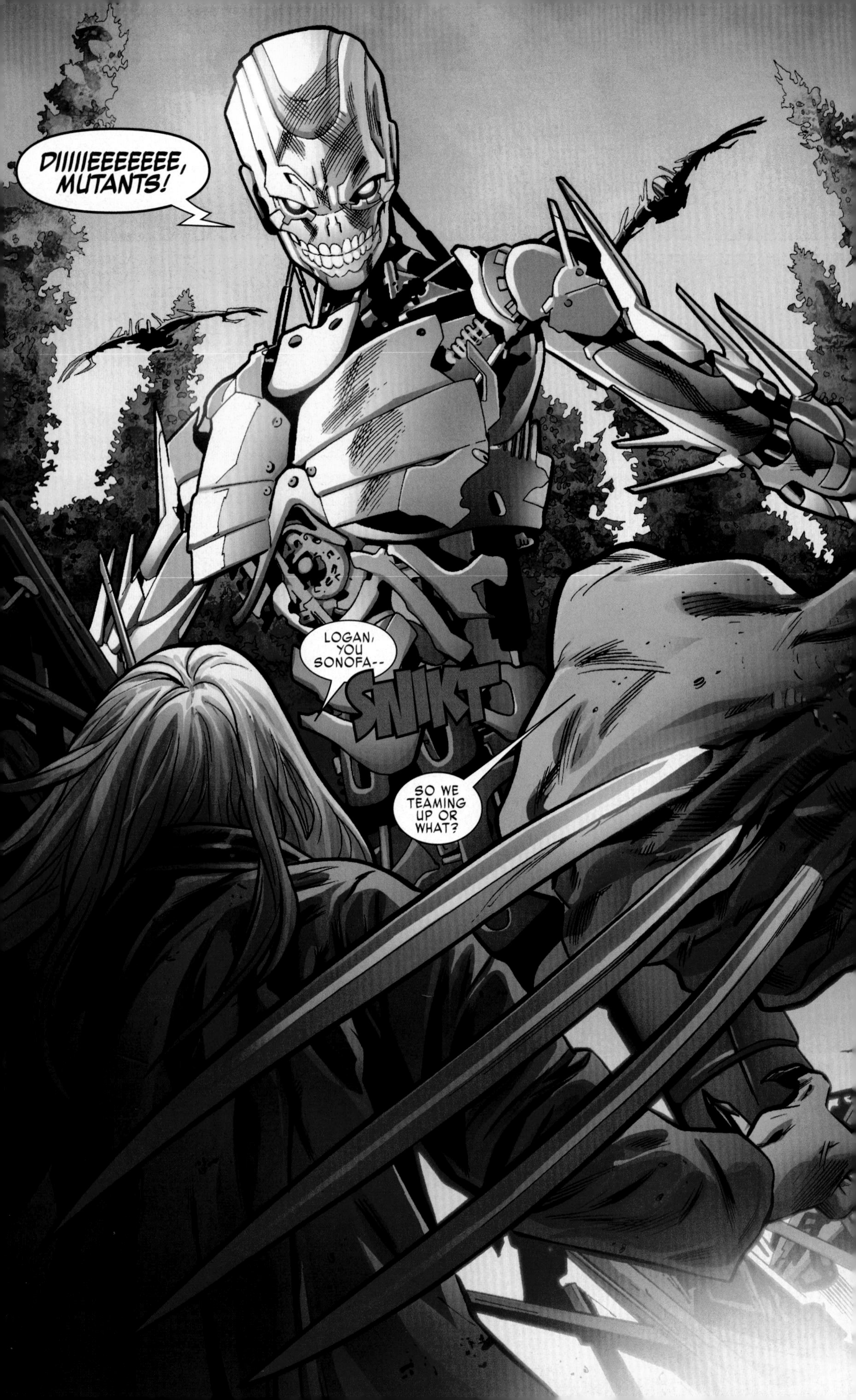
DIIIIIEEEEEEEE, MUTANTS!
LOGAN, YOU SONOFA--
SNIKT
SO WE TEAMING UP OR WHAT?

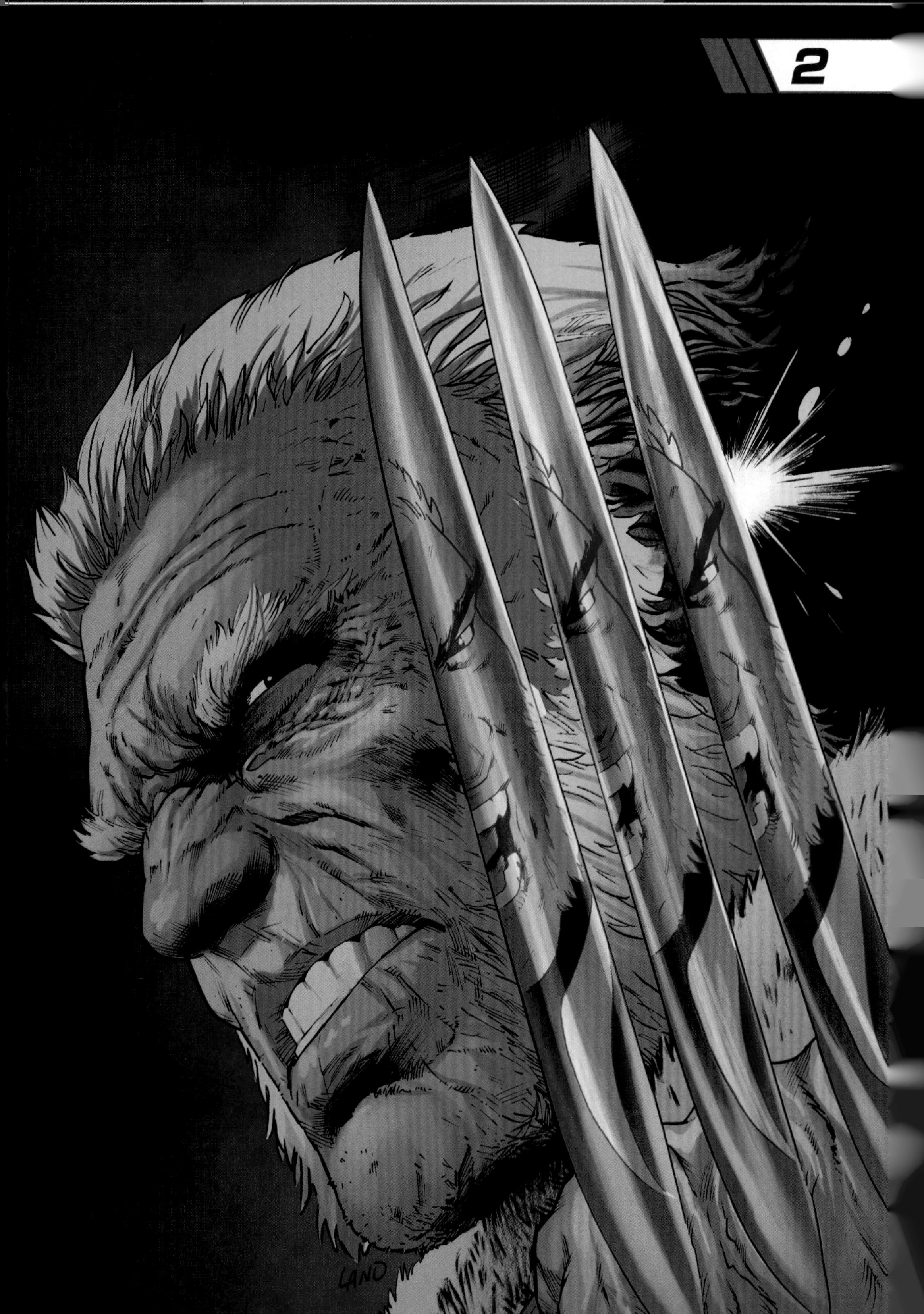
2
LAND

MY GRANDPA BROUGHT ME UP HERE WHEN I WAS NINE...

...JUST A COUPLE MONTHS BEFORE THE *CANCER* KILLED HIM.

TOLD ME EVEN THOUGH I WAS NEVER MUCH FOR *PRAYING*...

...SOMETIMES YOU NEED A QUIET SPOT TO SIT AND *THINK* A WHILE.

SO HERE I AM--

BLEEP

DANG IT.

Cousin Bobby

where u at, fam

THAT'S THE QUESTION, ISN'T IT?

I'M *JAMES PROUDSTAR*, DIL'ZHE'E APACHE, BORN EIGHTY MILES SOUTH ON THE CAMP VERDE REZ.

I'M ALSO *WARPATH*, ONE OF THE STRONGEST MUTANTS ON THE PLANET.

SO I GOT LOTTA PLAC I COULD BE

I COULD BE HELPING THE FOLKS *REBUILDING* BACK HOME.

OR I COULD BE FIGHTING THE GOOD FIGHT WITH THE *X-MEN*.

OR HELL, I COULD BE SCREWING AROUND WITH *COUSIN BOBBY* IN FLAGSTAFF.

BUT SOMEHOW... WHATEVER I DO...

...FOLKS SEEM TO GET *KILLED*.

WELL, LOOK AT THAT...

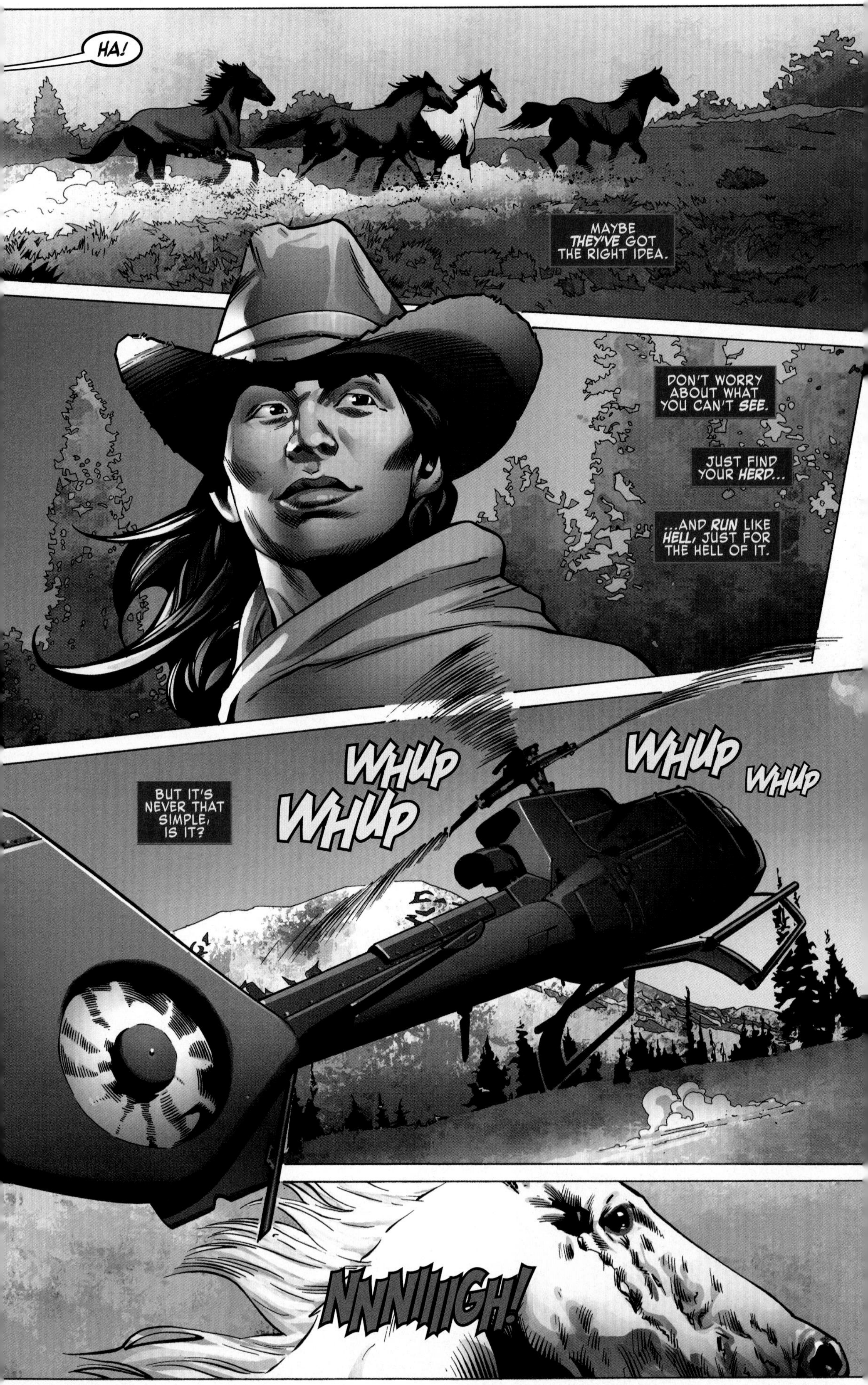
HA!
MAYBE THEY'VE GOT THE RIGHT IDEA.
DON'T WORRY ABOUT WHAT YOU CAN'T SEE.
JUST FIND YOUR HERD...
...AND RUN LIKE HELL, JUST FOR THE HELL OF IT.
BUT IT'S NEVER THAT SIMPLE, IS IT?
WHUP WHUP
WHUP WHUP
NNNIIIIGH!

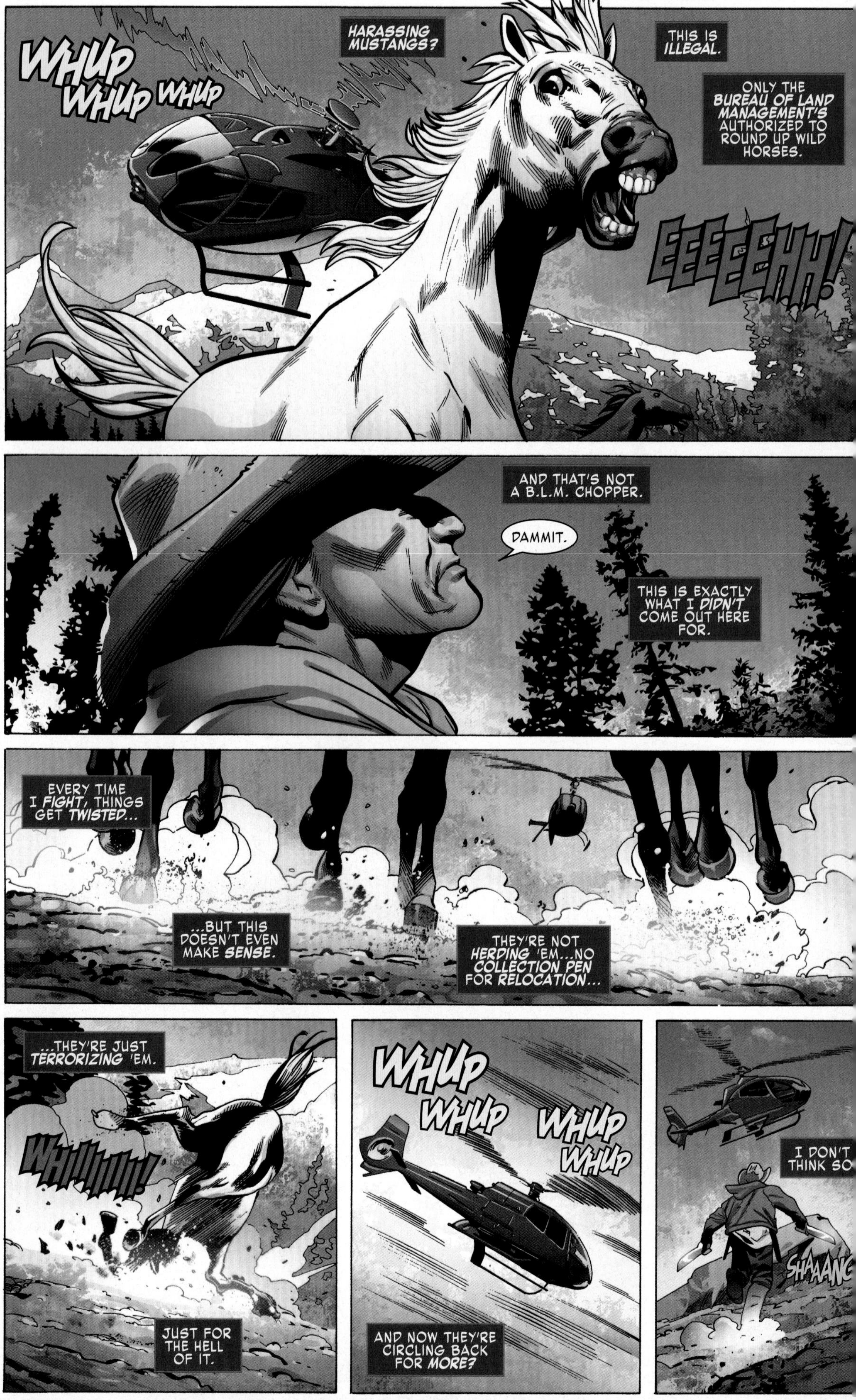
WHUP WHUP WHUP
HARASSING MUSTANGS?
THIS IS ILLEGAL.
ONLY THE BUREAU OF LAND MANAGEMENT'S AUTHORIZED TO ROUND UP WILD HORSES.
EEEEEHH!
AND THAT'S NOT A B.L.M. CHOPPER.
DAMMIT.
THIS IS EXACTLY WHAT I DIDN'T COME OUT HERE FOR.
EVERY TIME I FIGHT, THINGS GET TWISTED...
...BUT THIS DOESN'T EVEN MAKE SENSE.
THEY'RE NOT HERDING 'EM...NO COLLECTION PEN FOR RELOCATION...
...THEY'RE JUST TERRORIZING 'EM.
WHIIIIIII!
JUST FOR THE HELL OF IT.
WHUP WHUP WHUP WHUP
AND NOW THEY'RE CIRCLING BACK FOR MORE?
I DON'T THINK SO
SHAAANG

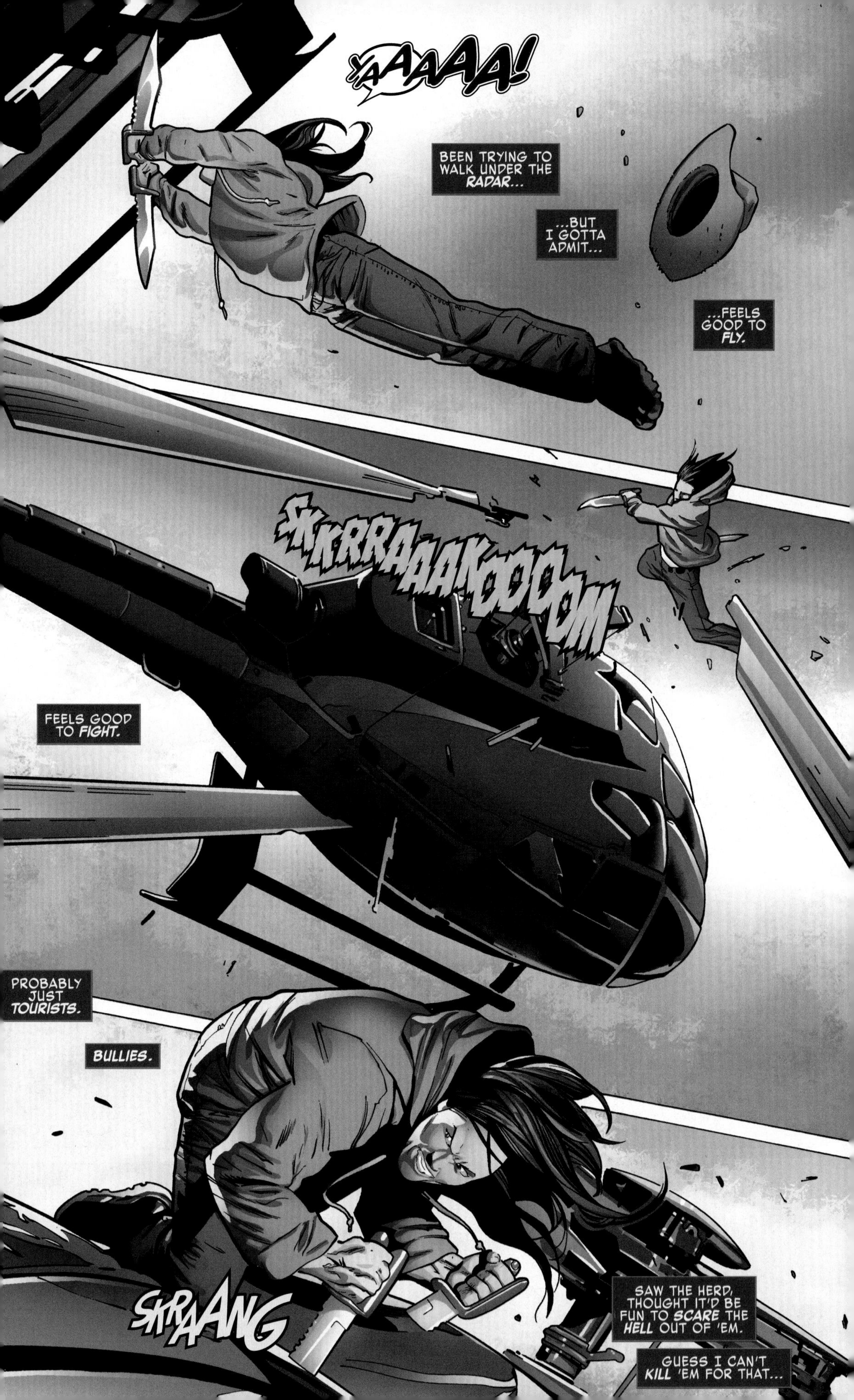
YAAAAA!
BEEN TRYING TO WALK UNDER THE RADAR...
...BUT I GOTTA ADMIT...
...FEELS GOOD TO FLY.
SKKRRAAAKOOOOM
FEELS GOOD TO FIGHT.
PROBABLY JUST TOURISTS.
BULLIES.
SKRAANG
SAW THE HERD, THOUGHT IT'D BE FUN TO SCARE THE HELL OUT OF 'EM.
GUESS I CAN'T KILL 'EM FOR THAT...

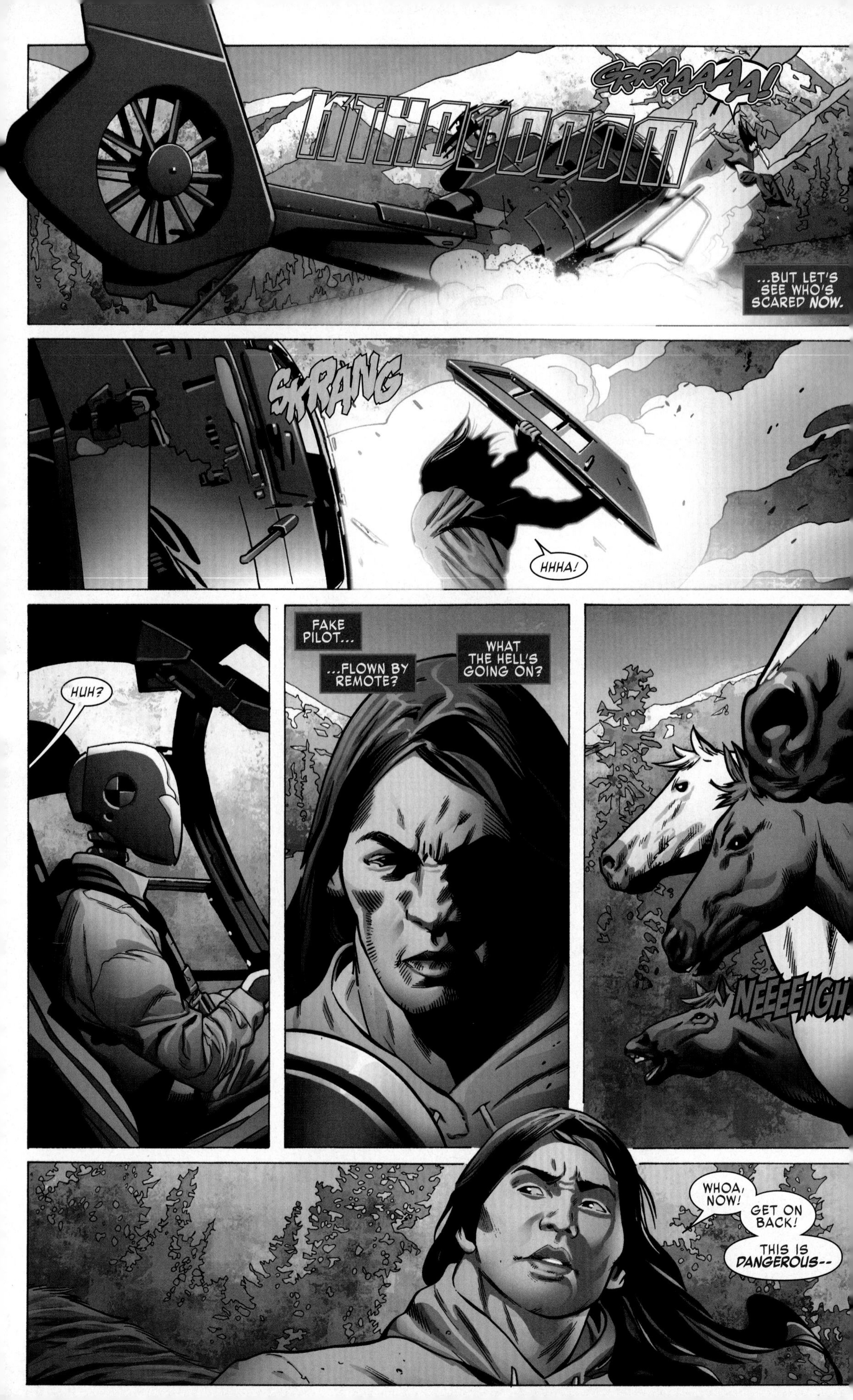
KTHOOOOOOM
GRRAAAAA!
...BUT LET'S SEE WHO'S SCARED NOW.
SKRANG
HHHA!
HUH?
FAKE PILOT...
...FLOWN BY REMOTE?
WHAT THE HELL'S GOING ON?
NEEEEIIGH
WHOA, NOW!
GET ON BACK!
THIS IS DANGEROUS--

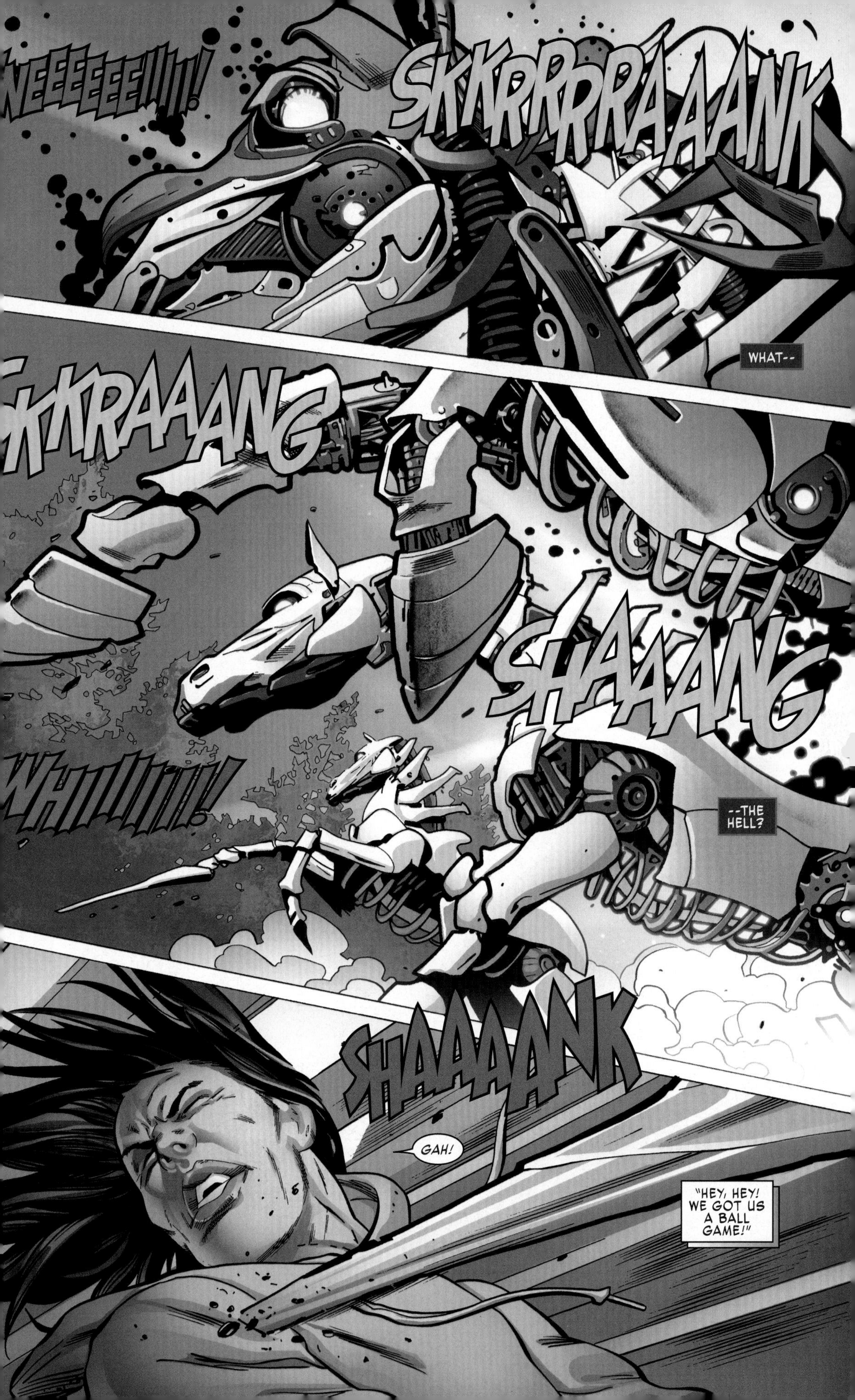
NEEEEEE!!!!!!!
SKKRRRRRAAANK
WHAT--
SKKRAAAANG
SHAAAANG
WHIIIIIII!
--THE HELL?
SHAAAANK
GAH!
"HEY, HEY! WE GOT US A BALL GAME!"

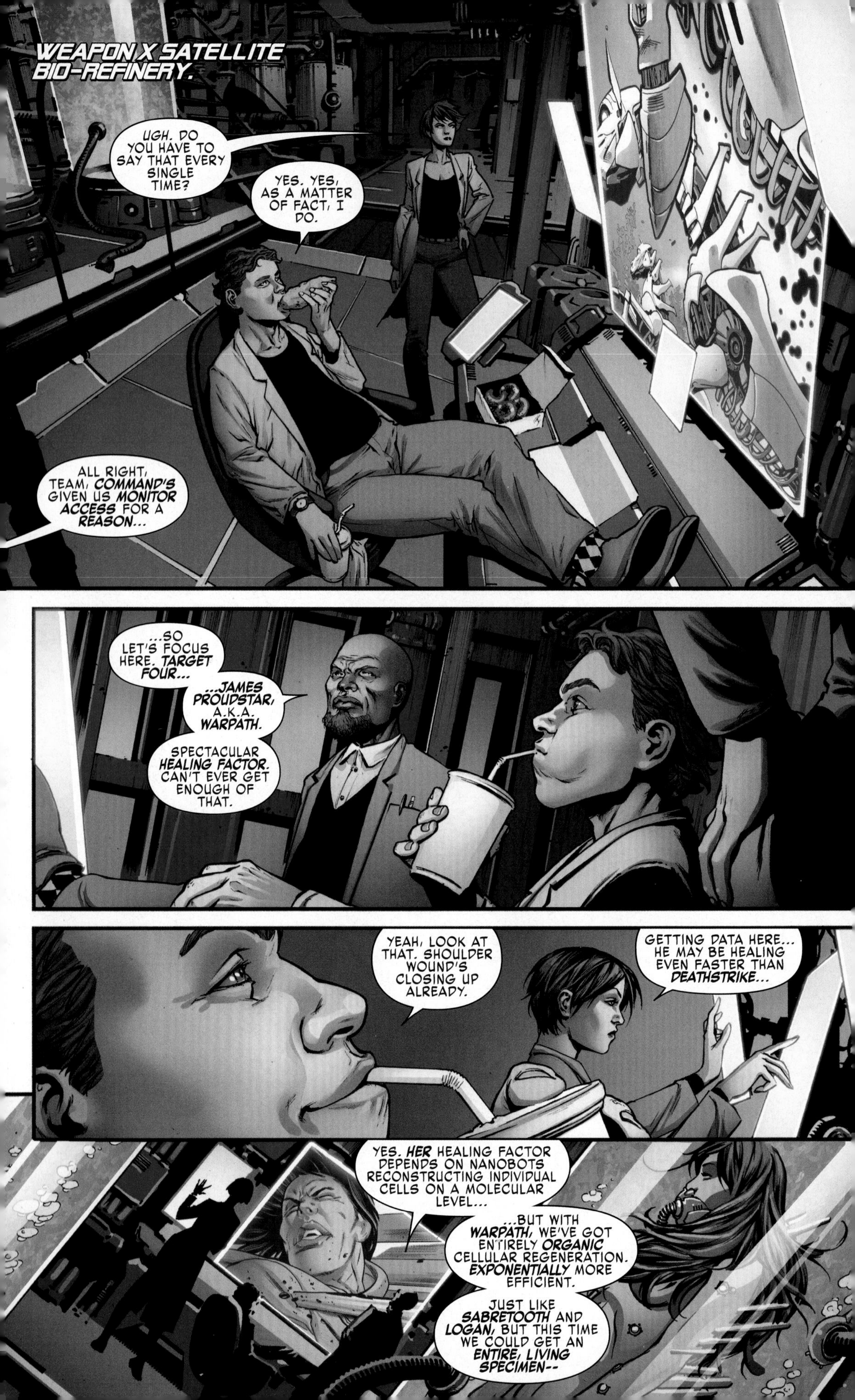
WEAPON X SATELLITE BIO-REFINERY.
UGH. DO YOU HAVE TO SAY THAT EVERY SINGLE TIME?
YES. YES, AS A MATTER OF FACT, I DO.
ALL RIGHT, TEAM, COMMAND'S GIVEN US MONITOR ACCESS FOR A REASON...
...SO LET'S FOCUS HERE. TARGET FOUR...
...JAMES PROUDSTAR, A.K.A. WARPATH.
SPECTACULAR HEALING FACTOR. CAN'T EVER GET ENOUGH OF THAT.
YEAH, LOOK AT THAT. SHOULDER WOUND'S CLOSING UP ALREADY.
GETTING DATA HERE... HE MAY BE HEALING EVEN FASTER THAN DEATHSTRIKE...
YES. HER HEALING FACTOR DEPENDS ON NANOBOTS RECONSTRUCTING INDIVIDUAL CELLS ON A MOLECULAR LEVEL...
...BUT WITH WARPATH, WE'VE GOT ENTIRELY ORGANIC CELLULAR REGENERATION. EXPONENTIALLY MORE EFFICIENT.
JUST LIKE SABRETOOTH AND LOGAN, BUT THIS TIME WE COULD GET AN ENTIRE, LIVING SPECIMEN--

GRRAAA!

SKRRAAAK

"WHOA! HE'S IN THE AIR!"

"YES. HE'S ALSO GOT TREMENDOUS **STRENGTH** AND **FLIGHT** POWERS..."

"...HUGE POTENTIAL HERE. BUT TOUGH TO **ISO** AND **EXTRACT**..."

"...SO WE'VE GOT A LOT OF WORK AHEAD OF US."

"I'M GONNA NEED EVERYONE TO WORK **DOUBLE SHIFTS.** TONIGHT'S AN **ALL-NIGHTER.**"

"WAIT A MINUTE, WHAT? THIS IS MY **CUSTODY DAY**--I'VE GOT TO PICK UP MY KID AT **FOUR.**"

"YEAH, AND WE'RE JUST PREPPING **ONE TANK,** RIGHT? THAT SHOULDN'T TAKE ALL NIGHT--"

"OH, NO NO NO..."

LOGAN   SABRETOOTH   WARRATH

...GOOD THINGS COME IN **THREES.**

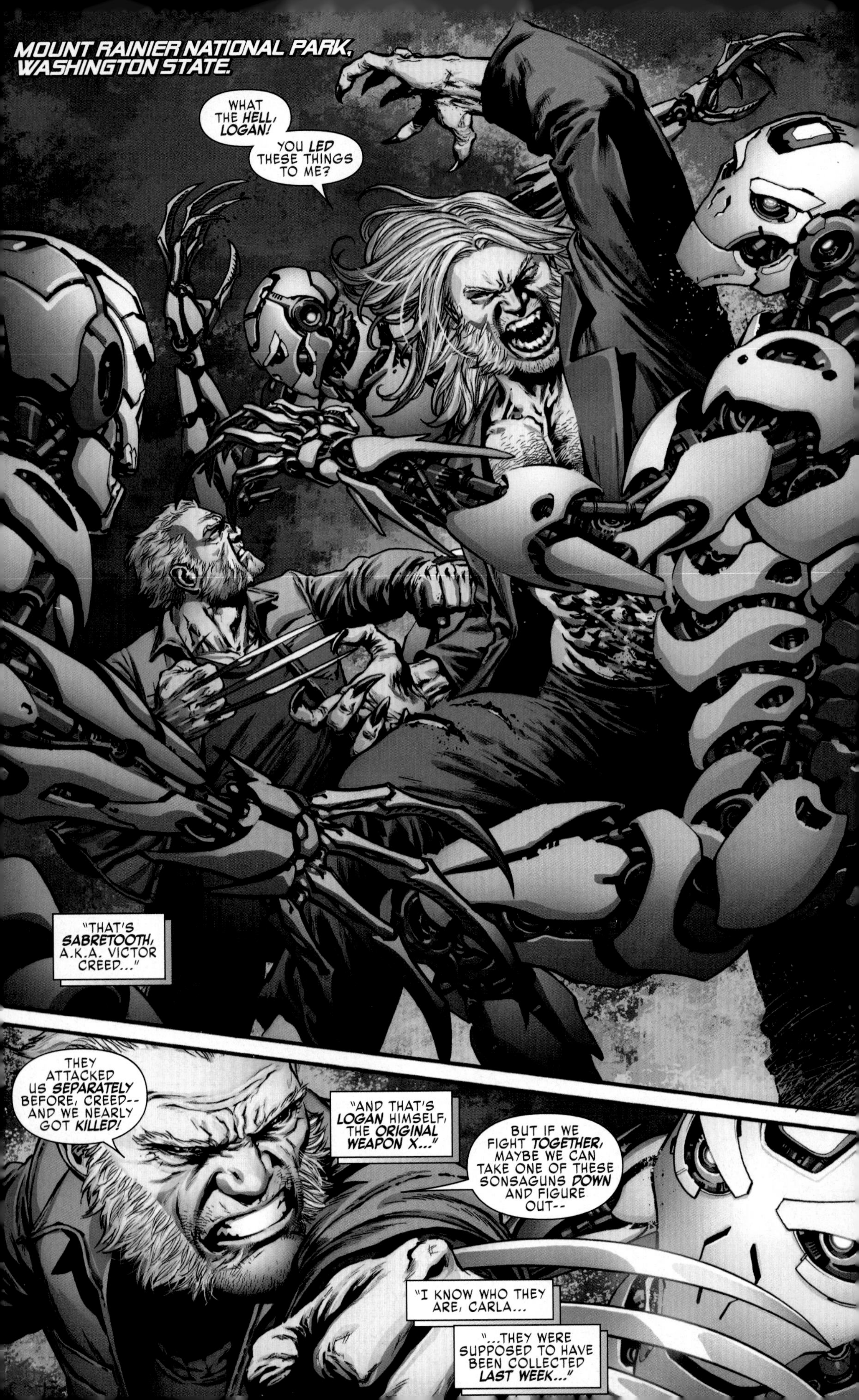
MOUNT RAINIER NATIONAL PARK, WASHINGTON STATE.
WHAT THE HELL, LOGAN!
YOU LED THESE THINGS TO ME?
"THAT'S SABRETOOTH, A.K.A. VICTOR CREED..."
THEY ATTACKED US SEPARATELY BEFORE, CREED--AND WE NEARLY GOT KILLED!
"AND THAT'S LOGAN HIMSELF, THE ORIGINAL WEAPON X..."
BUT IF WE FIGHT TOGETHER, MAYBE WE CAN TAKE ONE OF THESE SONSAGUNS DOWN AND FIGURE OUT--
"I KNOW WHO THEY ARE, CARLA...
"...THEY WERE SUPPOSED TO HAVE BEEN COLLECTED LAST WEEK..."

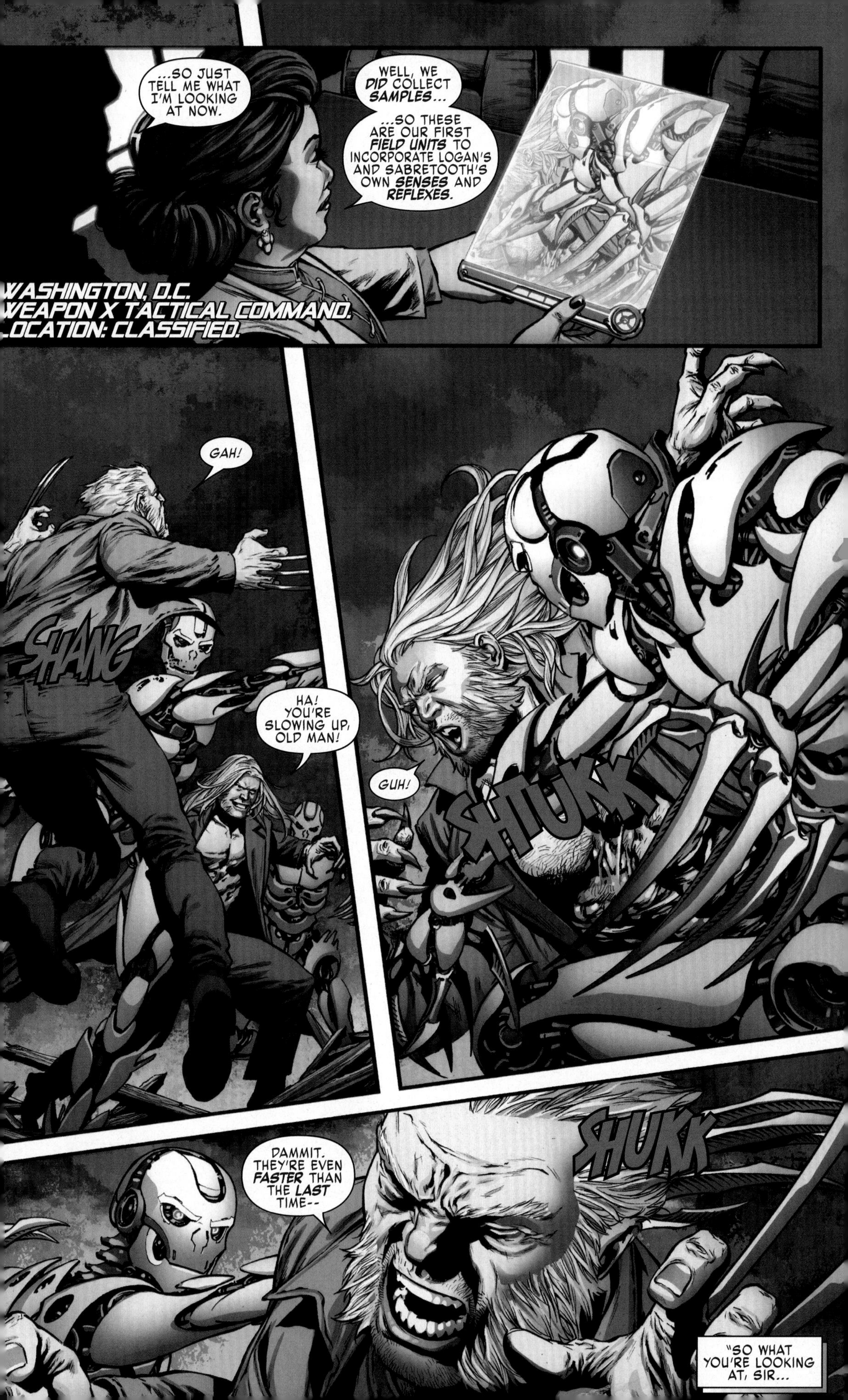
...SO JUST TELL ME WHAT I'M LOOKING AT NOW.
WELL, WE DID COLLECT SAMPLES...
...SO THESE ARE OUR FIRST FIELD UNITS TO INCORPORATE LOGAN'S AND SABRETOOTH'S OWN SENSES AND REFLEXES.
WASHINGTON, D.C.
WEAPON X TACTICAL COMMAND.
LOCATION: CLASSIFIED.
GAH!
SHANG
HA! YOU'RE SLOWING UP, OLD MAN!
GUH!
SHUKK
SHUKK
DAMMIT. THEY'RE EVEN FASTER THAN THE LAST TIME--
"SO WHAT YOU'RE LOOKING AT, SIR...

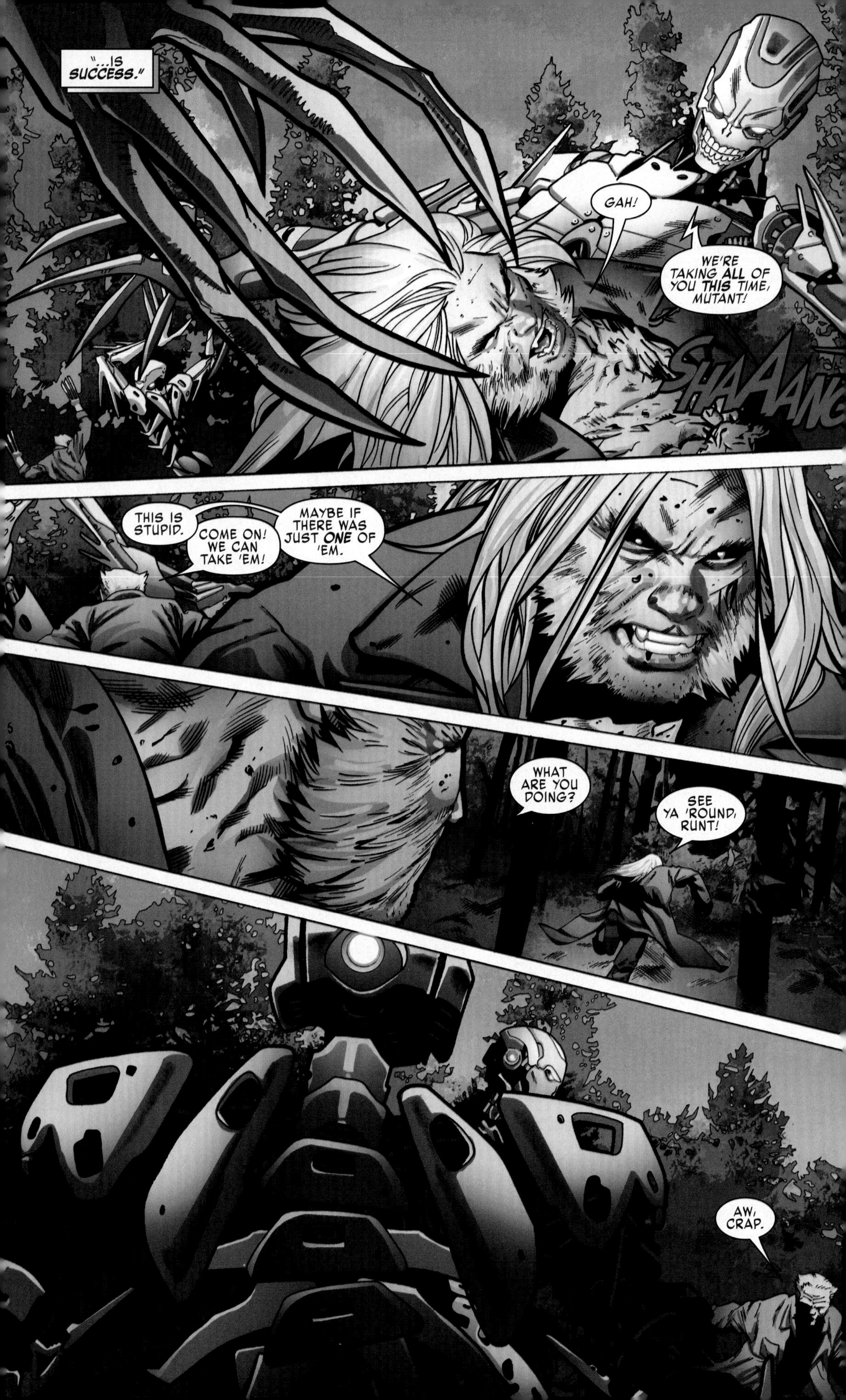
"...IS SUCCESS."
GAH!
WE'RE TAKING ALL OF YOU THIS TIME, MUTANT!
SHAAANG
THIS IS STUPID.
COME ON! WE CAN TAKE 'EM!
MAYBE IF THERE WAS JUST ONE OF 'EM.
WHAT ARE YOU DOING?
SEE YA 'ROUND, RUNT!
AW, CRAP.

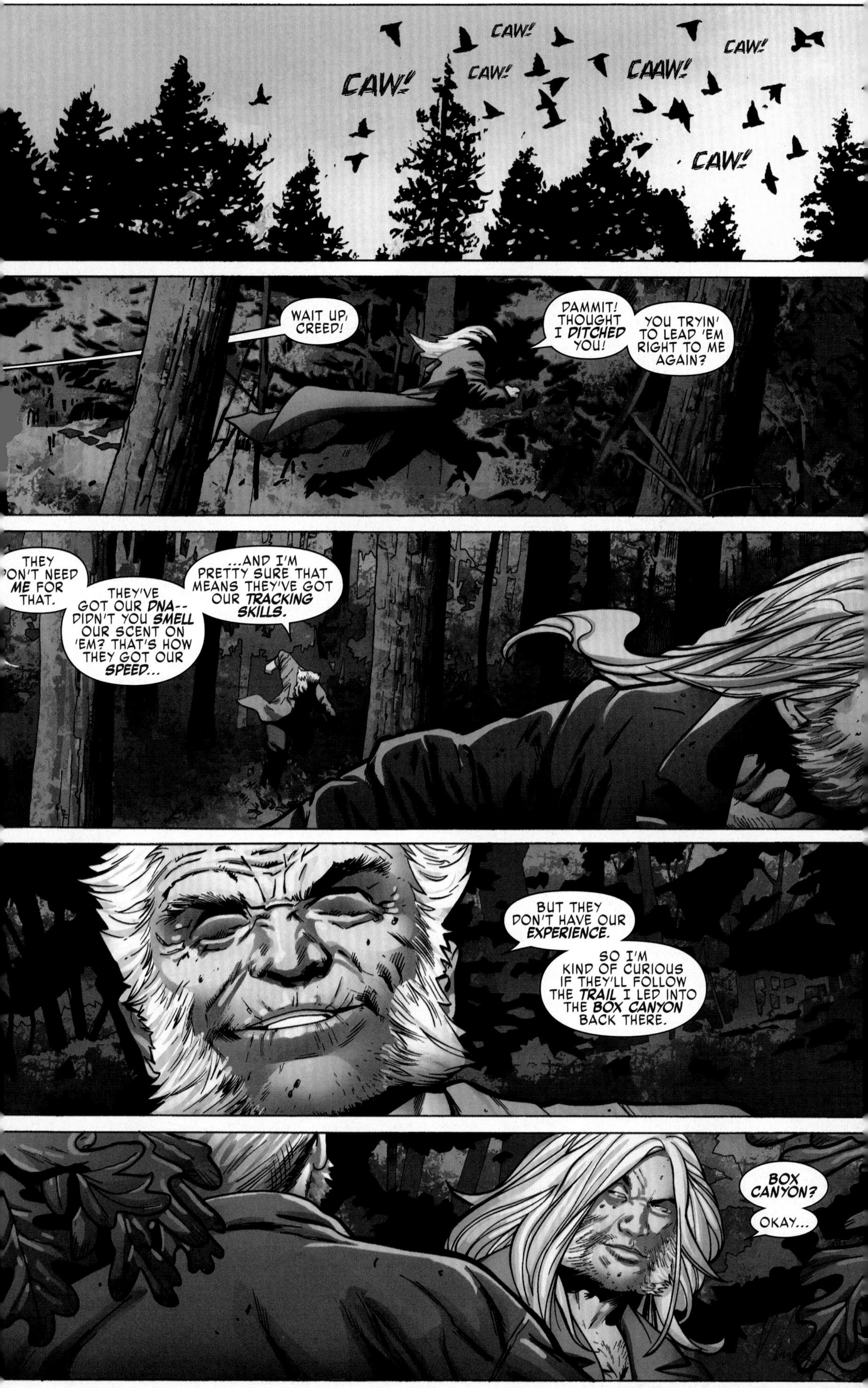
CAW!
CAW!
CAW!
CAAW!
CAW!
CAW!
WAIT UP, CREED!
DAMMIT! THOUGHT I DITCHED YOU!
YOU TRYIN' TO LEAD 'EM RIGHT TO ME AGAIN?
THEY DON'T NEED ME FOR THAT.
THEY'VE GOT OUR DNA-- DIDN'T YOU SMELL OUR SCENT ON 'EM? THAT'S HOW THEY GOT OUR SPEED...
...AND I'M PRETTY SURE THAT MEANS THEY'VE GOT OUR TRACKING SKILLS.
BUT THEY DON'T HAVE OUR EXPERIENCE.
SO I'M KIND OF CURIOUS IF THEY'LL FOLLOW THE TRAIL I LED INTO THE BOX CANYON BACK THERE.
BOX CANYON?
OKAY...

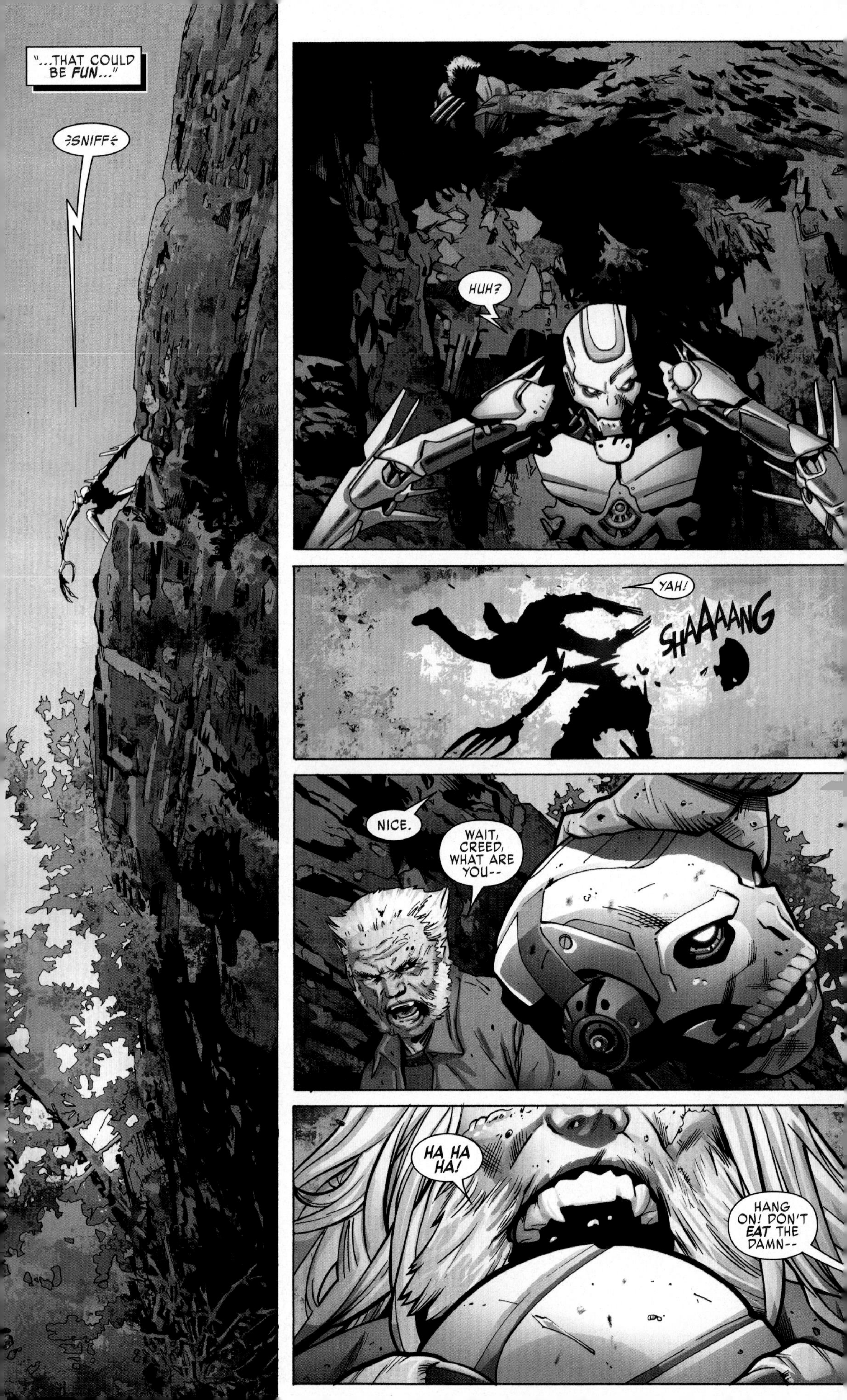
"...THAT COULD BE FUN..."
SNIFF
HUH?
YAH!
SHAAAANG
NICE.
WAIT, CREED, WHAT ARE YOU--
HA HA HA!
HANG ON! DON'T EAT THE DAMN--

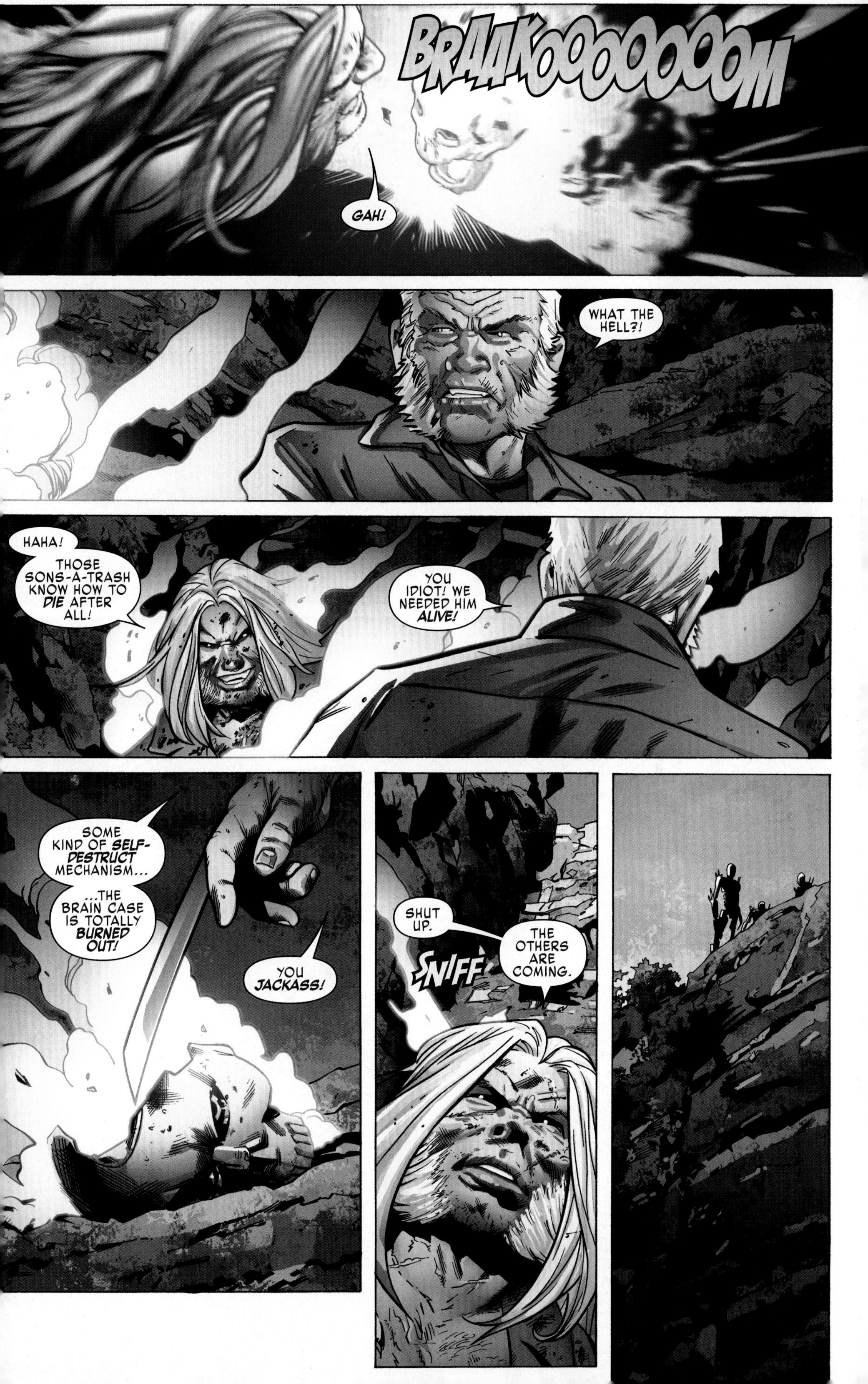
BRAAKOOOOOOOM
GAH!
WHAT THE HELL?!
HAHA! THOSE SONS-A-TRASH KNOW HOW TO DIE AFTER ALL!
YOU IDIOT! WE NEEDED HIM ALIVE!
SOME KIND OF SELF-DESTRUCT MECHANISM...
...THE BRAIN CASE IS TOTALLY BURNED OUT!
YOU JACKASS!
SHUT UP.
THE OTHERS ARE COMING.
SNIFF

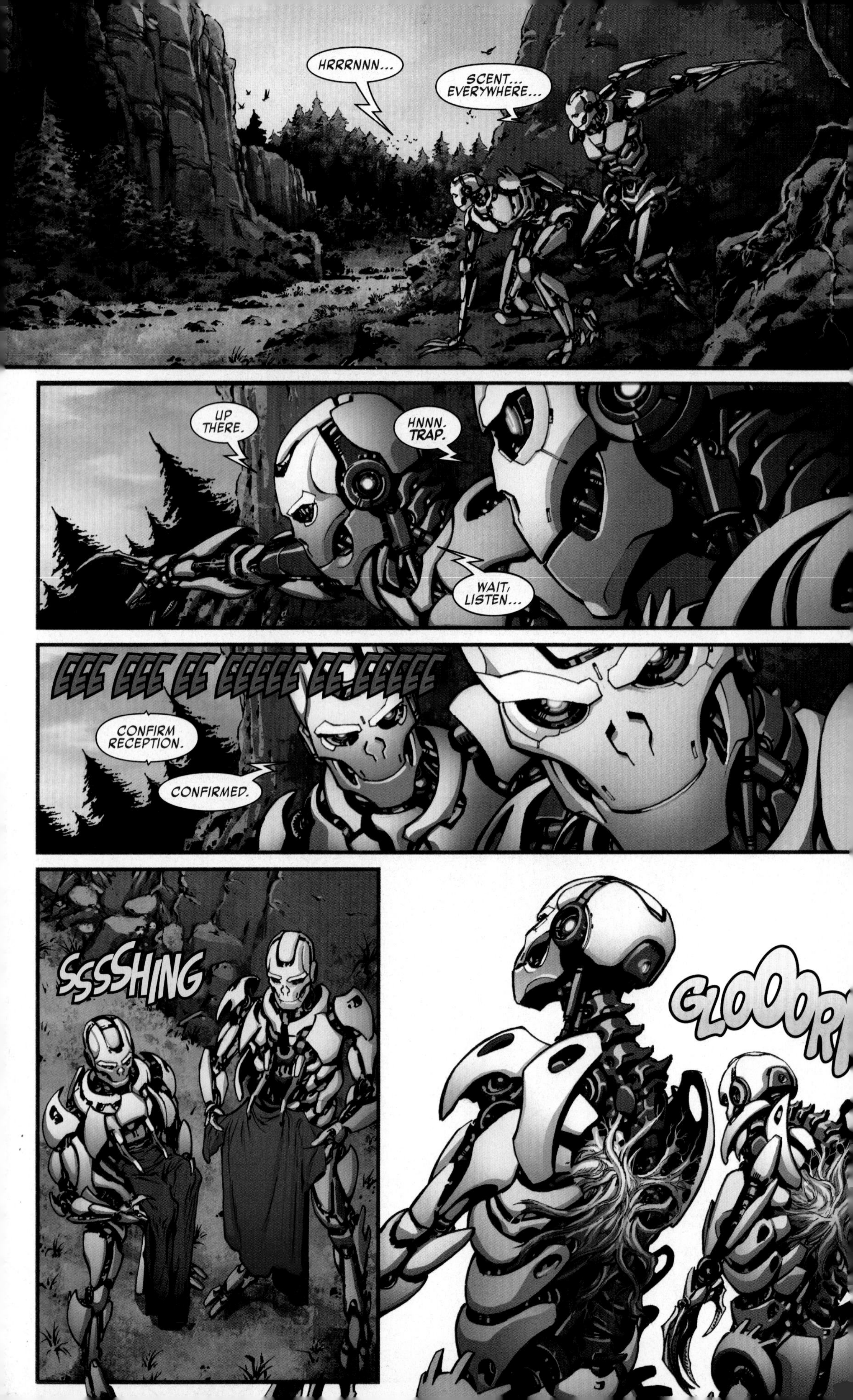
HRRRNNN...
SCENT... EVERYWHERE...
UP THERE.
HNNN. TRAP.
WAIT, LISTEN...
EEE EEE EE EEEEE EE EEEEE
CONFIRM RECEPTION.
CONFIRMED.
SSSSHING
GLOOOR

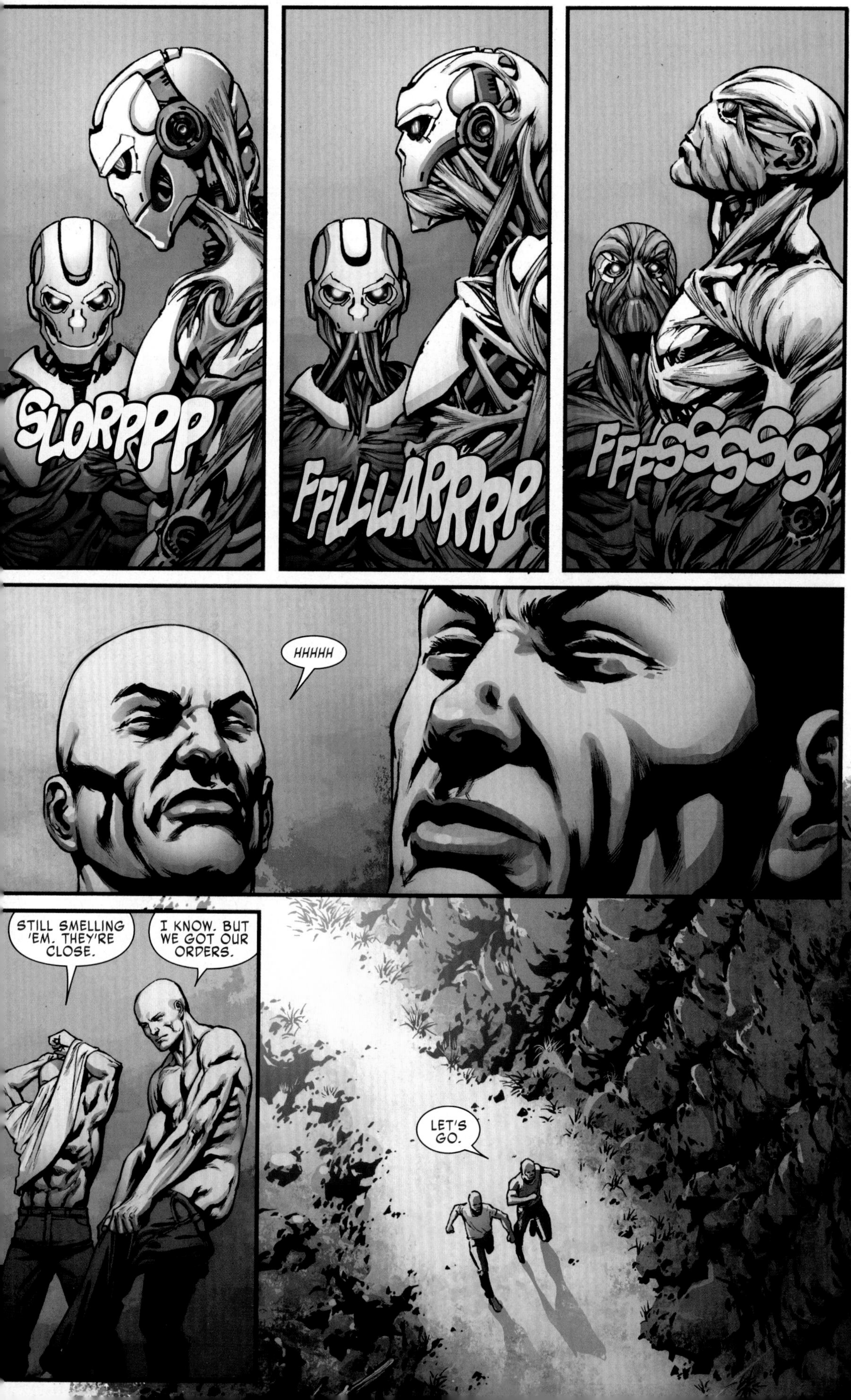
SLORPPP
FFLLLARRRP
FFFSSSSSS
HHHHH
STILL SMELLING 'EM. THEY'RE CLOSE.
I KNOW. BUT WE GOT OUR ORDERS.
LET'S GO.

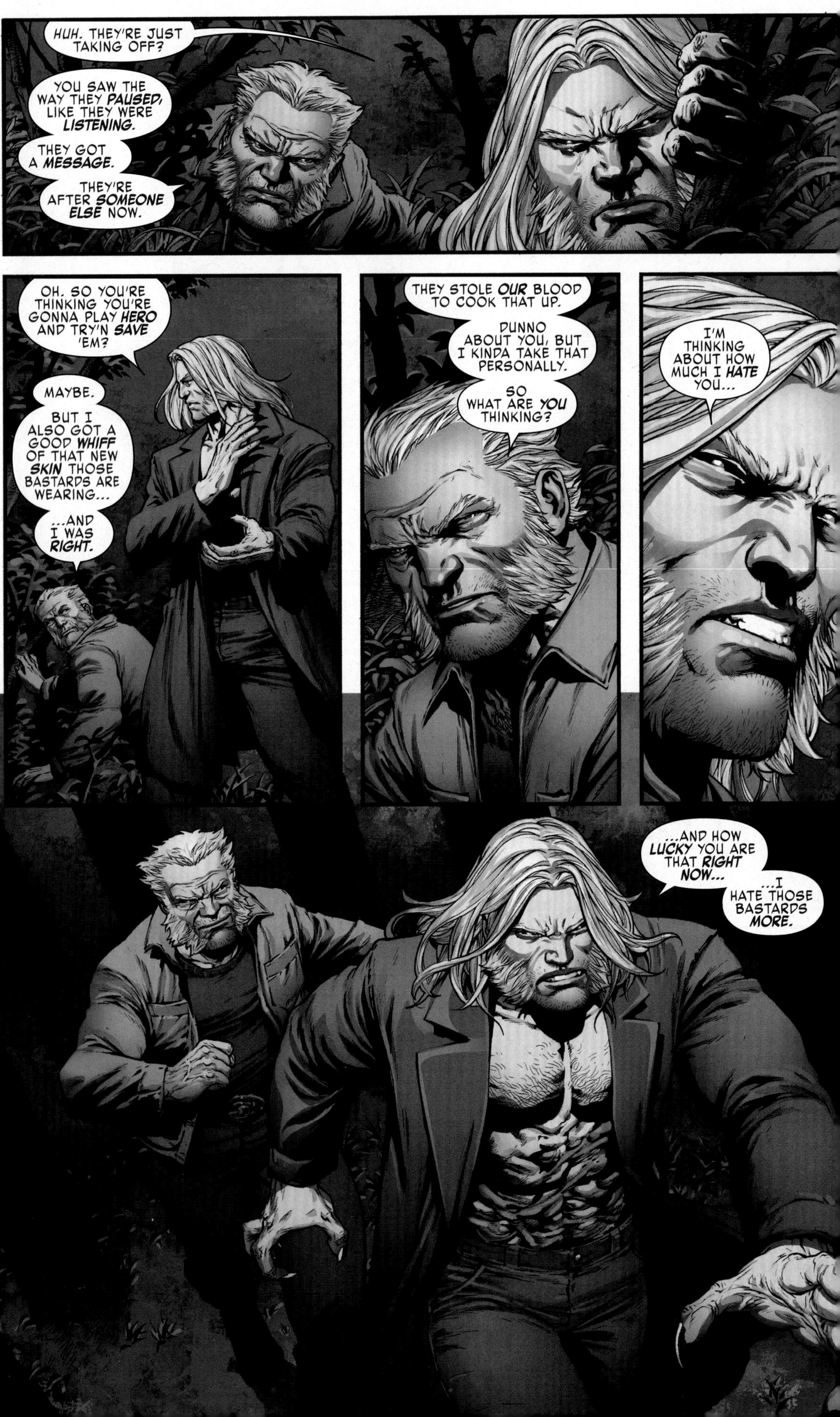
HUH. THEY'RE JUST TAKING OFF?
YOU SAW THE WAY THEY PAUSED, LIKE THEY WERE LISTENING.
THEY GOT A MESSAGE.
THEY'RE AFTER SOMEONE ELSE NOW.
OH. SO YOU'RE THINKING YOU'RE GONNA PLAY HERO AND TRY'N SAVE 'EM?
MAYBE.
BUT I ALSO GOT A GOOD WHIFF OF THAT NEW SKIN THOSE BASTARDS ARE WEARING...
...AND I WAS RIGHT.
THEY STOLE OUR BLOOD TO COOK THAT UP.
DUNNO ABOUT YOU, BUT I KINDA TAKE THAT PERSONALLY.
SO WHAT ARE YOU THINKING?
I'M THINKING ABOUT HOW MUCH I HATE YOU...
...AND HOW LUCKY YOU ARE THAT RIGHT NOW...
...I HATE THOSE BASTARDS MORE.

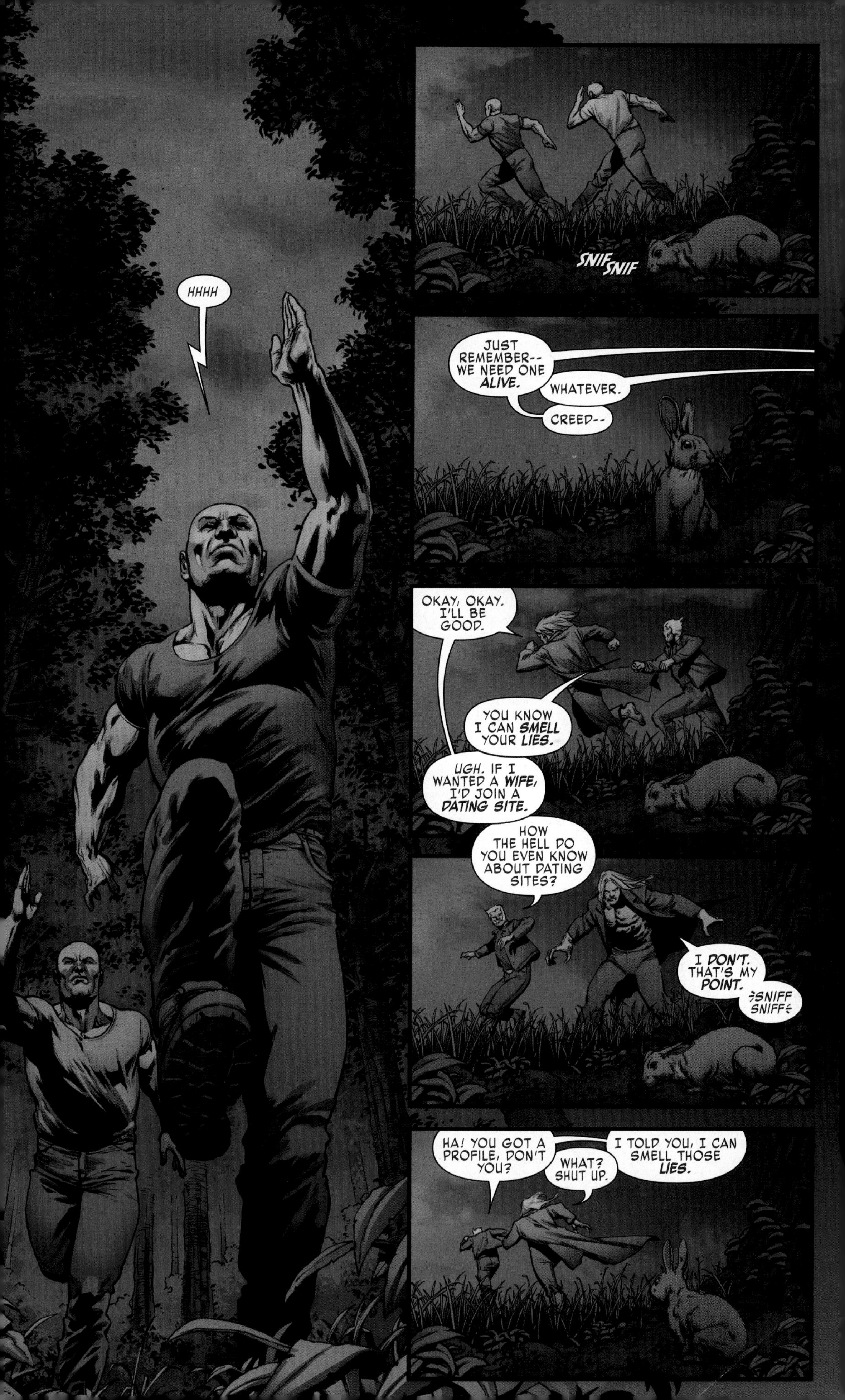
HHHH
SNIF SNIF
JUST REMEMBER-- WE NEED ONE ALIVE.
WHATEVER.
CREED--
OKAY, OKAY. I'LL BE GOOD.
YOU KNOW I CAN SMELL YOUR LIES.
UGH. IF I WANTED A WIFE, I'D JOIN A DATING SITE.
HOW THE HELL DO YOU EVEN KNOW ABOUT DATING SITES?
I DON'T. THAT'S MY POINT.
SNIFF SNIFF
HA! YOU GOT A PROFILE, DON'T YOU?
WHAT? SHUT UP.
I TOLD YOU, I CAN SMELL THOSE LIES.

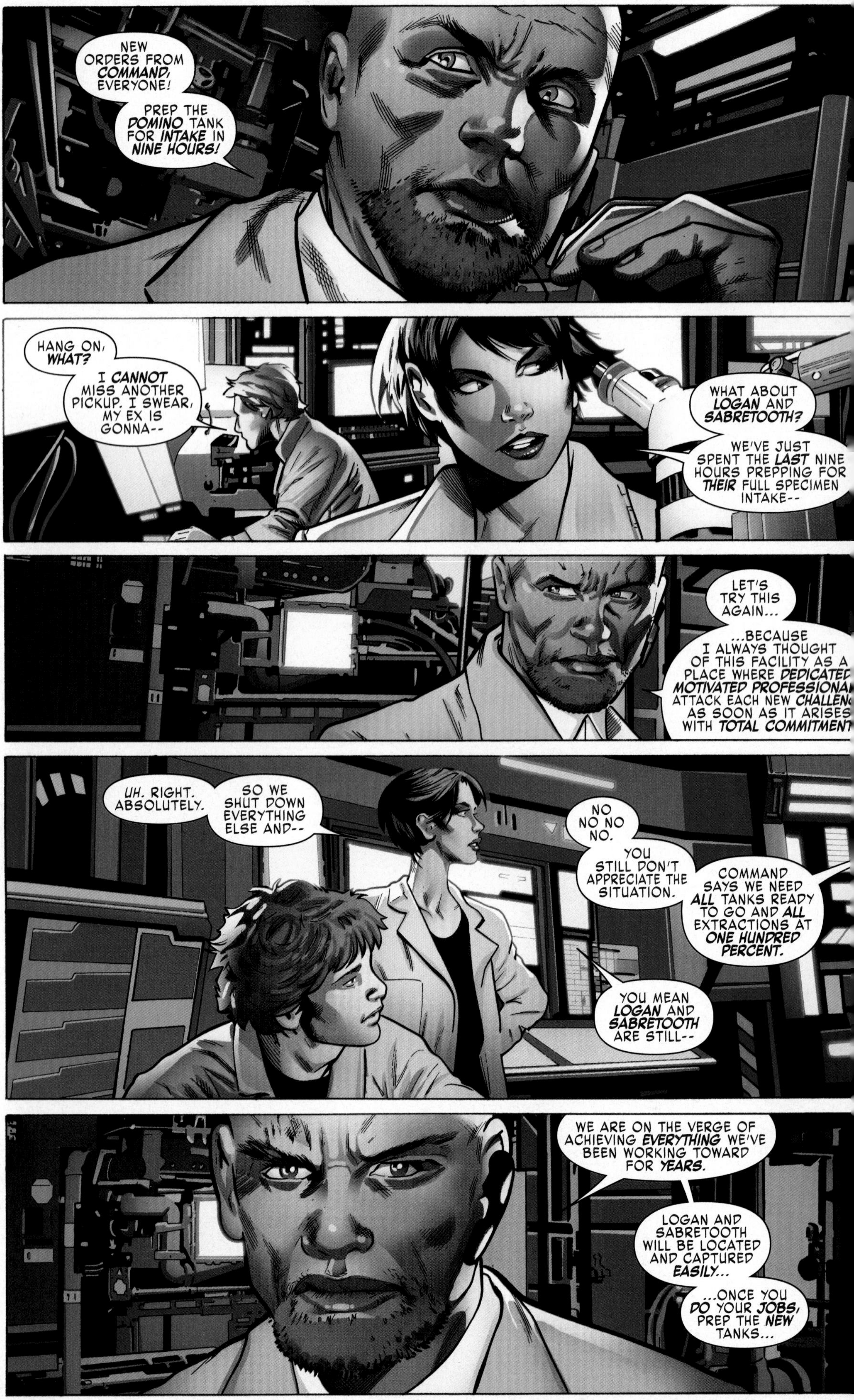

NEW ORDERS FROM COMMAND, EVERYONE!
PREP THE DOMINO TANK FOR INTAKE IN NINE HOURS!
HANG ON, WHAT?
I CANNOT MISS ANOTHER PICKUP. I SWEAR, MY EX IS GONNA--
WHAT ABOUT LOGAN AND SABRETOOTH?
WE'VE JUST SPENT THE LAST NINE HOURS PREPPING FOR THEIR FULL SPECIMEN INTAKE--
LET'S TRY THIS AGAIN...
...BECAUSE I ALWAYS THOUGHT OF THIS FACILITY AS A PLACE WHERE DEDICATED MOTIVATED PROFESSIONAL ATTACK EACH NEW CHALLEN AS SOON AS IT ARISES WITH TOTAL COMMITMENT
UH. RIGHT. ABSOLUTELY.
SO WE SHUT DOWN EVERYTHING ELSE AND--
NO NO NO NO.
YOU STILL DON'T APPRECIATE THE SITUATION.
COMMAND SAYS WE NEED ALL TANKS READY TO GO AND ALL EXTRACTIONS AT ONE HUNDRED PERCENT.
YOU MEAN LOGAN AND SABRETOOTH ARE STILL--
WE ARE ON THE VERGE OF ACHIEVING EVERYTHING WE'VE BEEN WORKING TOWARD FOR YEARS.
LOGAN AND SABRETOOTH WILL BE LOCATED AND CAPTURED EASILY...
...ONCE YOU DO YOUR JOBS, PREP THE NEW TANKS...

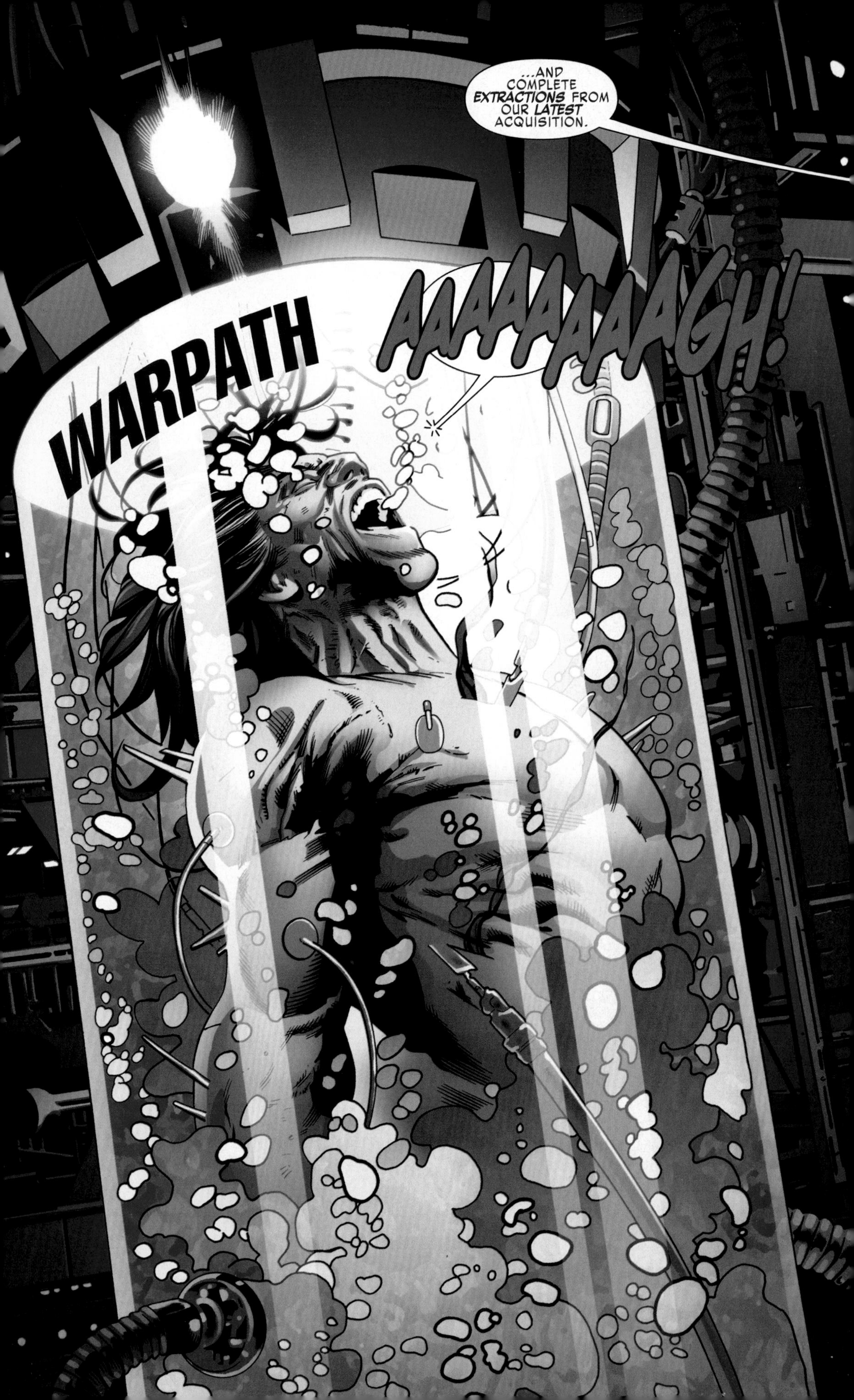
...AND COMPLETE EXTRACTIONS FROM OUR LATEST ACQUISITION.
WARPATH
AAAAAAAAGH!

3

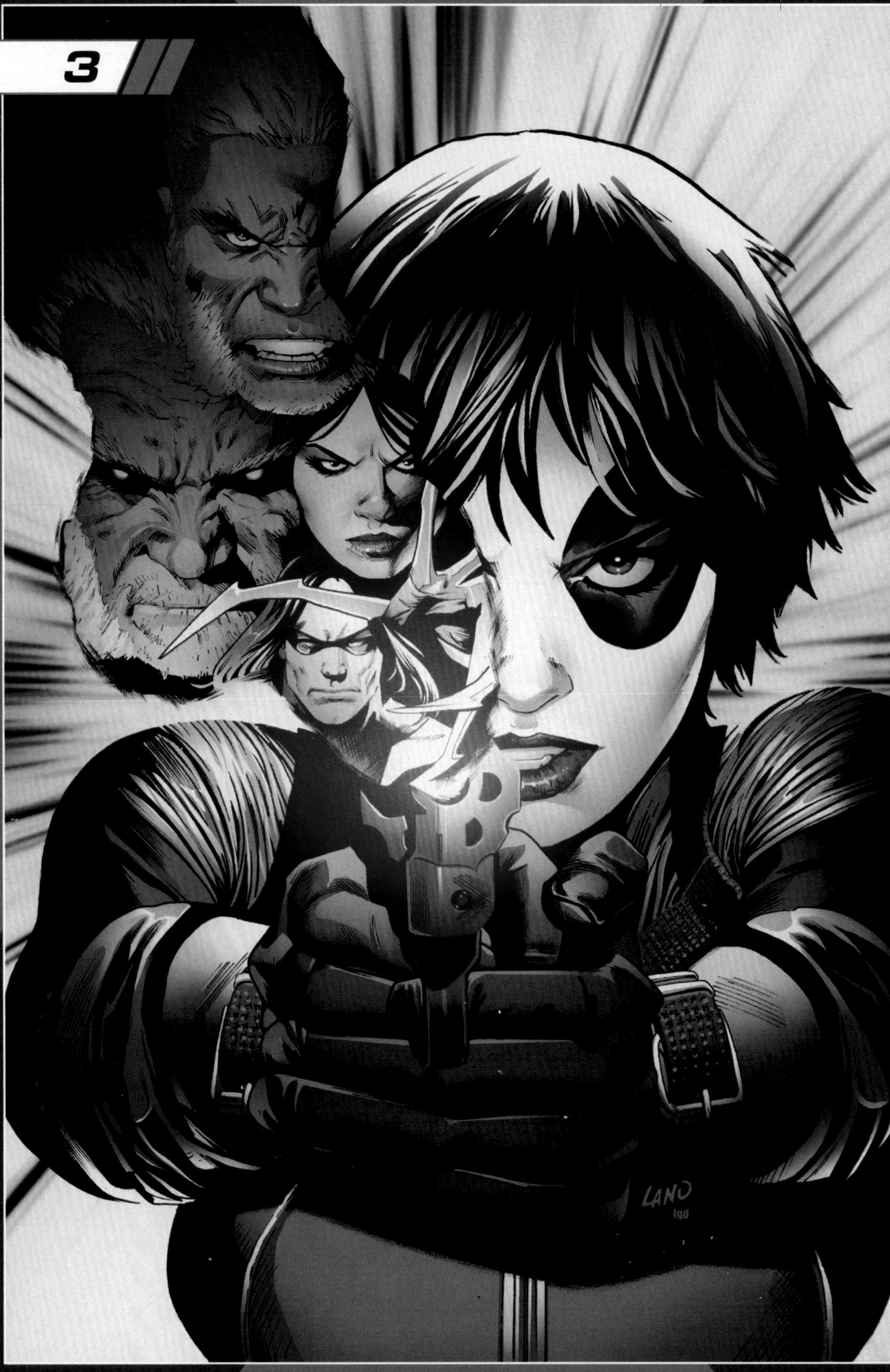

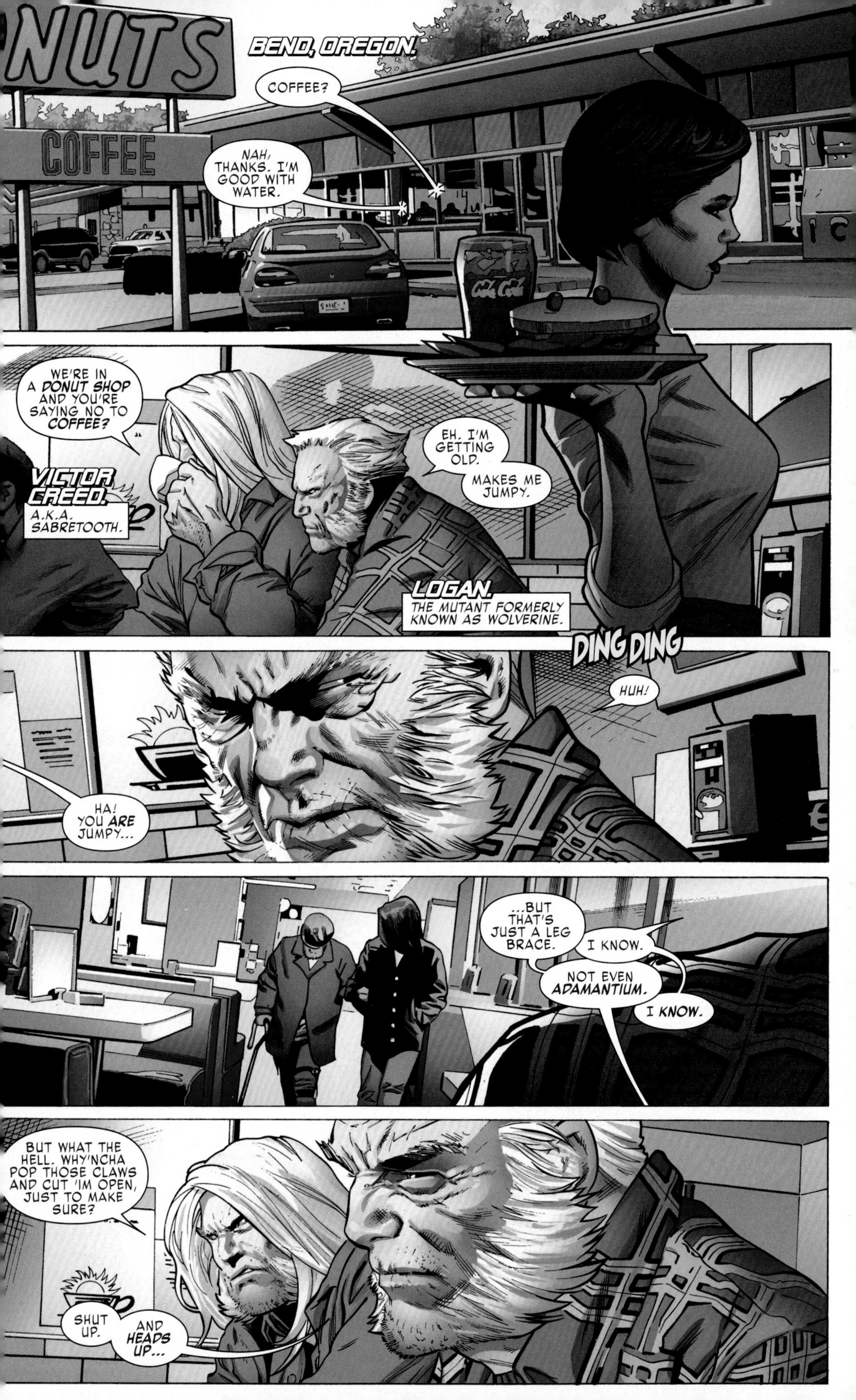

BEND, OREGON.
COFFEE?
NAH, THANKS. I'M GOOD WITH WATER.
WE'RE IN A DONUT SHOP AND YOU'RE SAYING NO TO COFFEE?
VICTOR CREED.
A.K.A. SABRETOOTH.
EH. I'M GETTING OLD.
MAKES ME JUMPY.
LOGAN.
THE MUTANT FORMERLY KNOWN AS WOLVERINE.
DING DING
HUH!
HA! YOU ARE JUMPY...
...BUT THAT'S JUST A LEG BRACE.
I KNOW.
NOT EVEN ADAMANTIUM.
I KNOW.
BUT WHAT THE HELL. WHY'NCHA POP THOSE CLAWS AND CUT 'IM OPEN, JUST TO MAKE SURE?
SHUT UP.
AND HEADS UP...

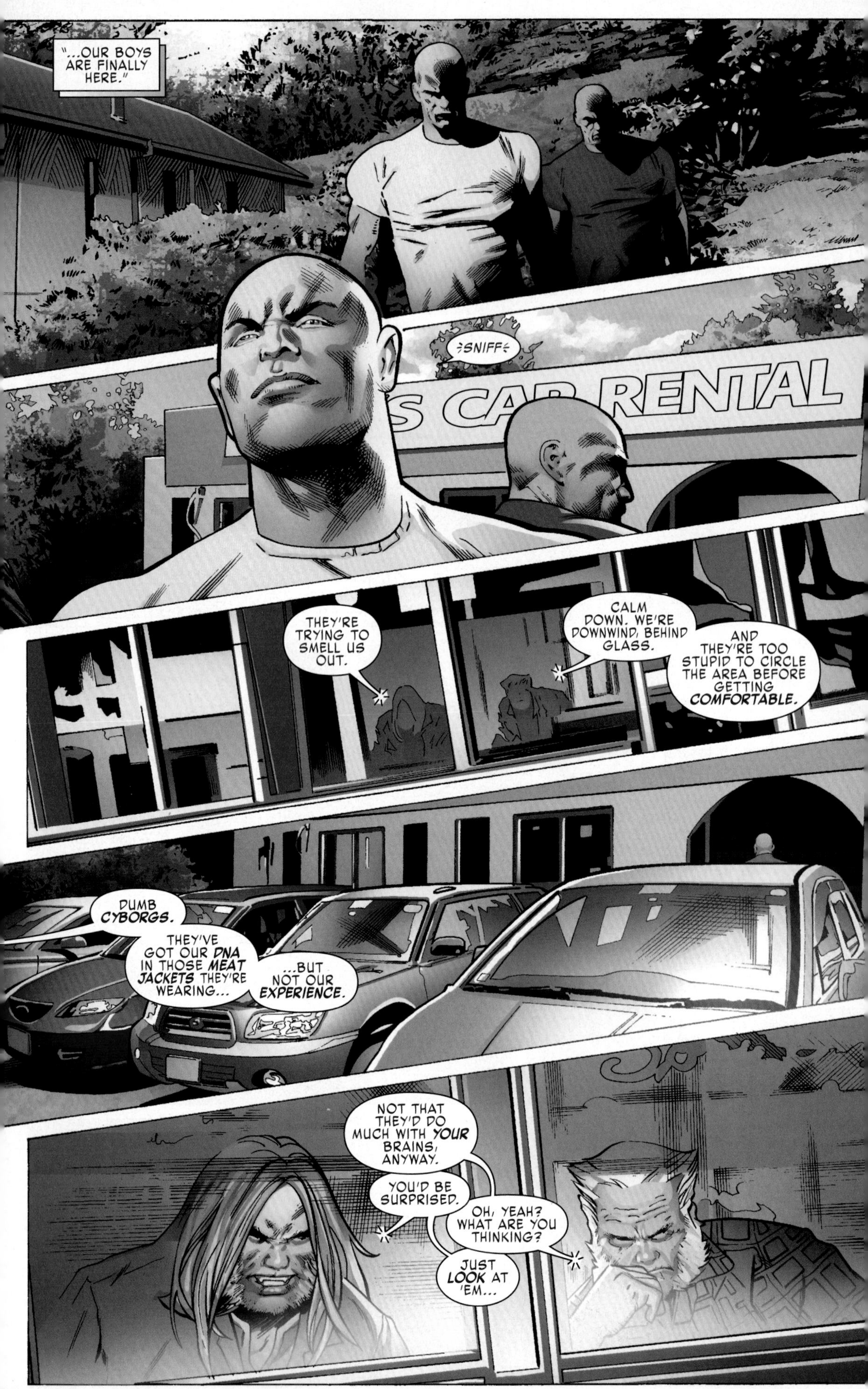
"...OUR BOYS ARE FINALLY HERE."
SNIFF
S CAR RENTAL
THEY'RE TRYING TO SMELL US OUT.
CALM DOWN. WE'RE DOWNWIND, BEHIND GLASS.
AND THEY'RE TOO STUPID TO CIRCLE THE AREA BEFORE GETTING COMFORTABLE.
DUMB CYBORGS.
THEY'VE GOT OUR DNA IN THOSE MEAT JACKETS THEY'RE WEARING...
...BUT NOT OUR EXPERIENCE.
NOT THAT THEY'D DO MUCH WITH YOUR BRAINS, ANYWAY.
YOU'D BE SURPRISED.
OH, YEAH? WHAT ARE YOU THINKING?
JUST LOOK AT 'EM...

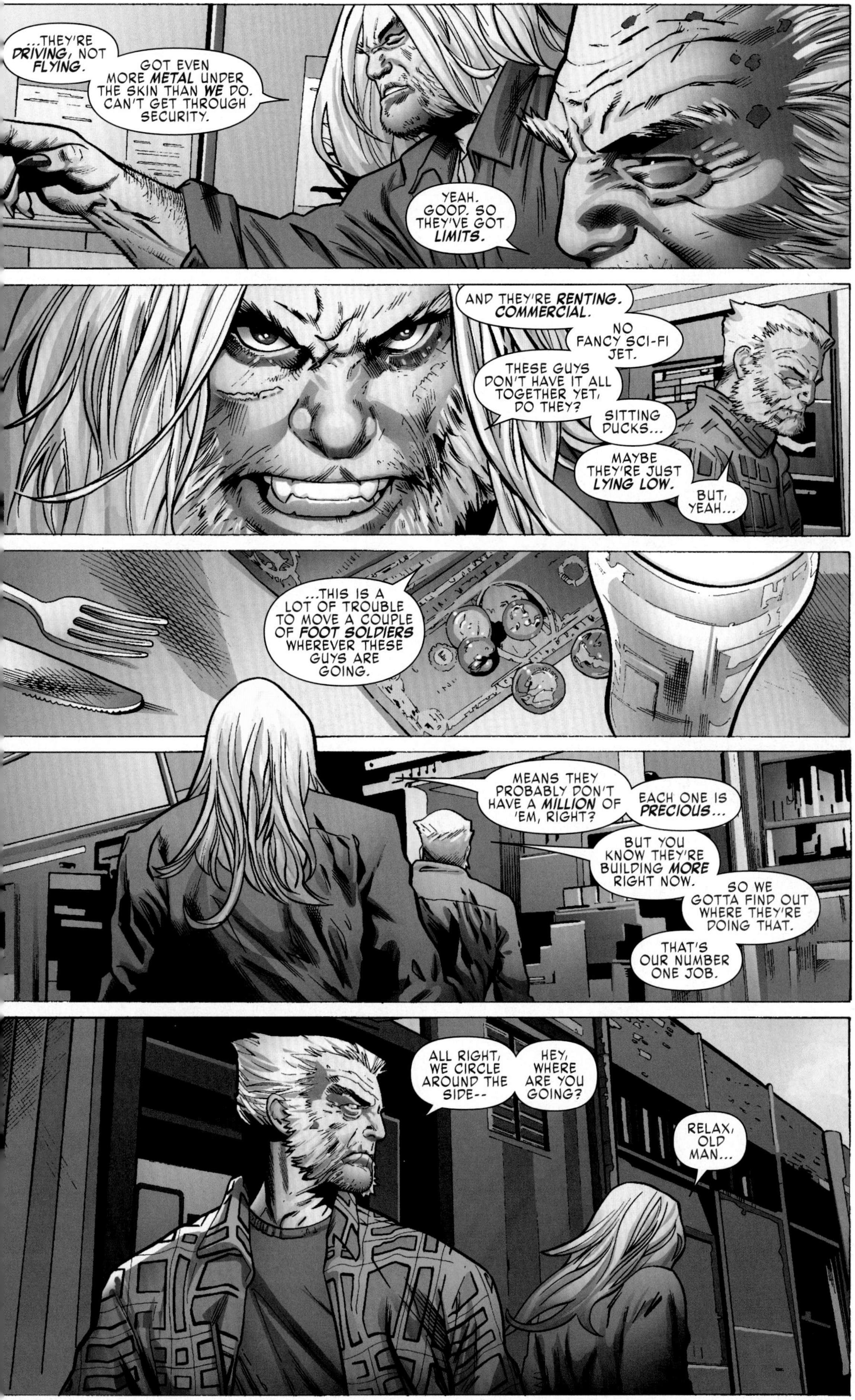
...THEY'RE DRIVING, NOT FLYING.
GOT EVEN MORE METAL UNDER THE SKIN THAN WE DO. CAN'T GET THROUGH SECURITY.
YEAH. GOOD. SO THEY'VE GOT LIMITS.
AND THEY'RE RENTING. COMMERCIAL.
NO FANCY SCI-FI JET.
THESE GUYS DON'T HAVE IT ALL TOGETHER YET, DO THEY?
SITTING DUCKS...
MAYBE THEY'RE JUST LYING LOW.
BUT, YEAH...
...THIS IS A LOT OF TROUBLE TO MOVE A COUPLE OF FOOT SOLDIERS WHEREVER THESE GUYS ARE GOING.
MEANS THEY PROBABLY DON'T HAVE A MILLION OF 'EM, RIGHT?
EACH ONE IS PRECIOUS...
BUT YOU KNOW THEY'RE BUILDING MORE RIGHT NOW.
SO WE GOTTA FIND OUT WHERE THEY'RE DOING THAT.
THAT'S OUR NUMBER ONE JOB.
ALL RIGHT, WE CIRCLE AROUND THE SIDE--
HEY, WHERE ARE YOU GOING?
RELAX, OLD MAN...

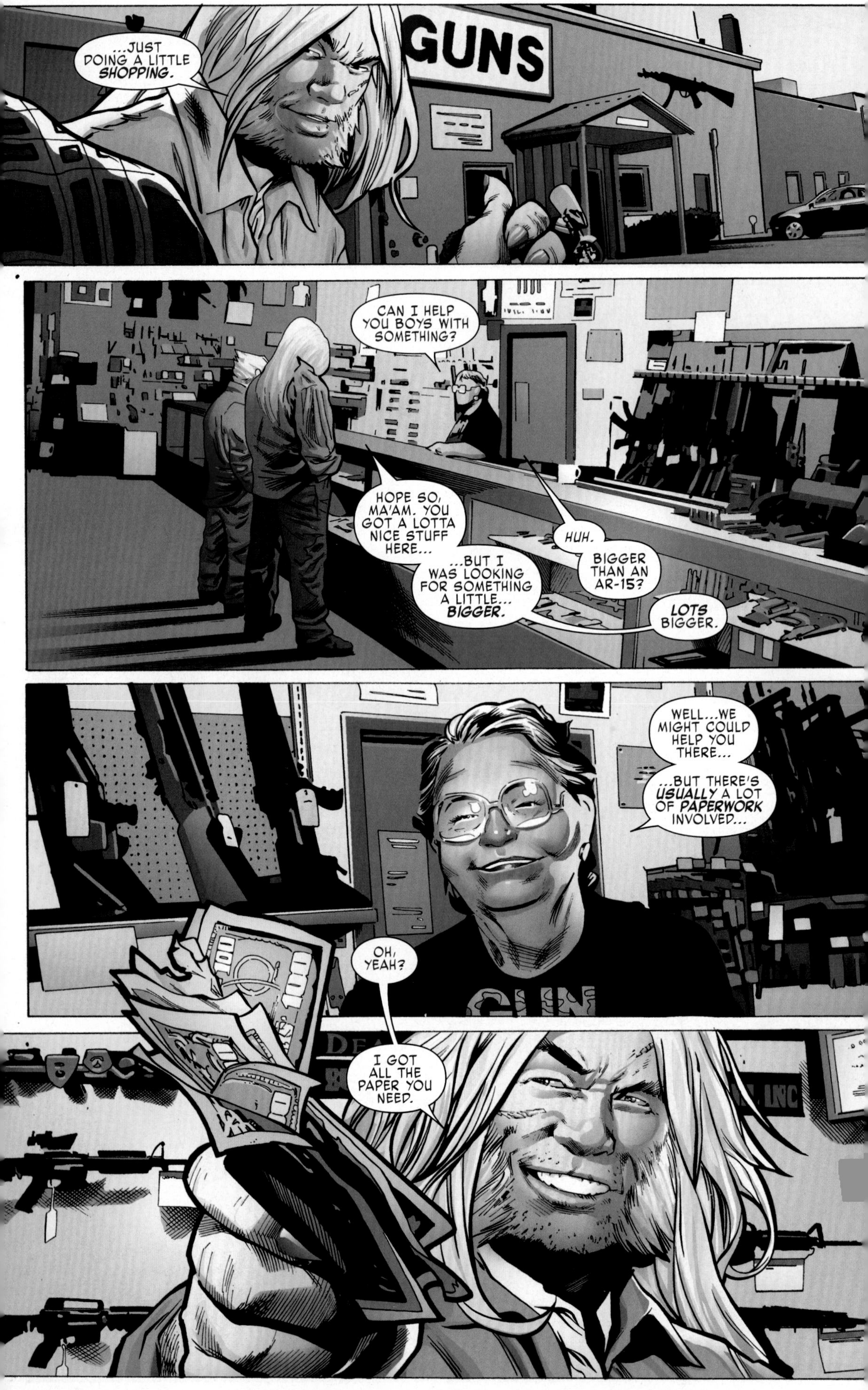
...JUST DOING A LITTLE SHOPPING.
GUNS
CAN I HELP YOU BOYS WITH SOMETHING?
HOPE SO, MA'AM. YOU GOT A LOTTA NICE STUFF HERE...
...BUT I WAS LOOKING FOR SOMETHING A LITTLE... BIGGER.
HUH.
BIGGER THAN AN AR-15?
LOTS BIGGER.
WELL...WE MIGHT COULD HELP YOU THERE...
...BUT THERE'S USUALLY A LOT OF PAPERWORK INVOLVED...
GUN
OH, YEAH?
I GOT ALL THE PAPER YOU NEED.

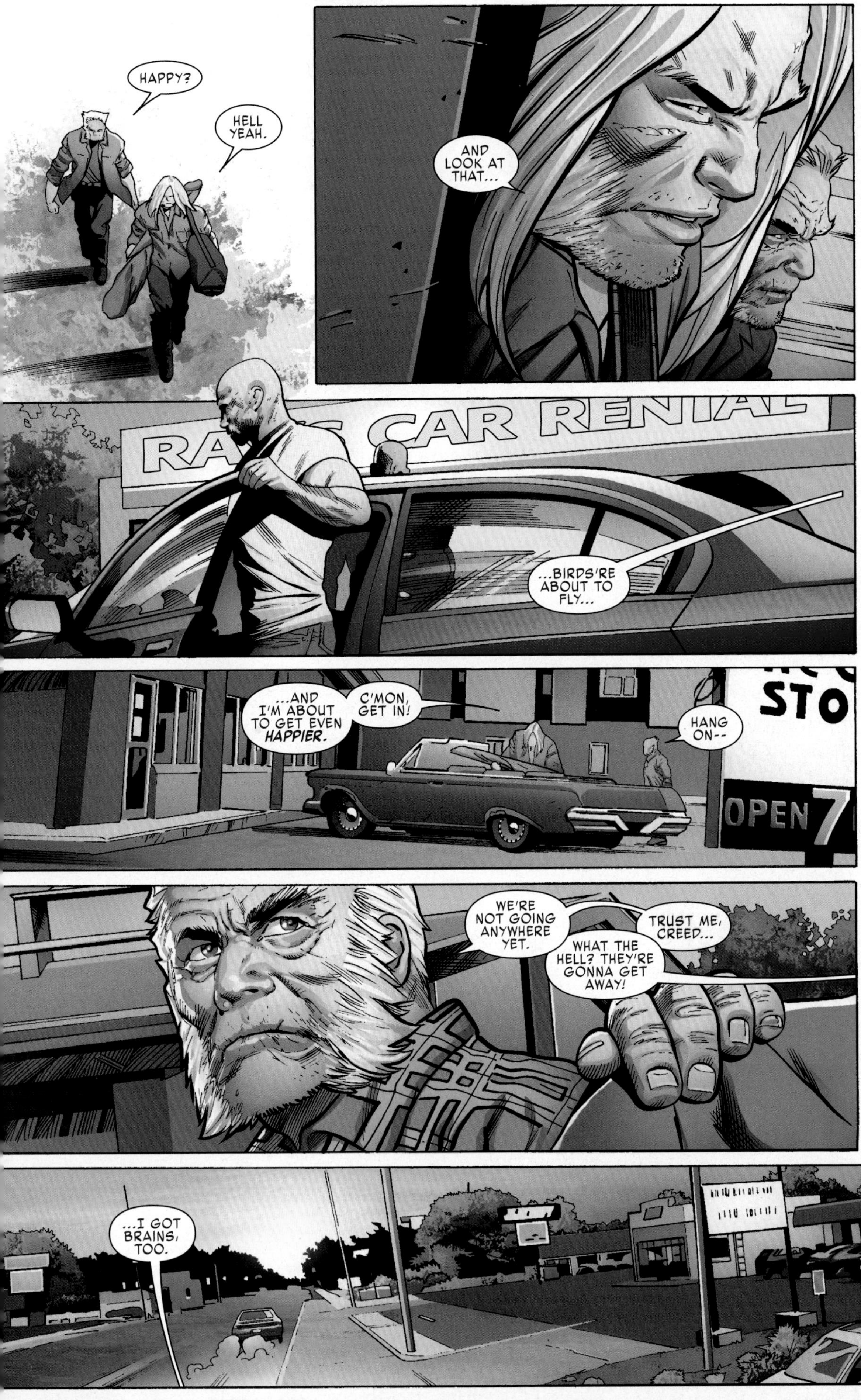
HAPPY?
HELL YEAH.
AND LOOK AT THAT...
RA CAR RENTAL
...BIRDS'RE ABOUT TO FLY...
...AND I'M ABOUT TO GET EVEN *HAPPIER.*
C'MON, GET IN!
HANG ON--
STO
OPEN 7
WE'RE NOT GOING ANYWHERE YET.
WHAT THE HELL? THEY'RE GONNA GET AWAY!
TRUST ME, CREED...
...I GOT BRAINS, TOO.

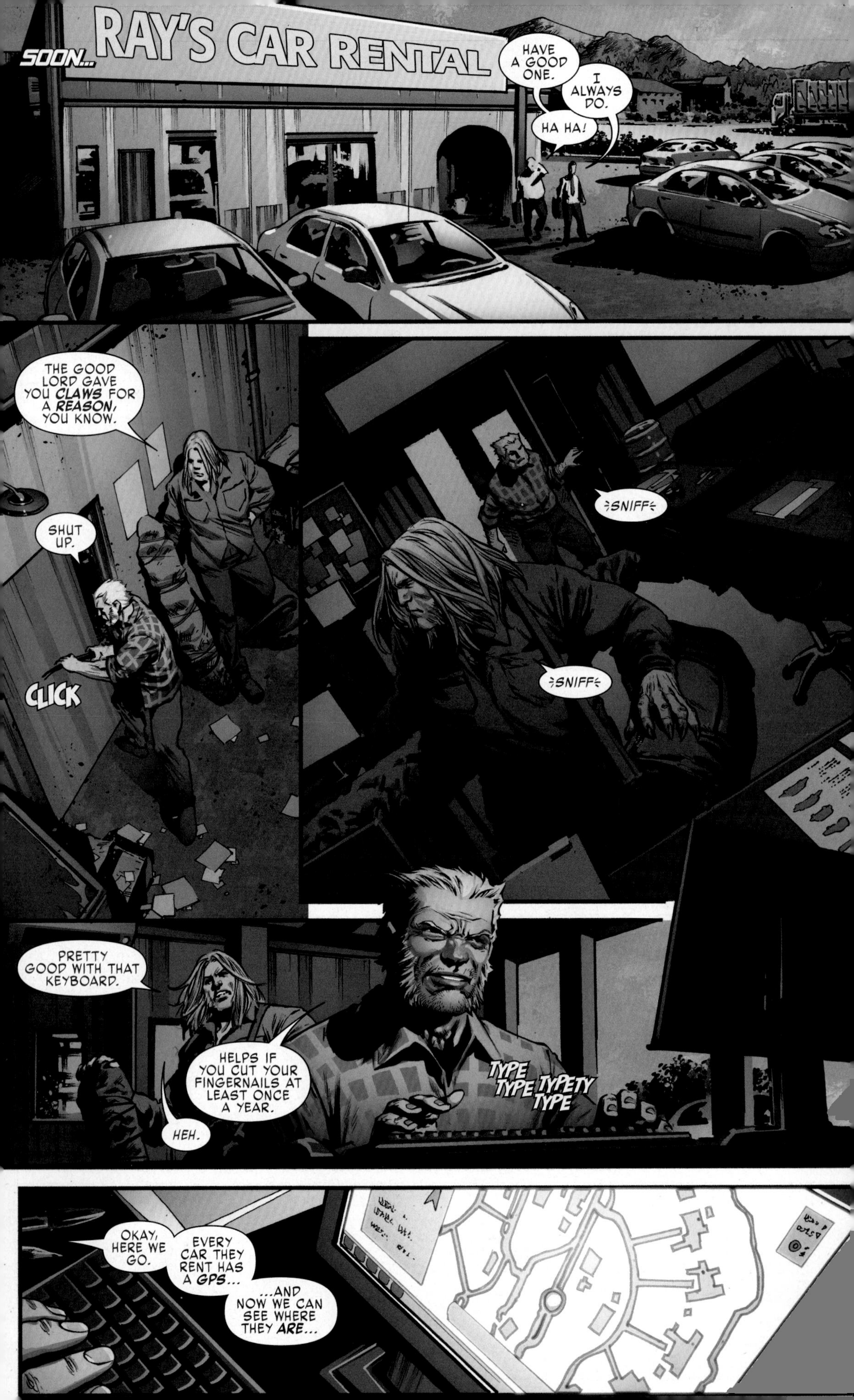
SOON...
RAY'S CAR RENTAL
HAVE A GOOD ONE.
I ALWAYS DO.
HA HA!
THE GOOD LORD GAVE YOU CLAWS FOR A REASON, YOU KNOW.
SHUT UP.
CLICK
SNIFF
SNIFF
PRETTY GOOD WITH THAT KEYBOARD.
HELPS IF YOU CUT YOUR FINGERNAILS AT LEAST ONCE A YEAR.
HEH.
TYPE TYPE TYPETY TYPE
OKAY, HERE WE GO.
EVERY CAR THEY RENT HAS A GPS...
...AND NOW WE CAN SEE WHERE THEY ARE...

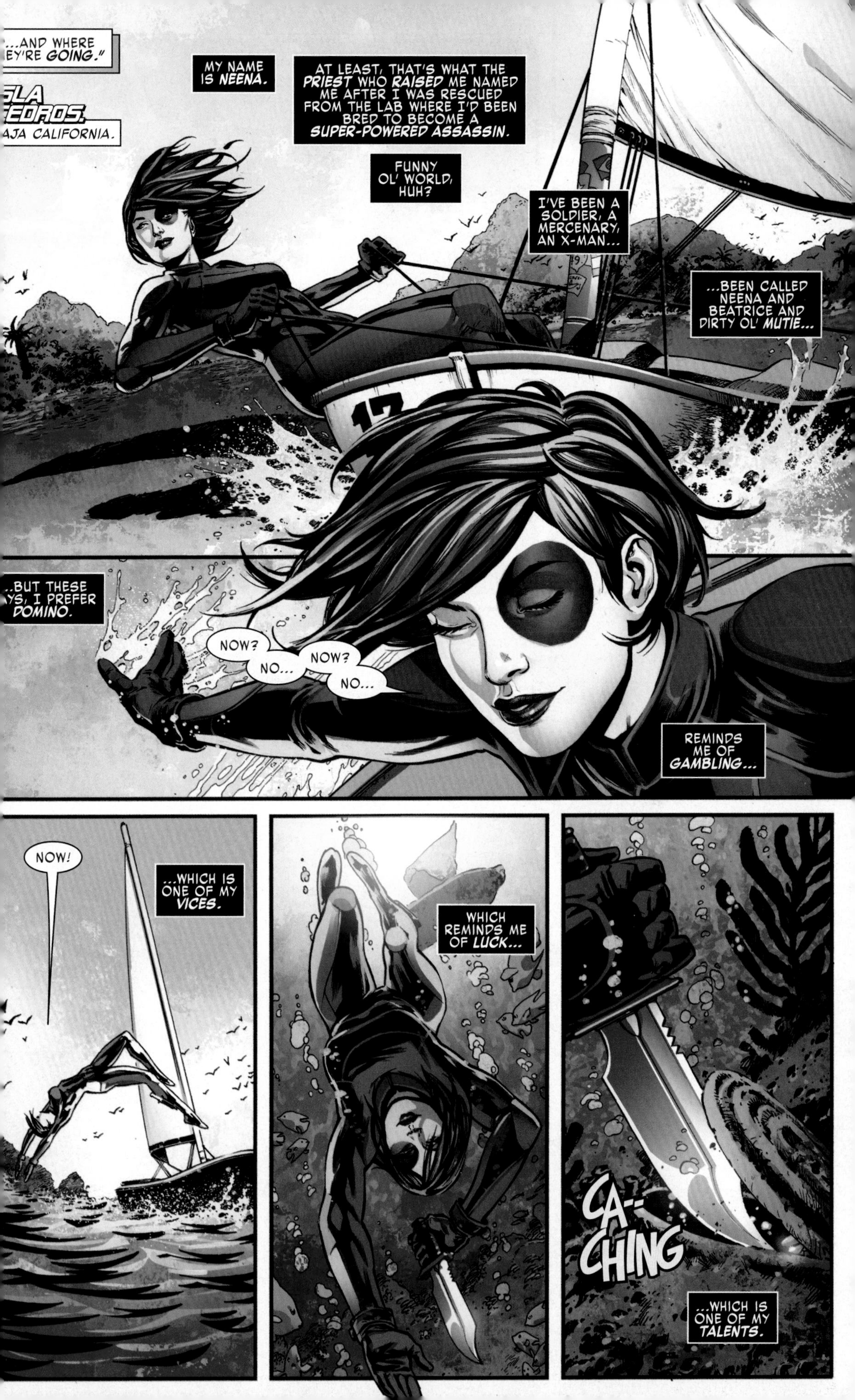
...AND WHERE
EY'RE GOING."
SLA
EDROS.
AJA CALIFORNIA.
MY NAME IS NEENA.
AT LEAST, THAT'S WHAT THE PRIEST WHO RAISED ME NAMED ME AFTER I WAS RESCUED FROM THE LAB WHERE I'D BEEN BRED TO BECOME A SUPER-POWERED ASSASSIN.
FUNNY OL' WORLD, HUH?
I'VE BEEN A SOLDIER, A MERCENARY, AN X-MAN...
...BEEN CALLED NEENA AND BEATRICE AND DIRTY OL' MUTIE...
..BUT THESE
YS, I PREFER DOMINO.
NOW?
NO...
NOW?
NO...
REMINDS ME OF GAMBLING...
NOW!
...WHICH IS ONE OF MY VICES.
WHICH REMINDS ME OF LUCK...
CA-CHING
...WHICH IS ONE OF MY TALENTS.

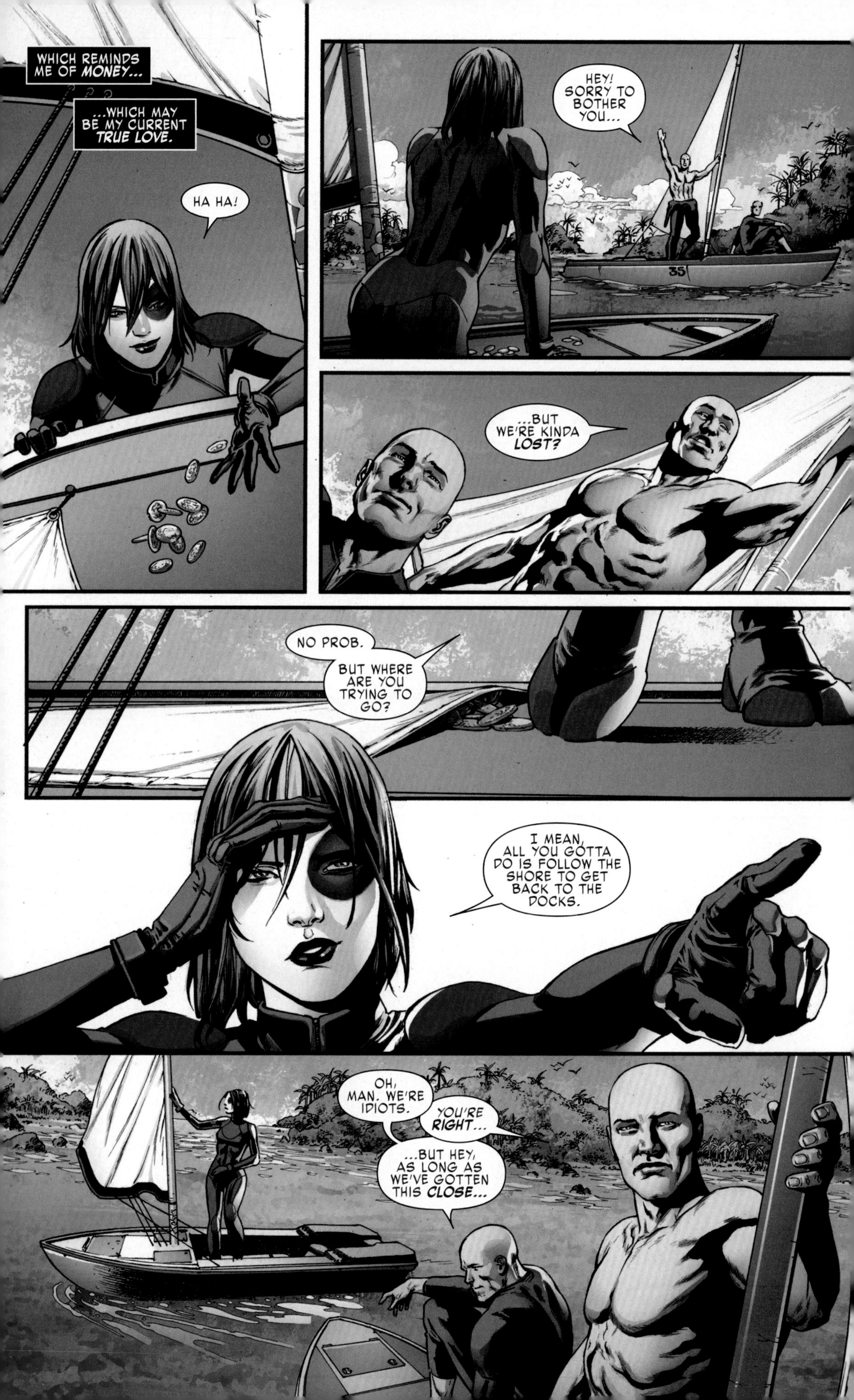
WHICH REMINDS ME OF MONEY...
...WHICH MAY BE MY CURRENT TRUE LOVE.
HA HA!
HEY! SORRY TO BOTHER YOU...
35
...BUT WE'RE KINDA LOST?
NO PROB.
BUT WHERE ARE YOU TRYING TO GO?
I MEAN, ALL YOU GOTTA DO IS FOLLOW THE SHORE TO GET BACK TO THE DOCKS.
OH, MAN. WE'RE IDIOTS.
YOU'RE RIGHT...
...BUT HEY, AS LONG AS WE'VE GOTTEN THIS CLOSE...

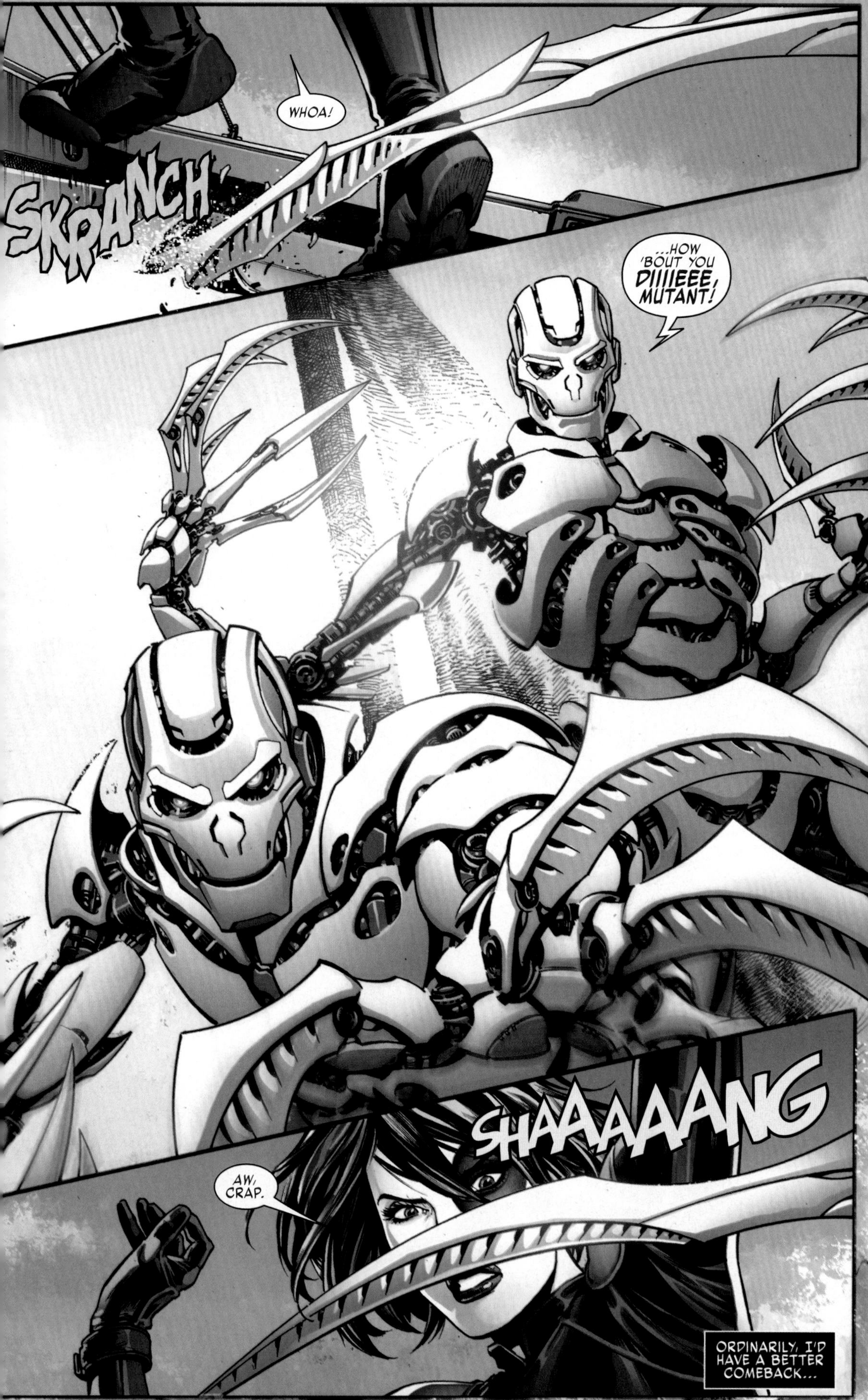
WHOA!
SKRANCH
...HOW 'BOUT YOU DIIIIEEE, MUTANT!
SHAAAAAANG
AW, CRAP.
ORDINARILY, I'D HAVE A BETTER COMEBACK...

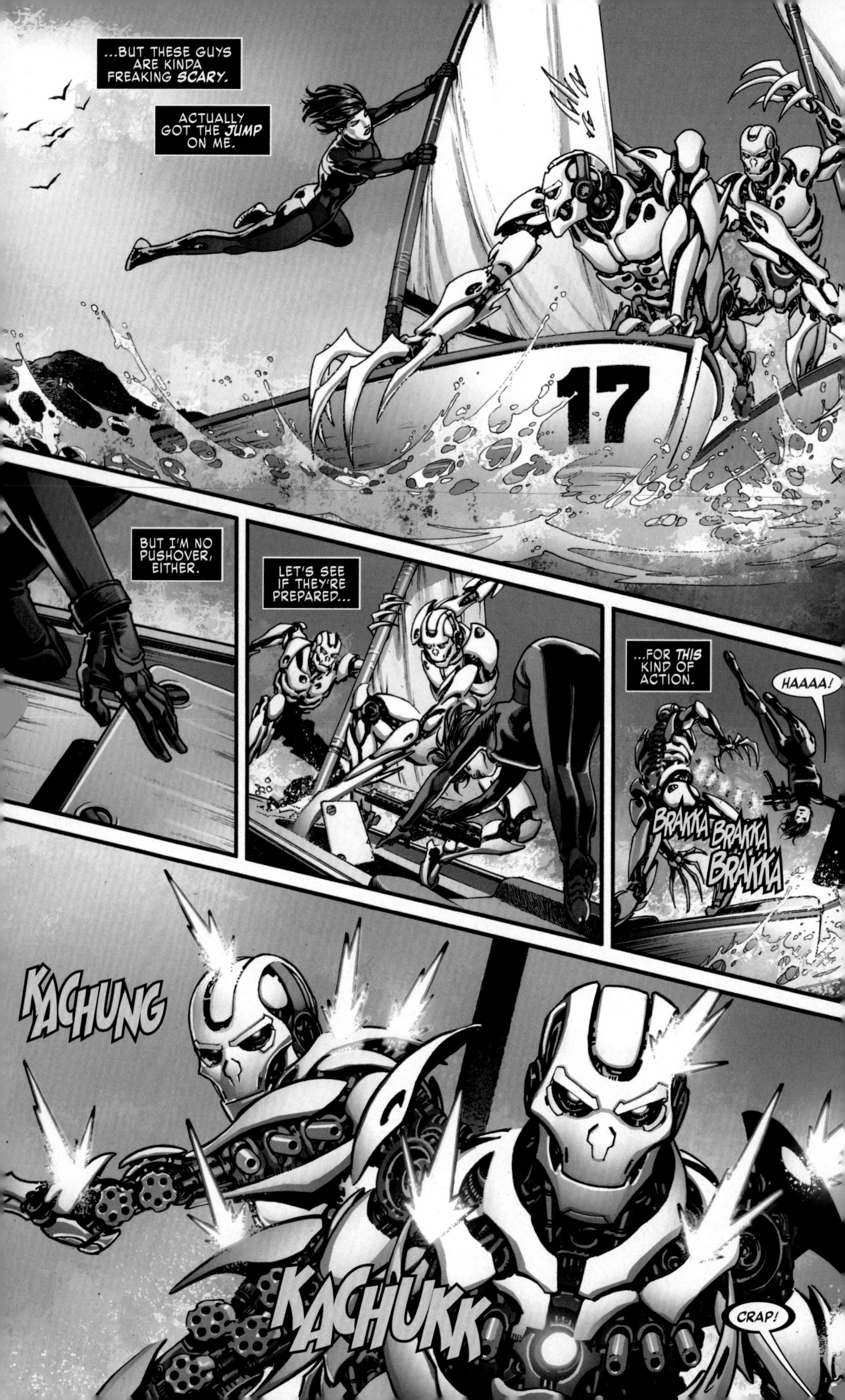
...BUT THESE GUYS ARE KINDA FREAKING SCARY.
ACTUALLY GOT THE JUMP ON ME.
17
BUT I'M NO PUSHOVER, EITHER.
LET'S SEE IF THEY'RE PREPARED...
...FOR THIS KIND OF ACTION.
HAAAA!
BRAKKA BRAKKA BRAKKA
KACHUNG
KACHUKK
CRAP!

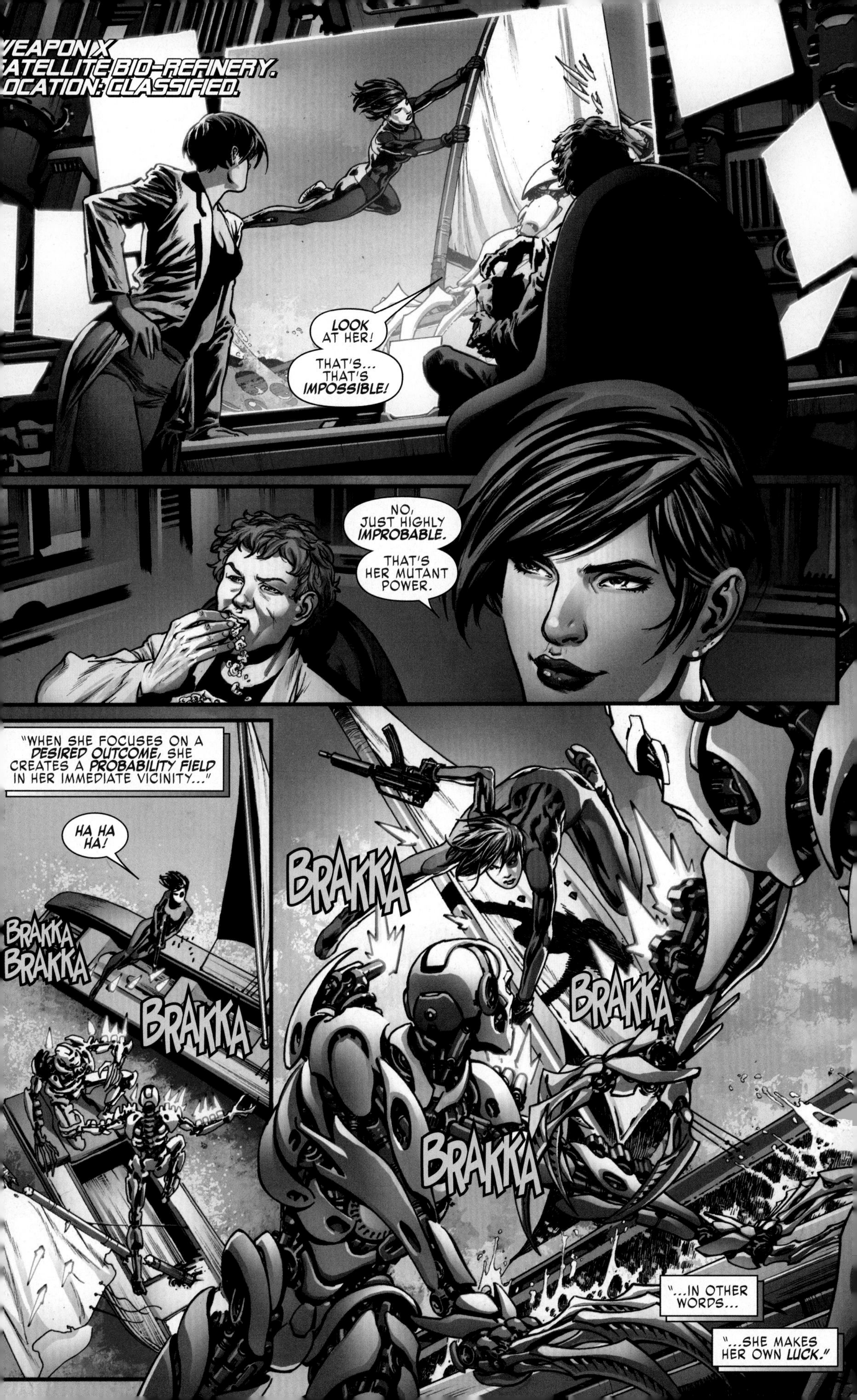
WEAPON X
SATELLITE BIO-REFINERY.
LOCATION: CLASSIFIED.
LOOK AT HER!
THAT'S... THAT'S IMPOSSIBLE!
NO, JUST HIGHLY IMPROBABLE.
THAT'S HER MUTANT POWER.
"WHEN SHE FOCUSES ON A DESIRED OUTCOME, SHE CREATES A PROBABILITY FIELD IN HER IMMEDIATE VICINITY..."
HA HA HA!
BRAKKA
BRAKKA BRAKKA
BRAKKA
BRAKKA
BRAKKA
"...IN OTHER WORDS...
"...SHE MAKES HER OWN LUCK."

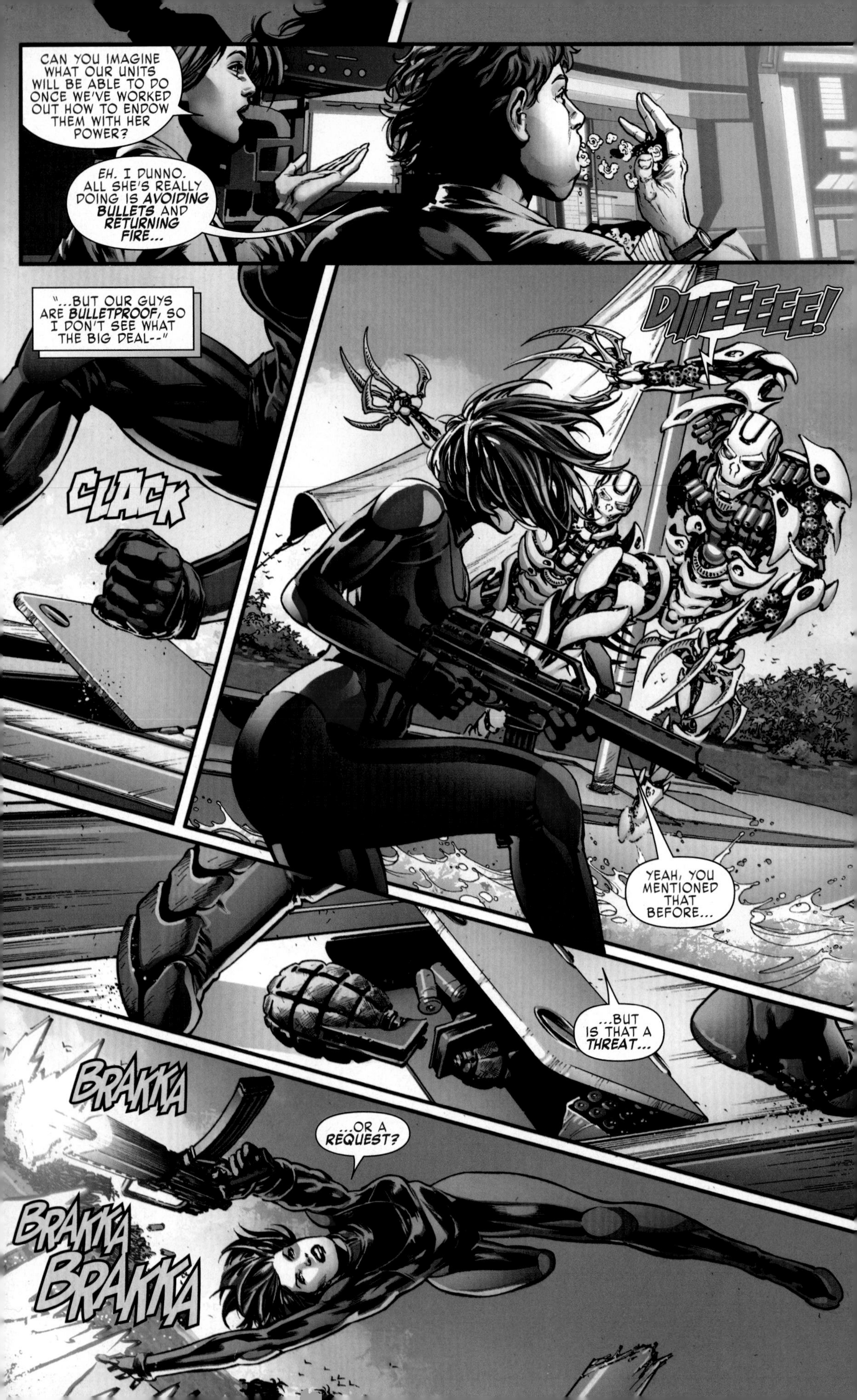
CAN YOU IMAGINE WHAT OUR UNITS WILL BE ABLE TO DO ONCE WE'VE WORKED OUT HOW TO ENDOW THEM WITH HER POWER?
EH. I DUNNO. ALL SHE'S REALLY DOING IS AVOIDING BULLETS AND RETURNING FIRE...
"...BUT OUR GUYS ARE BULLETPROOF, SO I DON'T SEE WHAT THE BIG DEAL--"
DIIIEEEEEE!
CLACK
YEAH, YOU MENTIONED THAT BEFORE...
...BUT IS THAT A THREAT...
BRAKKA
...OR A REQUEST?
BRAKKA BRAKKA

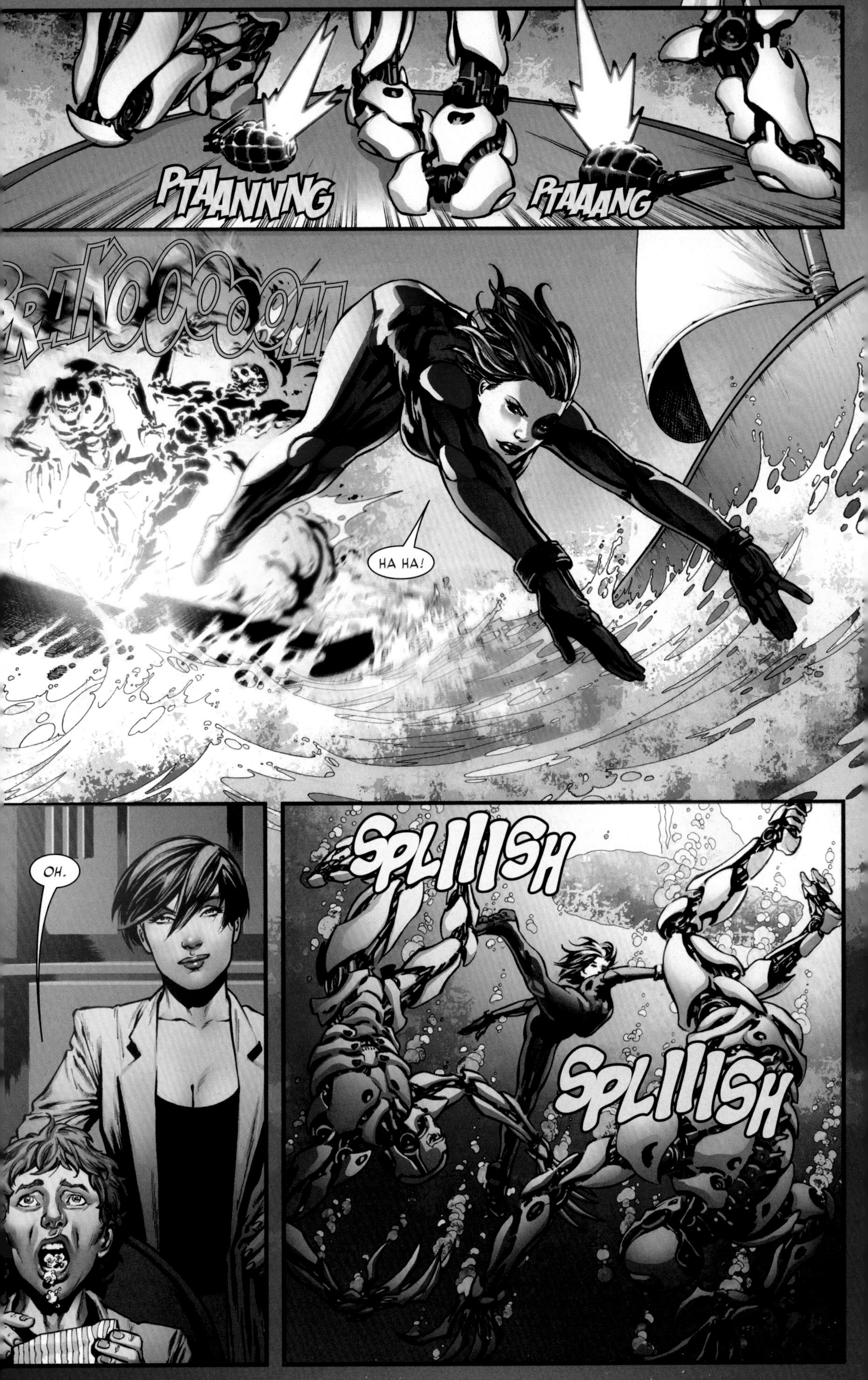
PTAANNNG
PTAAANG
HA HA!
OH.
SPLIIISH
SPLIIISH

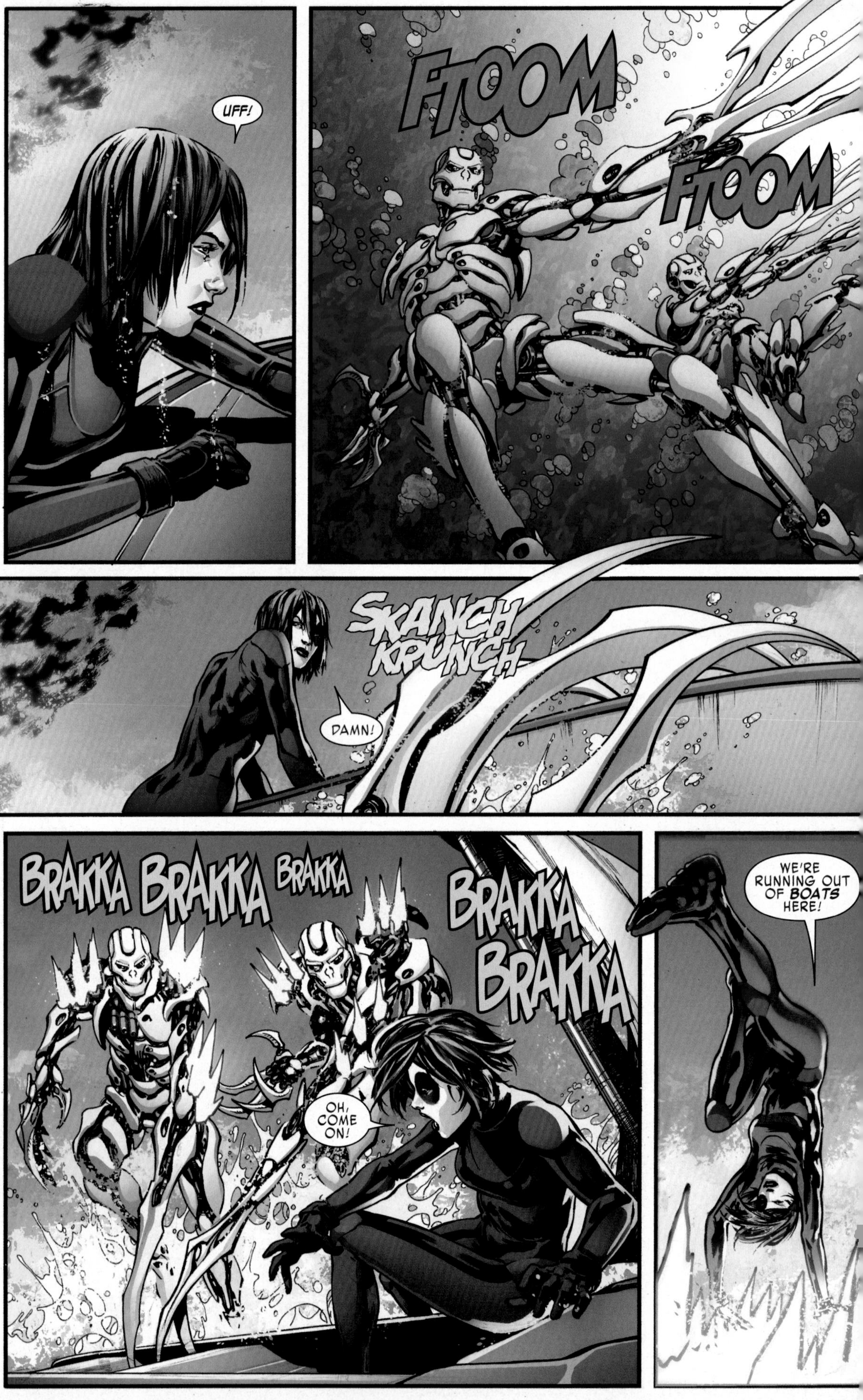
UFF!
FTOOM
FTOOM
SKANCH
KRUNCH
DAMN!
BRAKKA BRAKKA BRAKKA
BRAKKA BRAKKA
OH, COME ON!
WE'RE RUNNING OUT OF BOATS HERE!

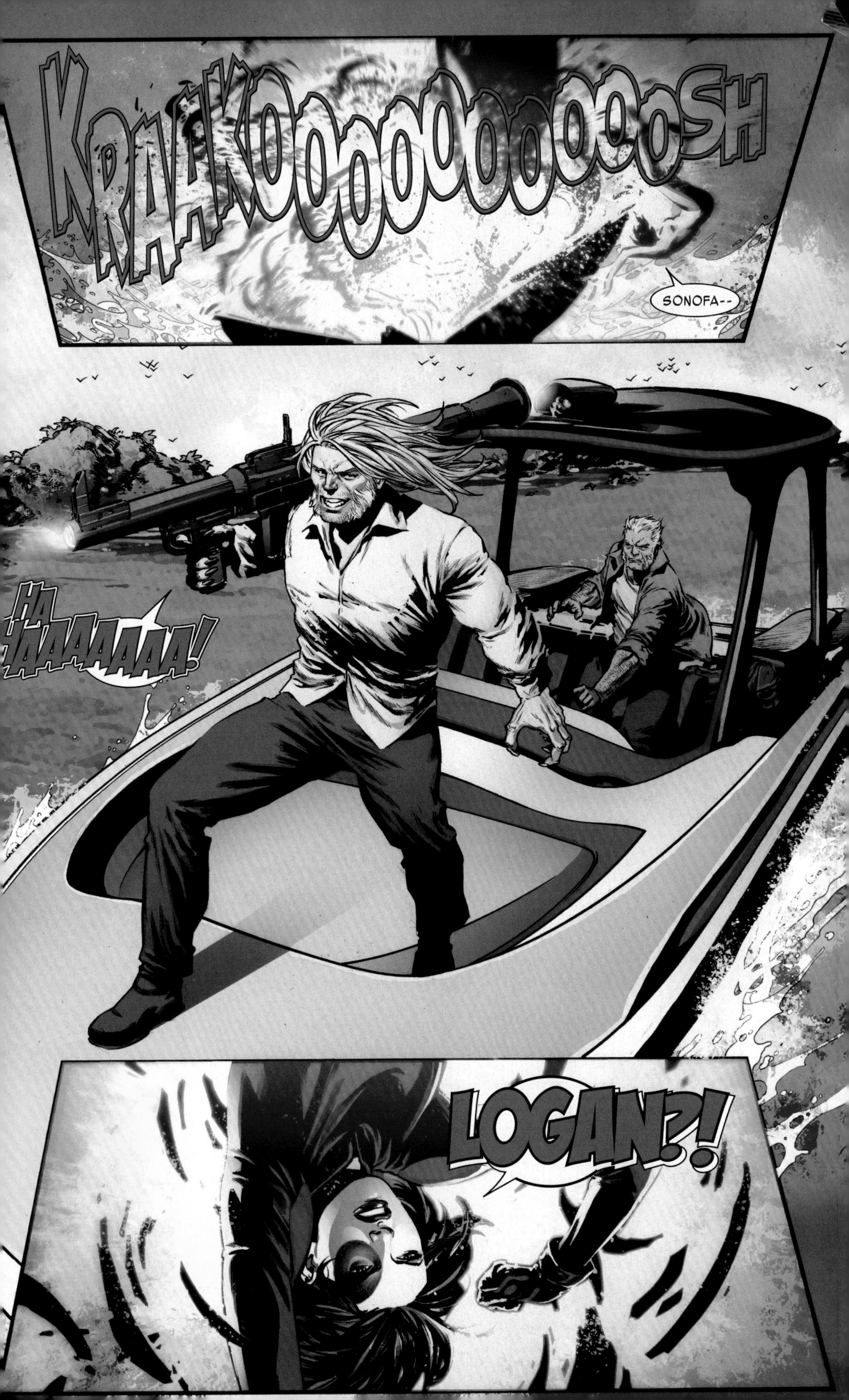
KRAAKOOOOOOOOOOOSH
SONOFA--
HA HAAAAAAA!
LOGAN?!

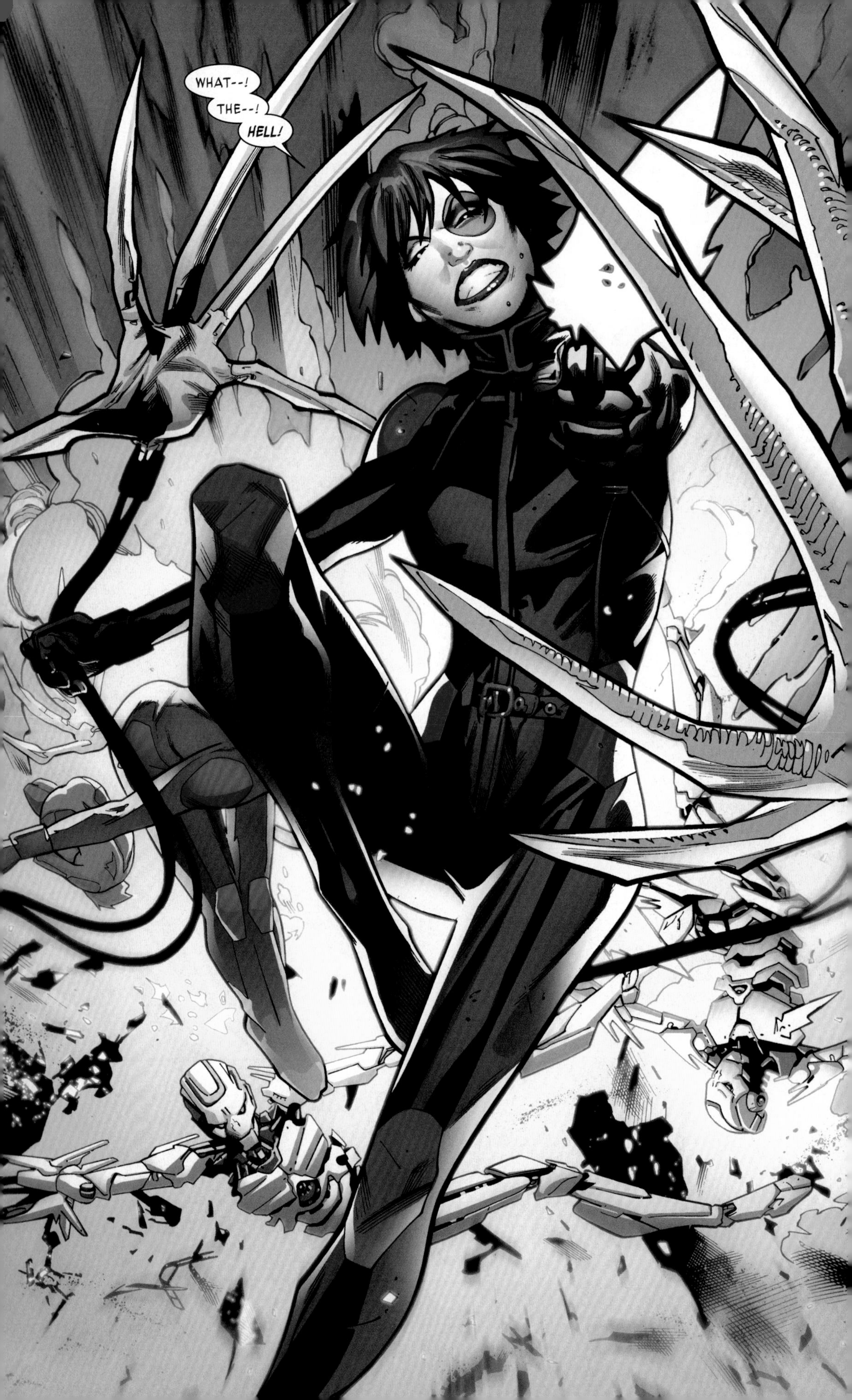
WHAT--!
THE--!
HELL!

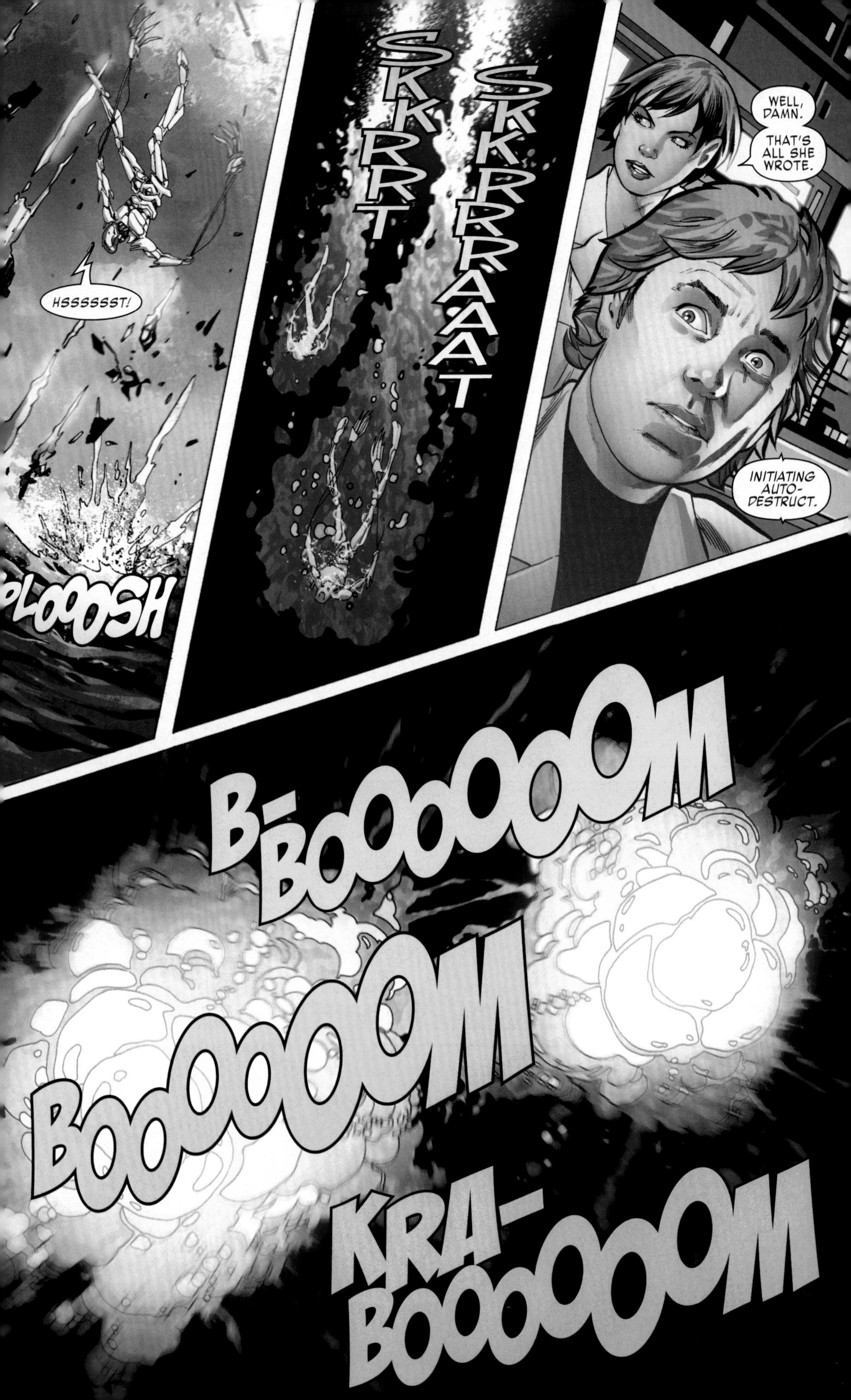
HSSSSSST!
PLOOOSH
SKKRRT
SKKRRRAAAT
WELL, DAMN.
THAT'S ALL SHE WROTE.
INITIATING AUTO-DESTRUCT.
B-BOOOOOOM
BOOOOOOOM
KRA-BOOOOOOM

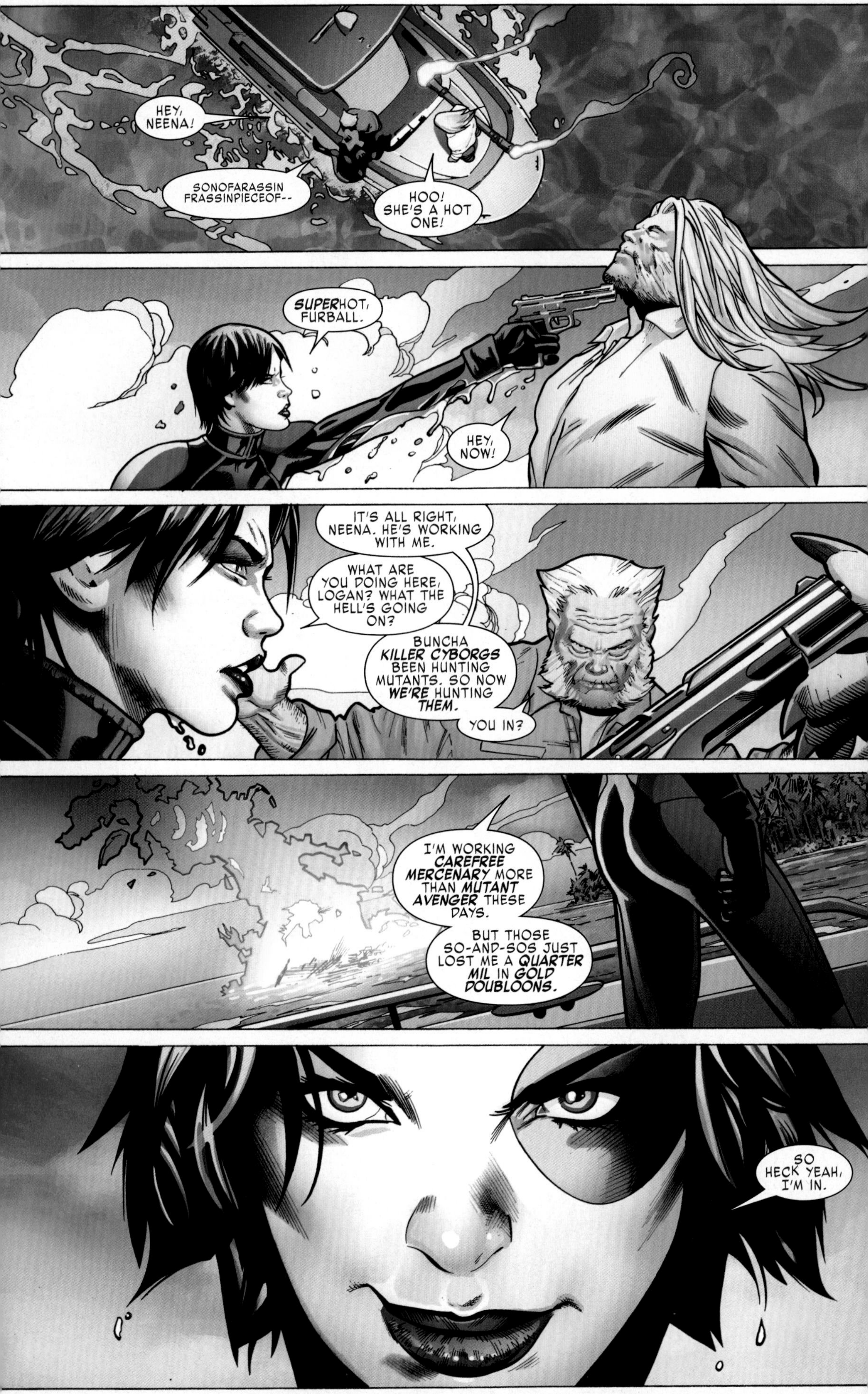
HEY, NEENA!
SONOFARASSIN FRASSINPIECEOF--
HOO! SHE'S A HOT ONE!
SUPERHOT, FURBALL.
HEY, NOW!
IT'S ALL RIGHT, NEENA. HE'S WORKING WITH ME.
WHAT ARE YOU DOING HERE, LOGAN? WHAT THE HELL'S GOING ON?
BUNCHA KILLER CYBORGS BEEN HUNTING MUTANTS. SO NOW WE'RE HUNTING THEM.
YOU IN?
I'M WORKING CAREFREE MERCENARY MORE THAN MUTANT AVENGER THESE DAYS.
BUT THOSE SO-AND-SOS JUST LOST ME A QUARTER MIL IN GOLD DOUBLOONS.
SO HECK YEAH, I'M IN.

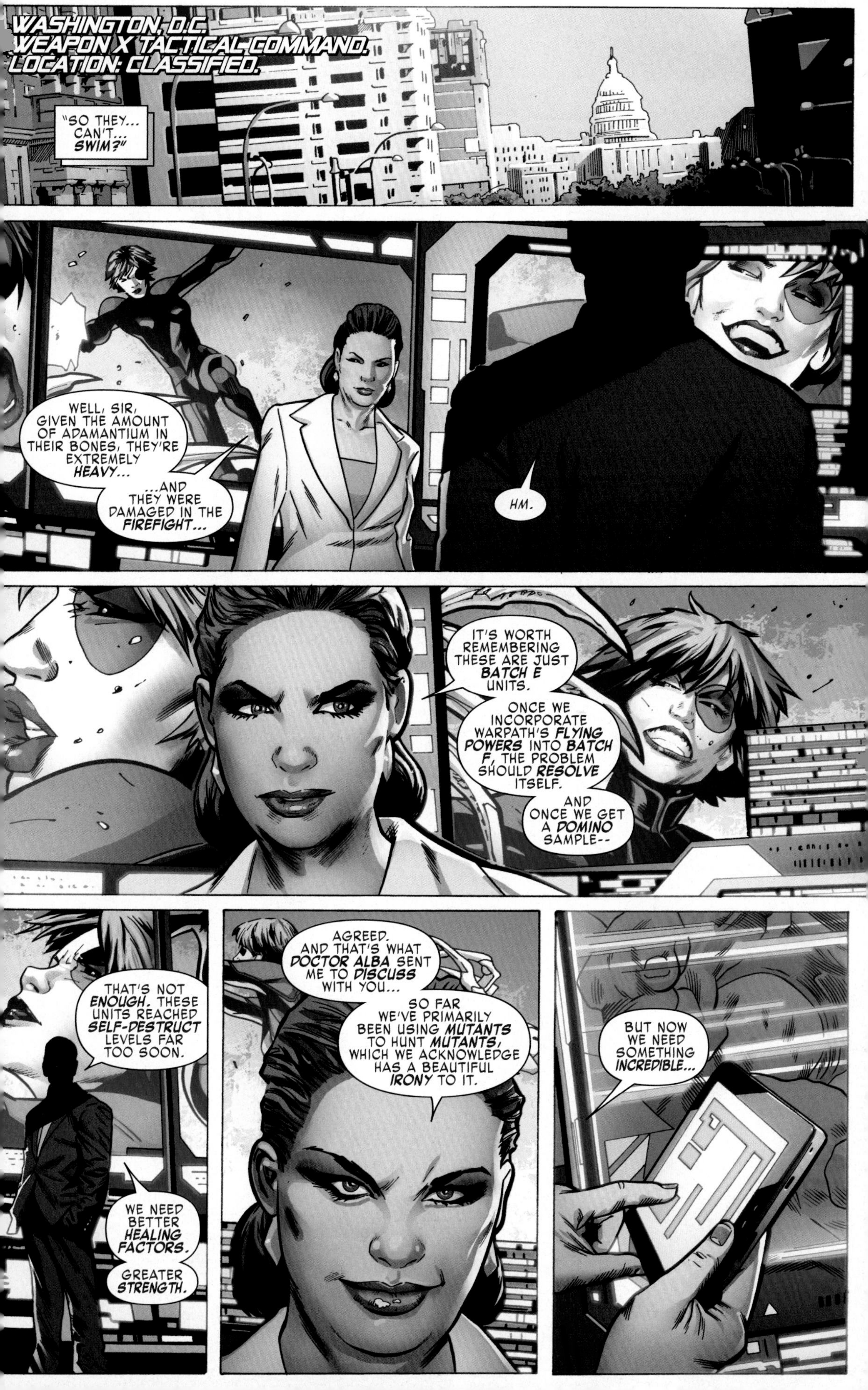
WASHINGTON, D.C.
WEAPON X TACTICAL COMMAND.
LOCATION: CLASSIFIED.
"SO THEY... CAN'T... SWIM?"
WELL, SIR, GIVEN THE AMOUNT OF ADAMANTIUM IN THEIR BONES, THEY'RE EXTREMELY HEAVY...
...AND THEY WERE DAMAGED IN THE FIREFIGHT...
HM.
IT'S WORTH REMEMBERING THESE ARE JUST BATCH E UNITS.
ONCE WE INCORPORATE WARPATH'S FLYING POWERS INTO BATCH F, THE PROBLEM SHOULD RESOLVE ITSELF.
AND ONCE WE GET A DOMINO SAMPLE--
THAT'S NOT ENOUGH. THESE UNITS REACHED SELF-DESTRUCT LEVELS FAR TOO SOON.
WE NEED BETTER HEALING FACTORS.
GREATER STRENGTH.
AGREED. AND THAT'S WHAT DOCTOR ALBA SENT ME TO DISCUSS WITH YOU...
SO FAR WE'VE PRIMARILY BEEN USING MUTANTS TO HUNT MUTANTS, WHICH WE ACKNOWLEDGE HAS A BEAUTIFUL IRONY TO IT.
BUT NOW WE NEED SOMETHING INCREDIBLE...

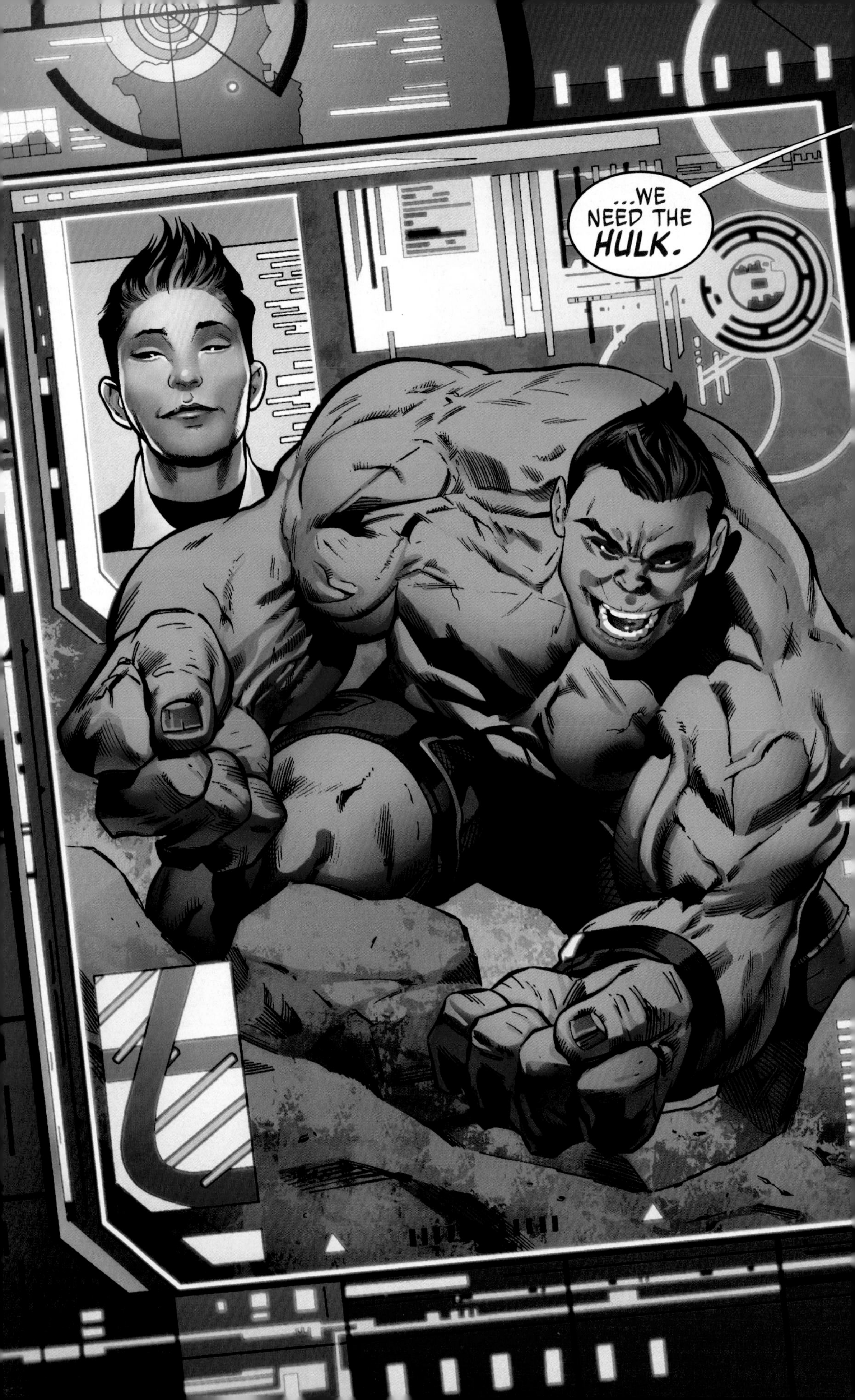
...WE NEED THE HULK.

THE TOTALLY AWESOME HULK #19

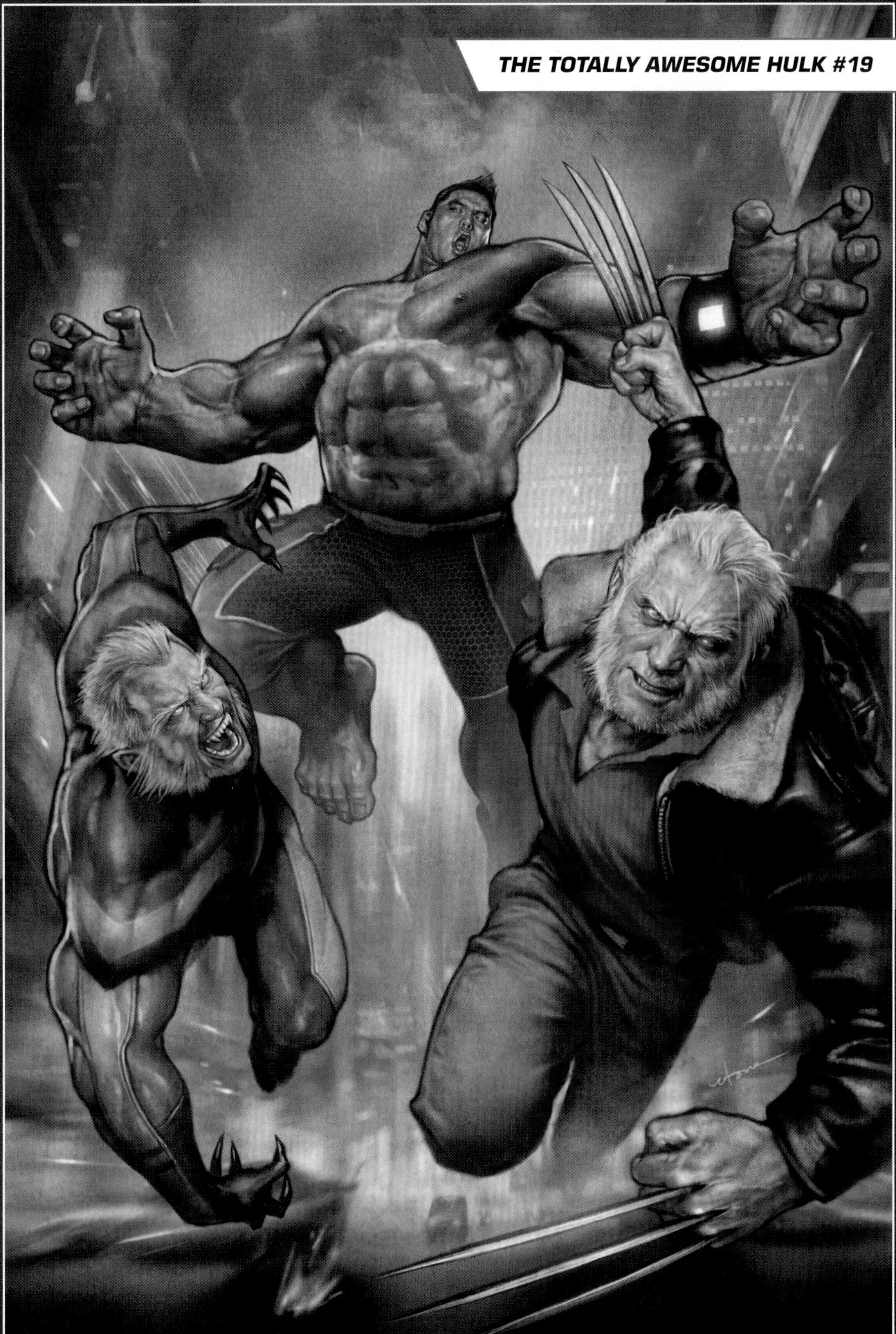

THE TOTALLY AWESOME HULK

HULK

OLD MAN LOGAN

DOMINO

SABRETOOTH

SUPER-GENIUS TEENAGER AMADEUS CHO CURED BRUCE BANNER AND TOOK ON THE POWERS AND MANTLE OF THE HULK!

PREVIOUSLY IN *THE TOTALLY AWESOME HULK...*

BEING THE HULK HAS HAD ITS UPS AND DOWNS: WHILE SAVING LIVES AND MAKING FRIENDS WITH OTHER HEROES HAS BEEN GREAT, AMADEUS HAS STRUGGLED TO KEEP HIS EMOTIONS IN CHECK, WHICH HAS CAUSED A SPLIT WITH HIS SISTER MADDY.

MEANWHILE, THE EVIL MINDS BEHIND THE WEAPON X PROGRAM HOPE TO CAPITALIZE ON THE GENETIC GIFTS OF MUTANTS TO WIPE OUT ALL OF MUTANT-KIND! USING ADAMANTIUM CYBORGS IMBUED WITH THE ABILITIES OF OLD MAN LOGAN, SABRETOOTH, WARPATH, AND LADY DEATHSTRIKE, THE WEAPON X PROGRAM HUNTS THEIR NEXT TARGET...

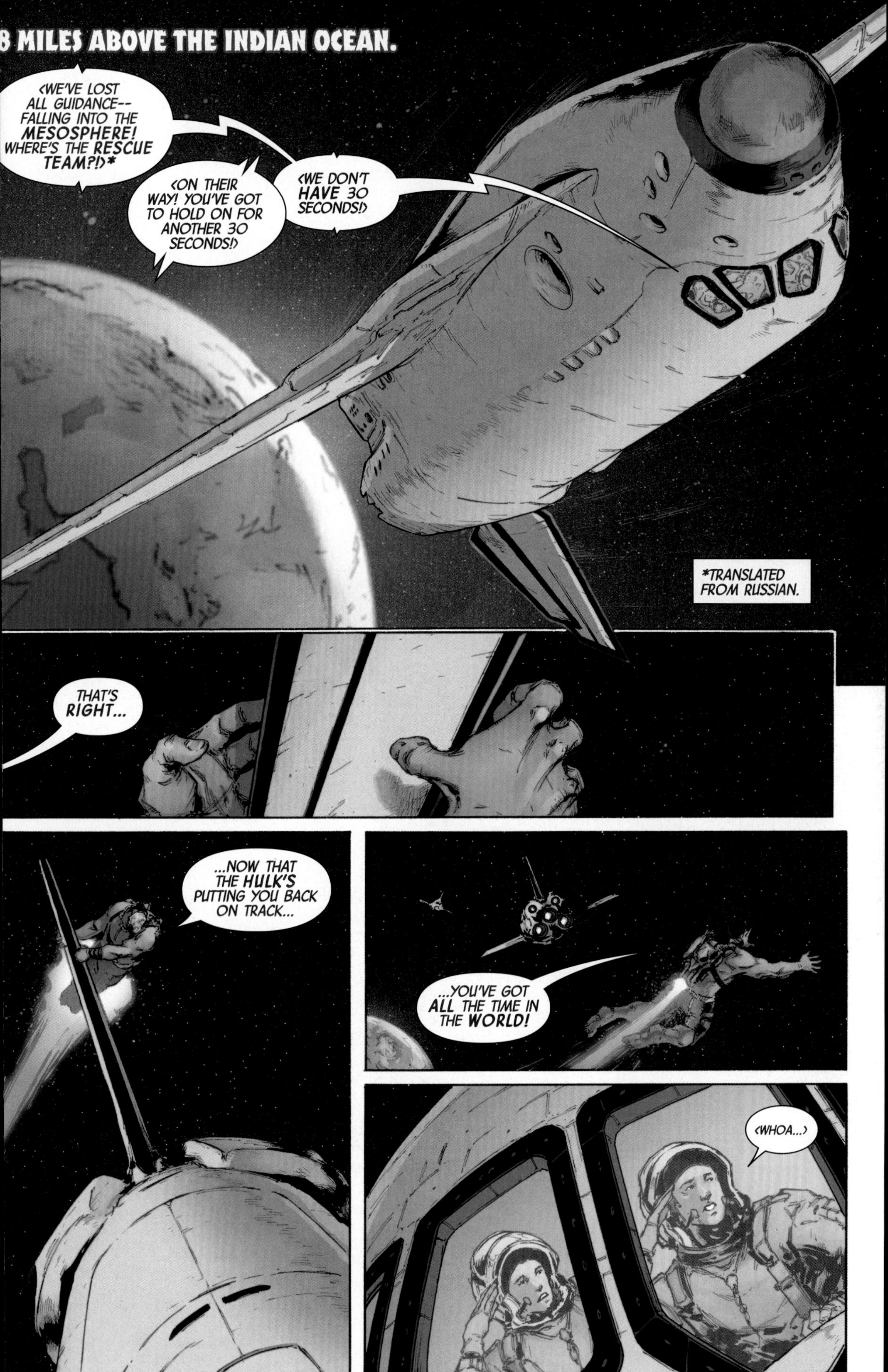

8 MILES ABOVE THE INDIAN OCEAN.
<WE'VE LOST ALL GUIDANCE-- FALLING INTO THE MESOSPHERE! WHERE'S THE RESCUE TEAM?!>*
<ON THEIR WAY! YOU'VE GOT TO HOLD ON FOR ANOTHER 30 SECONDS!>
<WE DON'T HAVE 30 SECONDS!>
*TRANSLATED FROM RUSSIAN.
THAT'S RIGHT...
...NOW THAT THE HULK'S PUTTING YOU BACK ON TRACK...
...YOU'VE GOT ALL THE TIME IN THE WORLD!
<WHOA...>

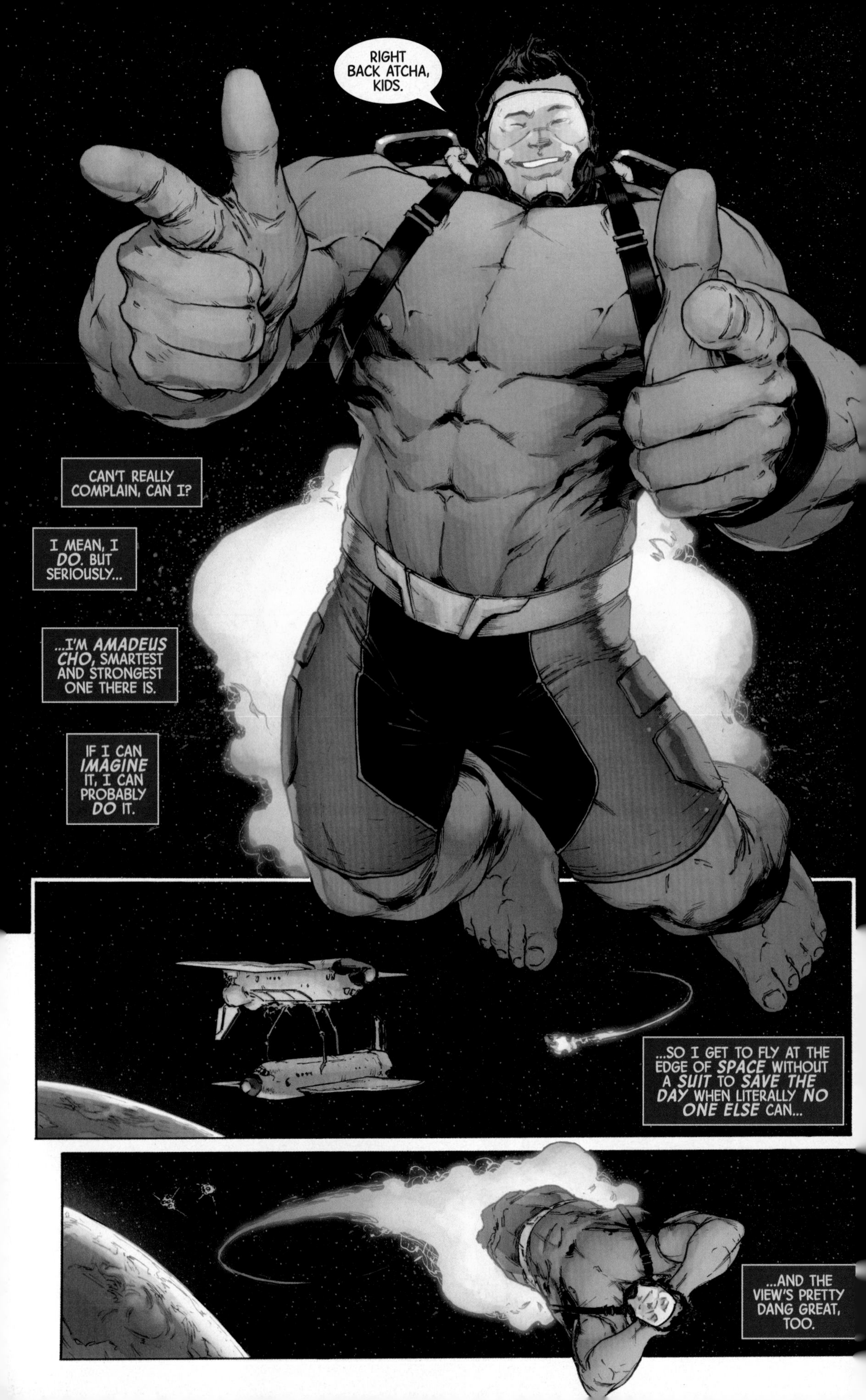
RIGHT BACK ATCHA, KIDS.
CAN'T REALLY COMPLAIN, CAN I?
I MEAN, I DO. BUT SERIOUSLY...
...I'M AMADEUS CHO, SMARTEST AND STRONGEST ONE THERE IS.
IF I CAN IMAGINE IT, I CAN PROBABLY DO IT.
...SO I GET TO FLY AT THE EDGE OF SPACE WITHOUT A SUIT TO SAVE THE DAY WHEN LITERALLY NO ONE ELSE CAN...
...AND THE VIEW'S PRETTY DANG GREAT, TOO.

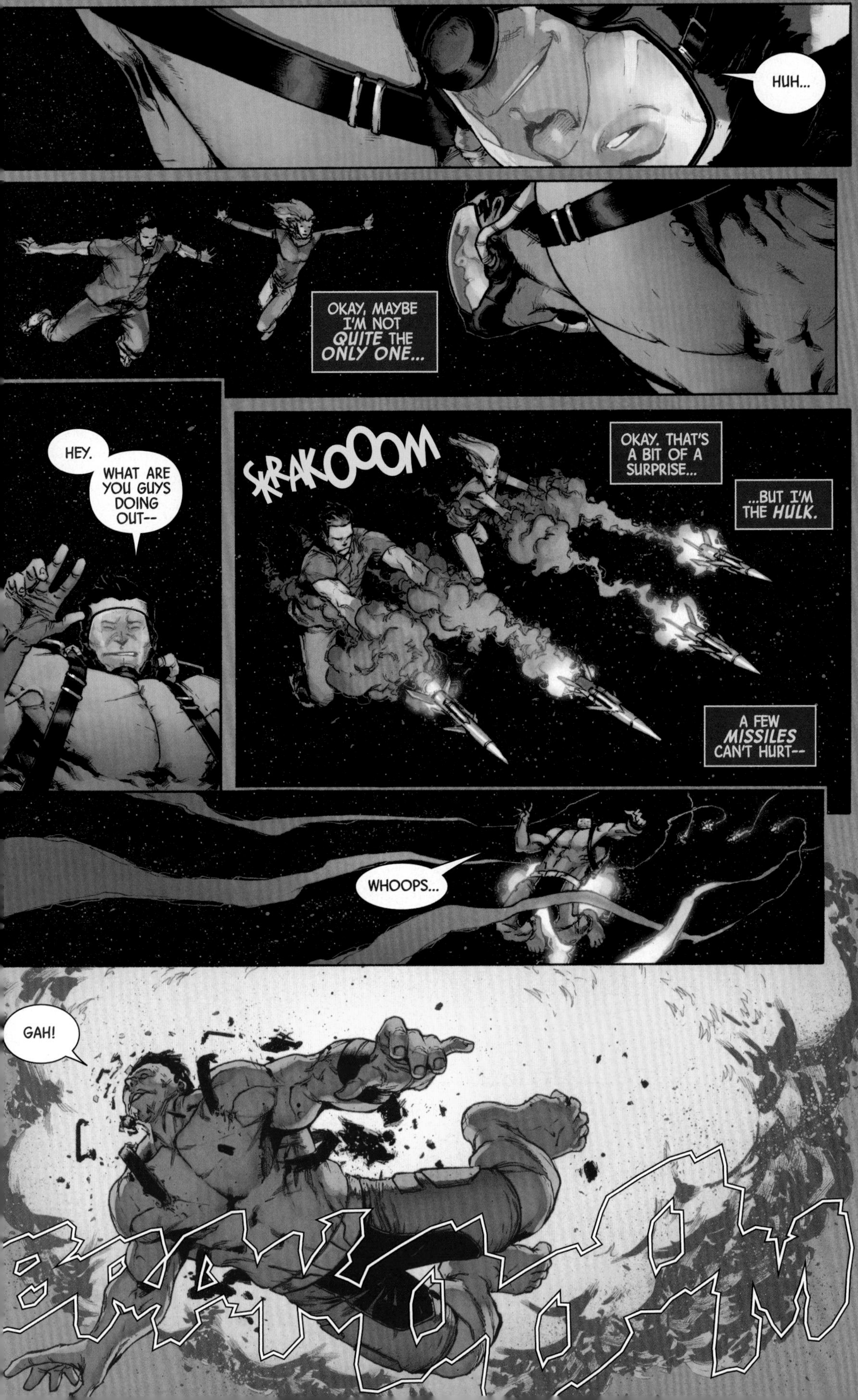
HUH...
OKAY, MAYBE I'M NOT QUITE THE ONLY ONE...
HEY.
WHAT ARE YOU GUYS DOING OUT--
SKRAKOOOM
OKAY, THAT'S A BIT OF A SURPRISE...
...BUT I'M THE HULK.
A FEW MISSILES CAN'T HURT--
WHOOPS...
GAH!

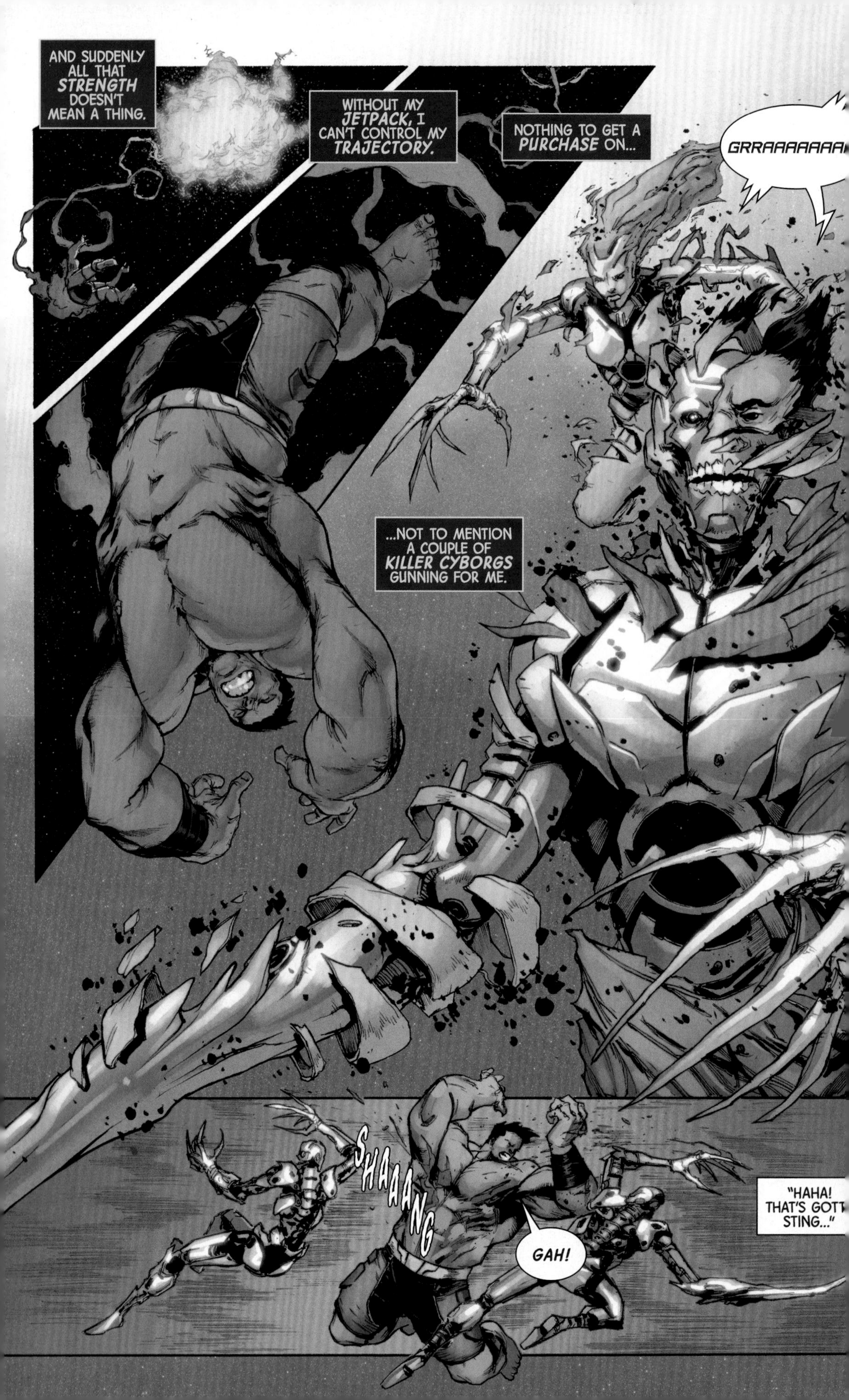
AND SUDDENLY ALL THAT STRENGTH DOESN'T MEAN A THING.
WITHOUT MY JETPACK, I CAN'T CONTROL MY TRAJECTORY.
NOTHING TO GET A PURCHASE ON...
GRRAAAAAAAA
...NOT TO MENTION A COUPLE OF KILLER CYBORGS GUNNING FOR ME.
SHAAAANG
GAH!
"HAHA! THAT'S GOTT STING..."

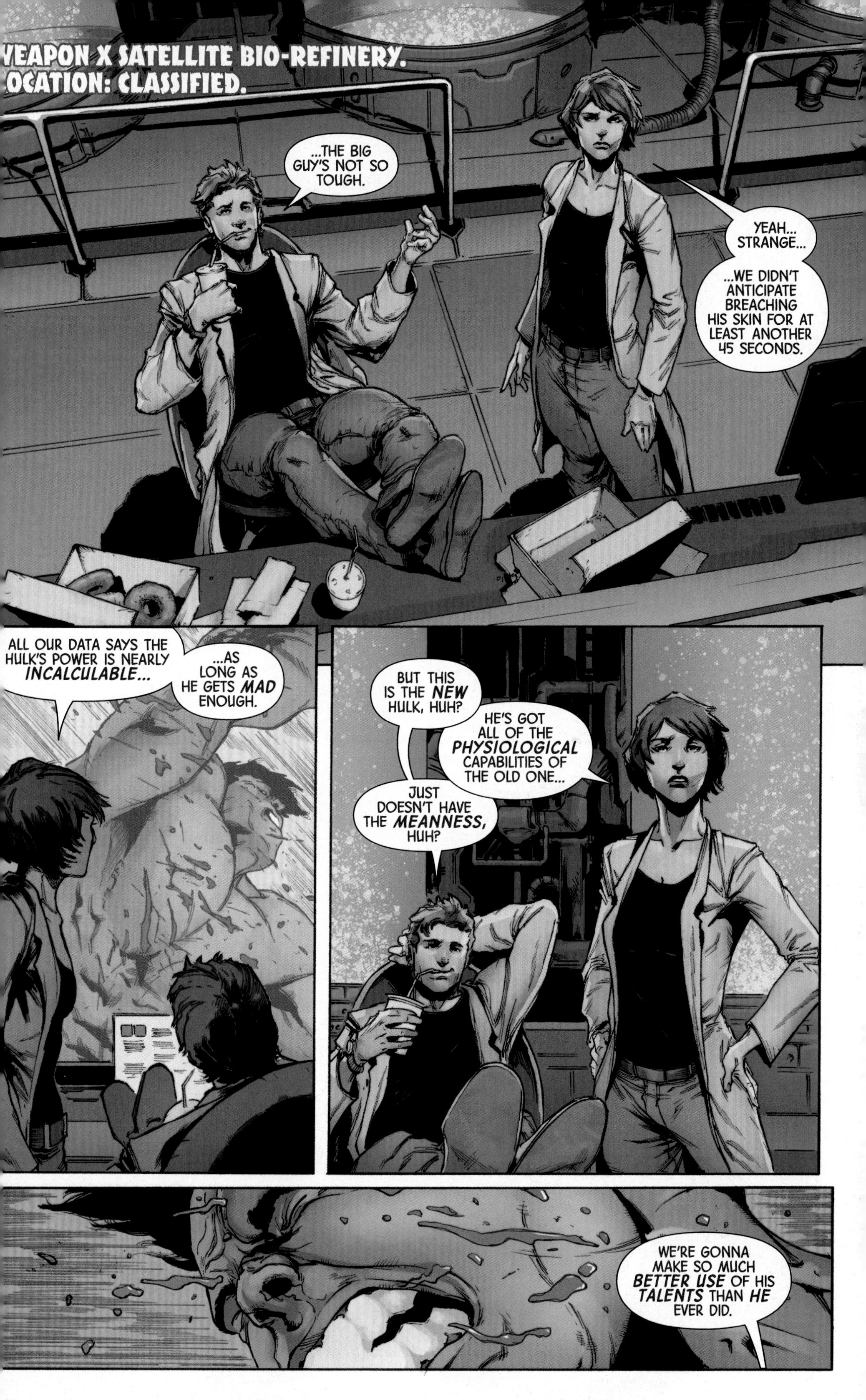

VEAPON X SATELLITE BIO-REFINERY. OCATION: CLASSIFIED.
...THE BIG GUY'S NOT SO TOUGH.
YEAH... STRANGE...
...WE DIDN'T ANTICIPATE BREACHING HIS SKIN FOR AT LEAST ANOTHER 45 SECONDS.
ALL OUR DATA SAYS THE HULK'S POWER IS NEARLY INCALCULABLE...
...AS LONG AS HE GETS MAD ENOUGH.
BUT THIS IS THE NEW HULK, HUH?
HE'S GOT ALL OF THE PHYSIOLOGICAL CAPABILITIES OF THE OLD ONE...
JUST DOESN'T HAVE THE MEANNESS, HUH?
WE'RE GONNA MAKE SO MUCH BETTER USE OF HIS TALENTS THAN HE EVER DID.

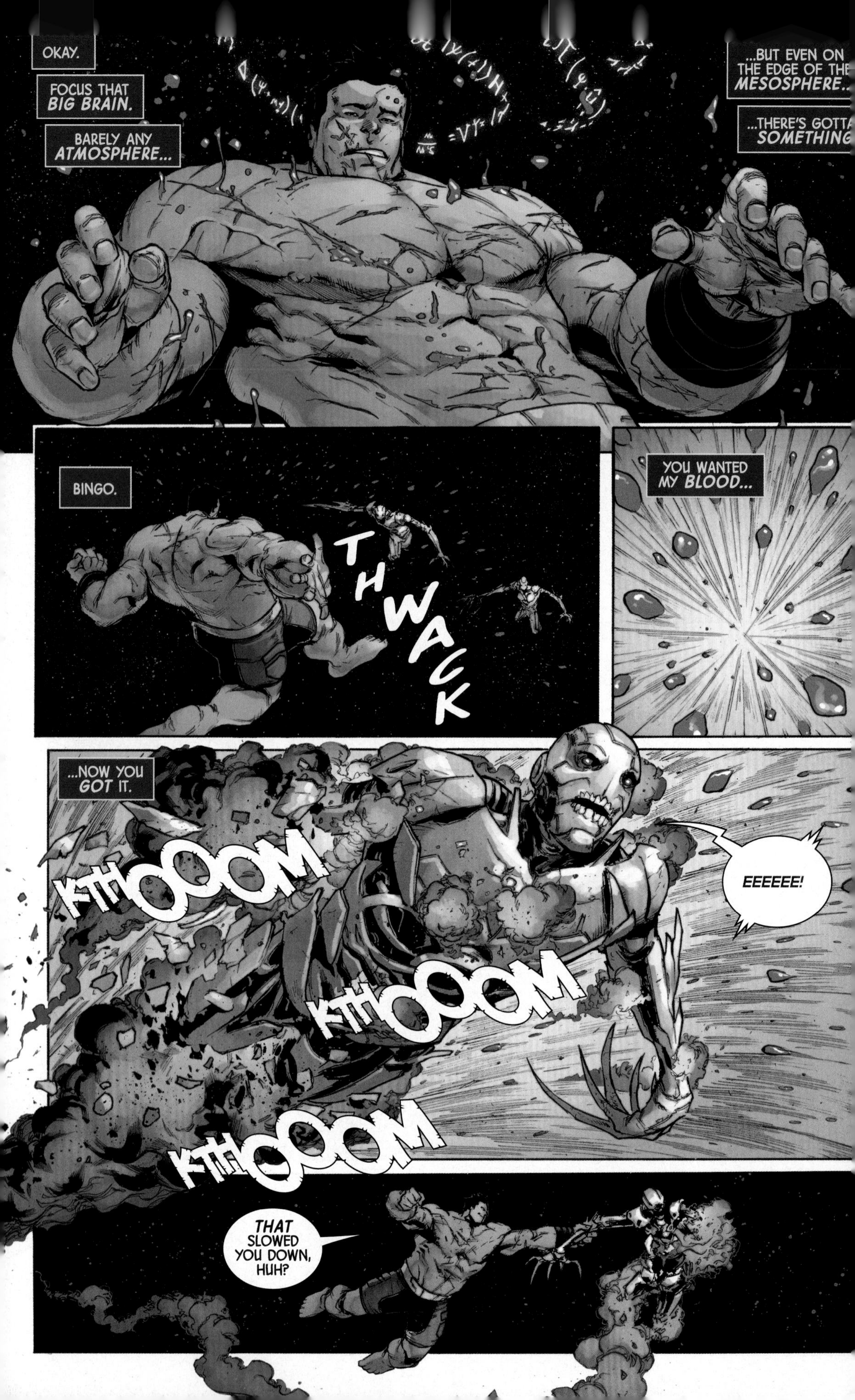
OKAY.
FOCUS THAT BIG BRAIN.
BARELY ANY ATMOSPHERE...
...BUT EVEN ON THE EDGE OF THE MESOSPHERE...
...THERE'S GOTTA SOMETHING
BINGO.
THWACK
YOU WANTED MY BLOOD...
...NOW YOU GOT IT.
KTHOOOM
EEEEEE!
KTHOOOM
KTHOOOM
THAT SLOWED YOU DOWN, HUH?

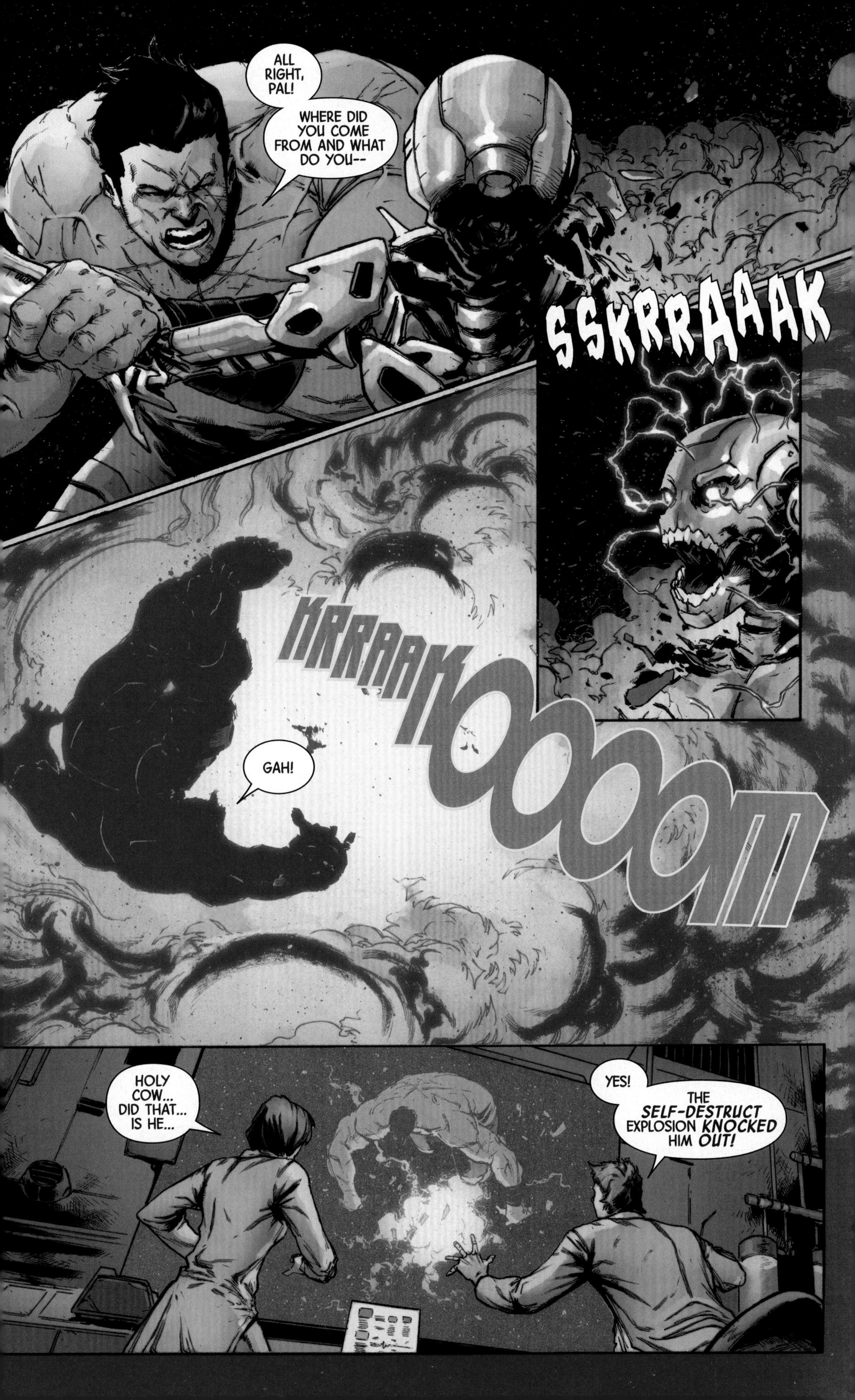
ALL RIGHT, PAL!
WHERE DID YOU COME FROM AND WHAT DO YOU--
SSKRRAAAK
KRRAAKOOOOM
GAH!
HOLY COW... DID THAT... IS HE...
YES!
THE *SELF-DESTRUCT* EXPLOSION *KNOCKED* HIM *OUT!*

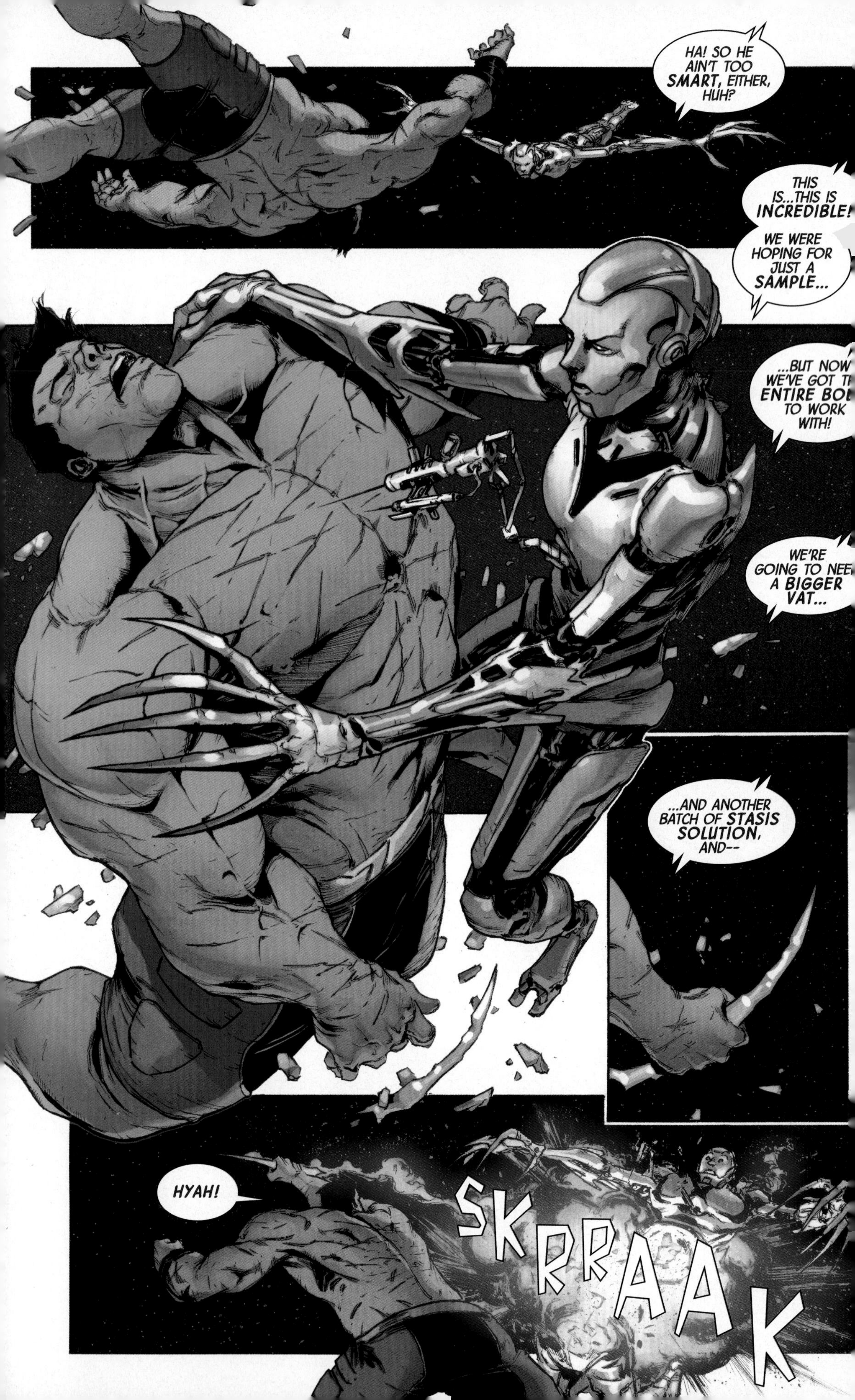
HA! SO HE AIN'T TOO SMART, EITHER, HUH?
THIS IS...THIS IS INCREDIBLE!
WE WERE HOPING FOR JUST A SAMPLE...
...BUT NOW WE'VE GOT TH ENTIRE BO TO WORK WITH!
WE'RE GOING TO NEE A BIGGER VAT...
...AND ANOTHER BATCH OF STASIS SOLUTION, AND--
HYAH!
SKRRAAK

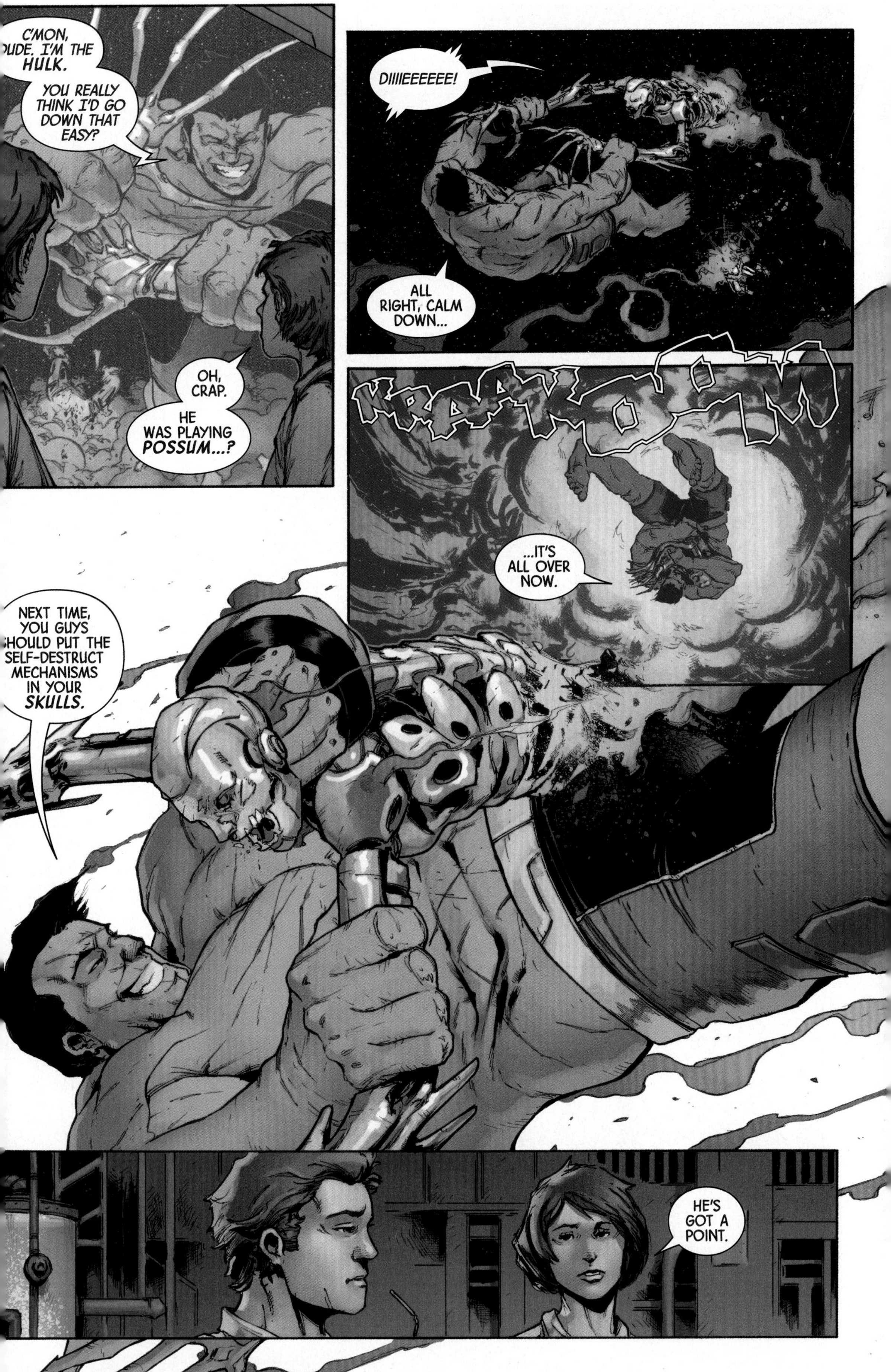
C'MON, DUDE. I'M THE HULK.
YOU REALLY THINK I'D GO DOWN THAT EASY?
OH, CRAP.
HE WAS PLAYING POSSUM...?
DIIIIEEEEEE!
ALL RIGHT, CALM DOWN...
KRAKOOOM
...IT'S ALL OVER NOW.
NEXT TIME, YOU GUYS SHOULD PUT THE SELF-DESTRUCT MECHANISMS IN YOUR SKULLS.
HE'S GOT A POINT.

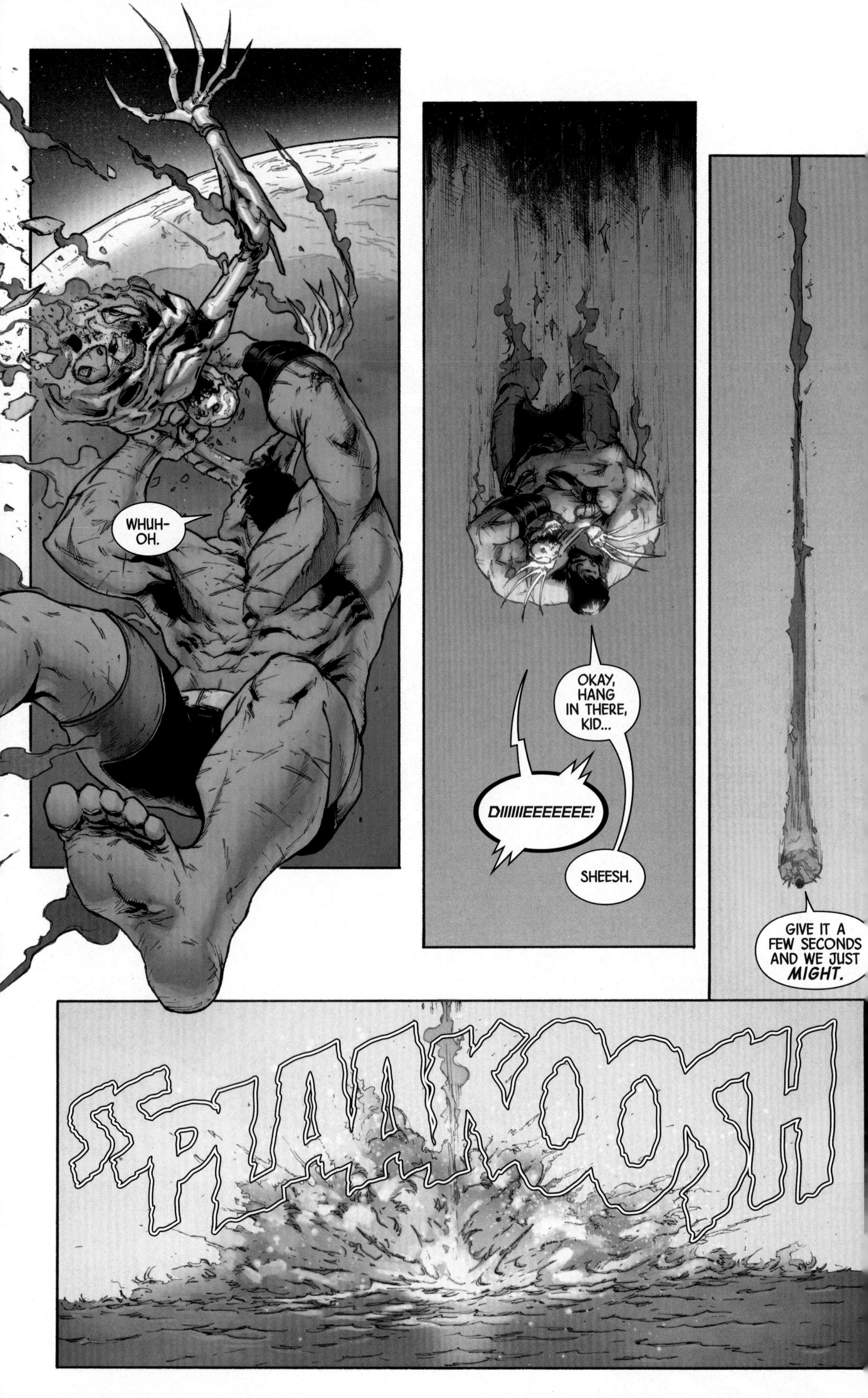

WHUH-OH.
OKAY, HANG IN THERE, KID...
DIIIIIEEEEEEE!
SHEESH.
GIVE IT A FEW SECONDS AND WE JUST *MIGHT.*
SPLAAKOOSH

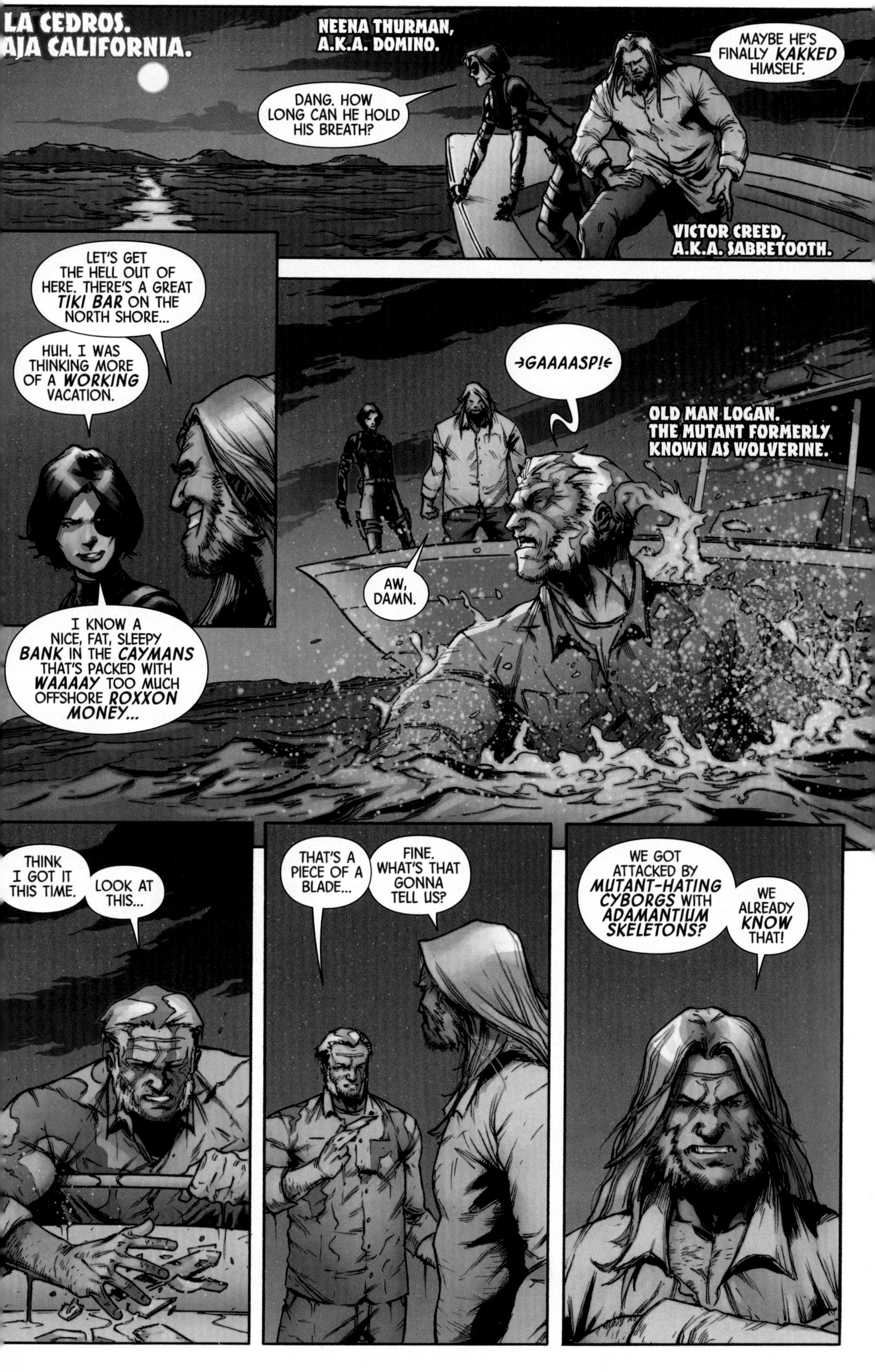
LA CEDROS.
AJA CALIFORNIA.
NEENA THURMAN,
A.K.A. DOMINO.
DANG. HOW LONG CAN HE HOLD HIS BREATH?
MAYBE HE'S FINALLY KAKKED HIMSELF.
VICTOR CREED,
A.K.A. SABRETOOTH.
LET'S GET THE HELL OUT OF HERE. THERE'S A GREAT TIKI BAR ON THE NORTH SHORE...
HUH. I WAS THINKING MORE OF A WORKING VACATION.
I KNOW A NICE, FAT, SLEEPY BANK IN THE CAYMANS THAT'S PACKED WITH WAAAAY TOO MUCH OFFSHORE ROXXON MONEY...
GAAAASP!
OLD MAN LOGAN.
THE MUTANT FORMERLY
KNOWN AS WOLVERINE.
AW, DAMN.
THINK I GOT IT THIS TIME.
LOOK AT THIS...
THAT'S A PIECE OF A BLADE...
FINE. WHAT'S THAT GONNA TELL US?
WE GOT ATTACKED BY MUTANT-HATING CYBORGS WITH ADAMANTIUM SKELETONS?
WE ALREADY KNOW THAT!

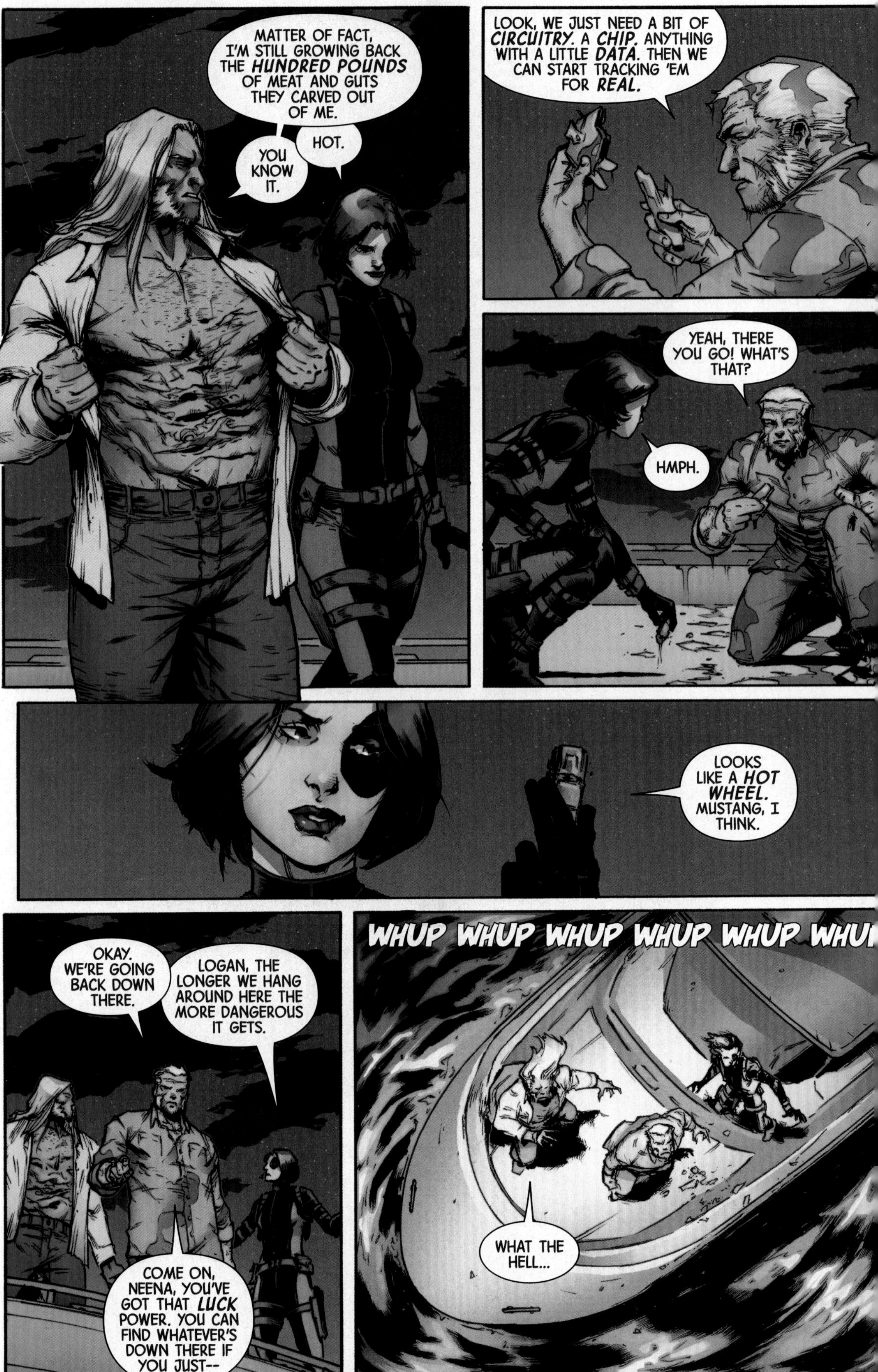
MATTER OF FACT, I'M STILL GROWING BACK THE HUNDRED POUNDS OF MEAT AND GUTS THEY CARVED OUT OF ME.
HOT.
YOU KNOW IT.
LOOK, WE JUST NEED A BIT OF CIRCUITRY. A CHIP. ANYTHING WITH A LITTLE DATA. THEN WE CAN START TRACKING 'EM FOR REAL.
YEAH, THERE YOU GO! WHAT'S THAT?
HMPH.
LOOKS LIKE A HOT WHEEL. MUSTANG, I THINK.
OKAY. WE'RE GOING BACK DOWN THERE.
LOGAN, THE LONGER WE HANG AROUND HERE THE MORE DANGEROUS IT GETS.
COME ON, NEENA, YOU'VE GOT THAT LUCK POWER. YOU CAN FIND WHATEVER'S DOWN THERE IF YOU JUST--
WHUP WHUP WHUP WHUP WHUP
WHAT THE HELL...

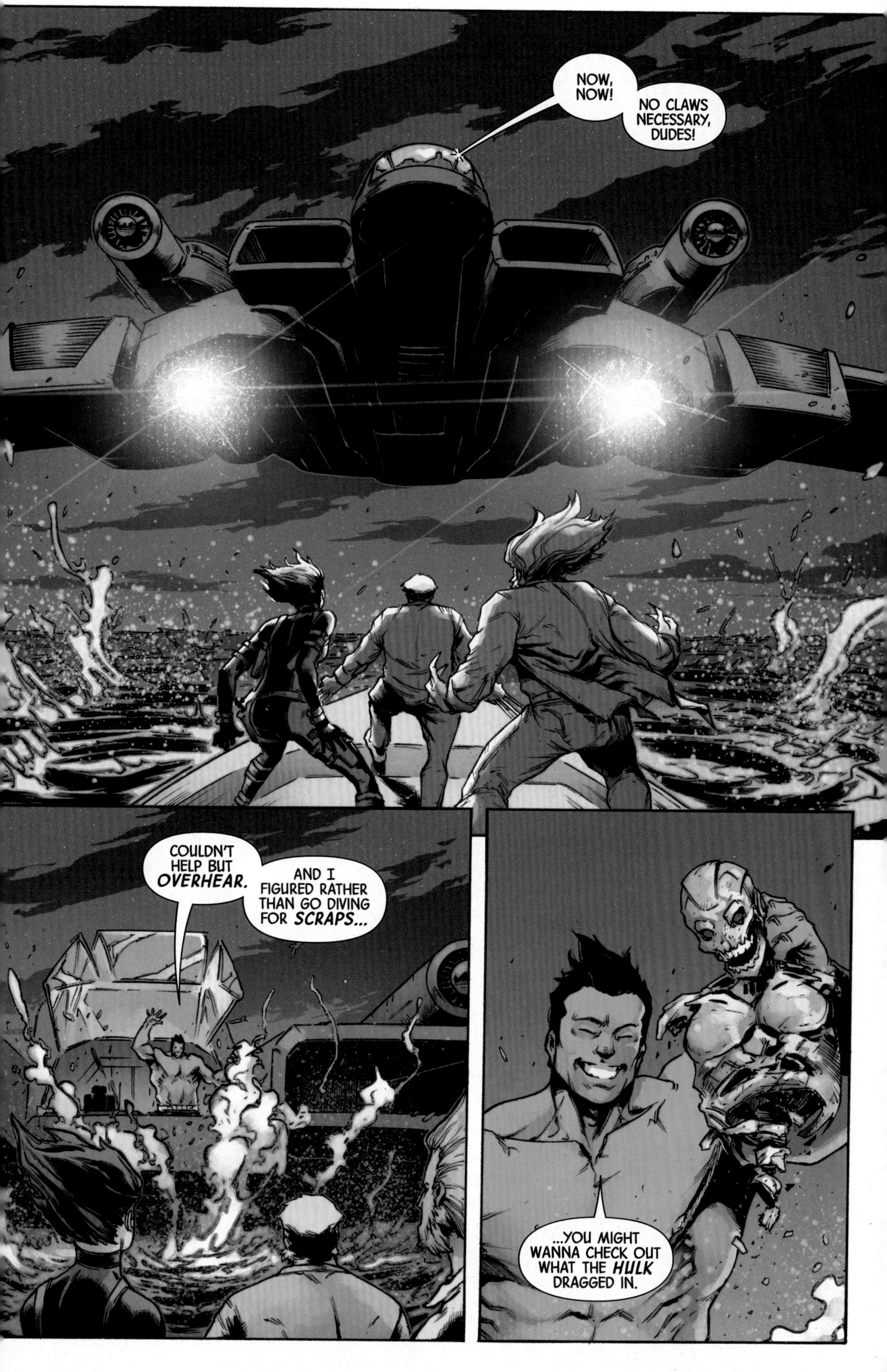
NOW, NOW!
NO CLAWS NECESSARY, DUDES!
COULDN'T HELP BUT *OVERHEAR.*
AND I FIGURED RATHER THAN GO DIVING FOR *SCRAPS...*
...YOU MIGHT WANNA CHECK OUT WHAT THE *HULK* DRAGGED IN.

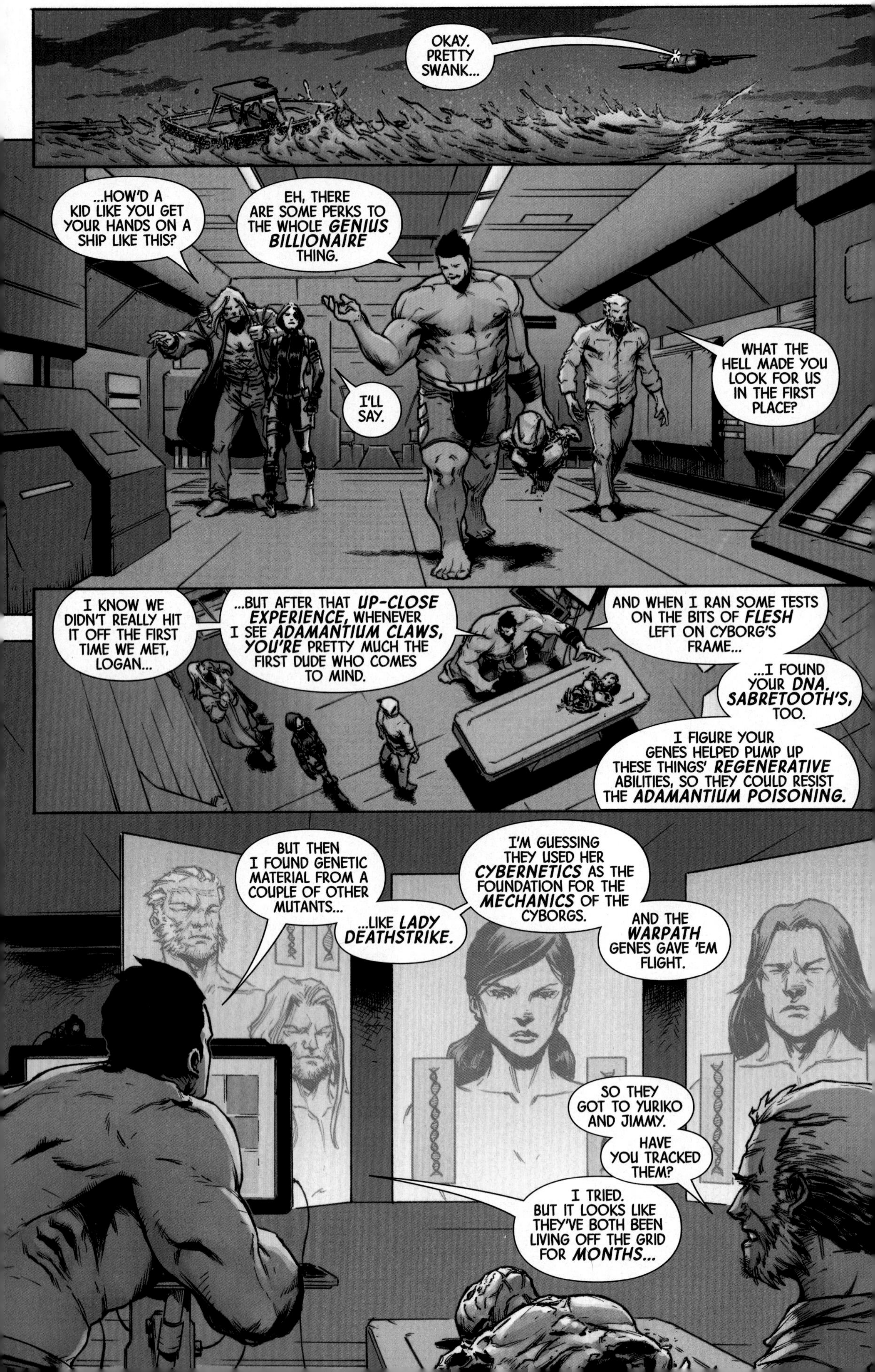
OKAY. PRETTY SWANK...
...HOW'D A KID LIKE YOU GET YOUR HANDS ON A SHIP LIKE THIS?
EH, THERE ARE SOME PERKS TO THE WHOLE GENIUS BILLIONAIRE THING.
I'LL SAY.
WHAT THE HELL MADE YOU LOOK FOR US IN THE FIRST PLACE?
I KNOW WE DIDN'T REALLY HIT IT OFF THE FIRST TIME WE MET, LOGAN...
...BUT AFTER THAT UP-CLOSE EXPERIENCE, WHENEVER I SEE ADAMANTIUM CLAWS, YOU'RE PRETTY MUCH THE FIRST DUDE WHO COMES TO MIND.
AND WHEN I RAN SOME TESTS ON THE BITS OF FLESH LEFT ON CYBORG'S FRAME...
...I FOUND YOUR DNA. SABRETOOTH'S, TOO.
I FIGURE YOUR GENES HELPED PUMP UP THESE THINGS' REGENERATIVE ABILITIES, SO THEY COULD RESIST THE ADAMANTIUM POISONING.
BUT THEN I FOUND GENETIC MATERIAL FROM A COUPLE OF OTHER MUTANTS...
...LIKE LADY DEATHSTRIKE.
I'M GUESSING THEY USED HER CYBERNETICS AS THE FOUNDATION FOR THE MECHANICS OF THE CYBORGS.
AND THE WARPATH GENES GAVE 'EM FLIGHT.
SO THEY GOT TO YURIKO AND JIMMY.
HAVE YOU TRACKED THEM?
I TRIED. BUT IT LOOKS LIKE THEY'VE BOTH BEEN LIVING OFF THE GRID FOR MONTHS...

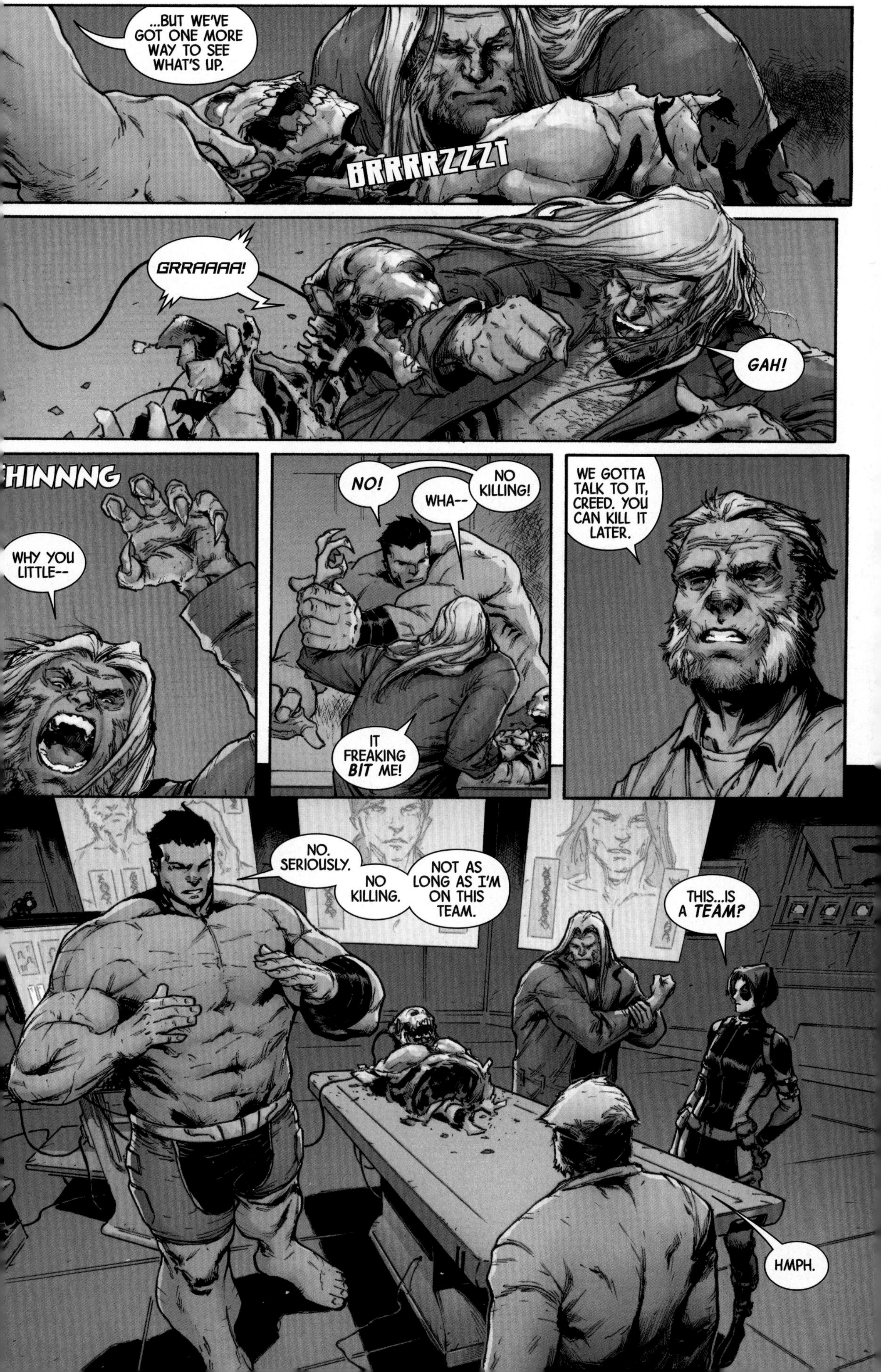
...BUT WE'VE GOT ONE MORE WAY TO SEE WHAT'S UP.
BRRRRZZZT
GRRAAAA!
GAH!
SHINNNG
WHY YOU LITTLE--
NO!
WHA--
NO KILLING!
IT FREAKING BIT ME!
WE GOTTA TALK TO IT, CREED. YOU CAN KILL IT LATER.
NO. SERIOUSLY.
NO KILLING.
NOT AS LONG AS I'M ON THIS TEAM.
THIS...IS A TEAM?
HMPH.

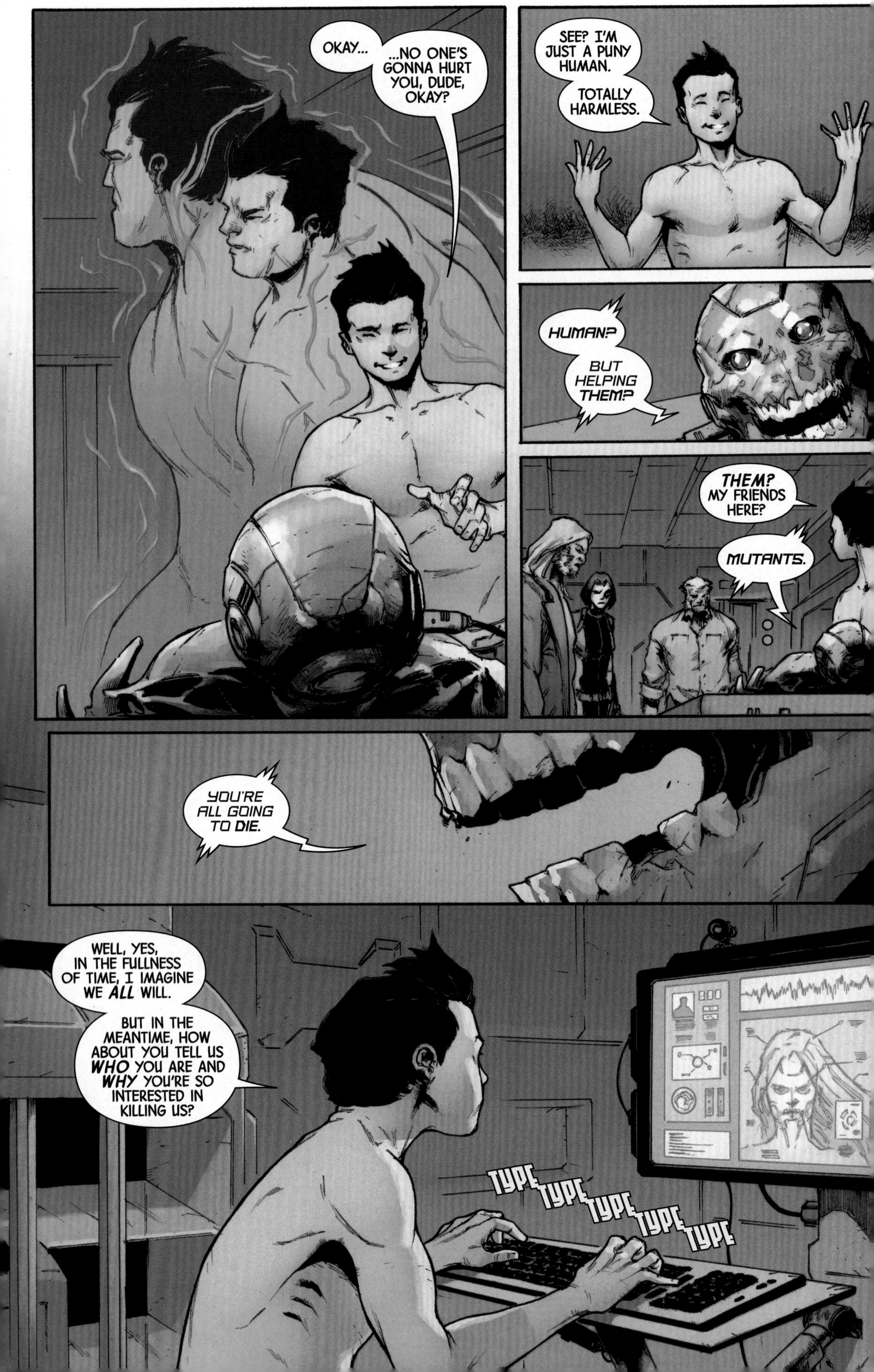

OKAY...
...NO ONE'S GONNA HURT YOU, DUDE, OKAY?
SEE? I'M JUST A PUNY HUMAN.
TOTALLY HARMLESS.
HUMAN?
BUT HELPING THEM?
THEM? MY FRIENDS HERE?
MUTANTS.
YOU'RE ALL GOING TO DIE.
WELL, YES, IN THE FULLNESS OF TIME, I IMAGINE WE ALL WILL.
BUT IN THE MEANTIME, HOW ABOUT YOU TELL US WHO YOU ARE AND WHY YOU'RE SO INTERESTED IN KILLING US?
TYPE TYPE TYPE TYPE TYPE

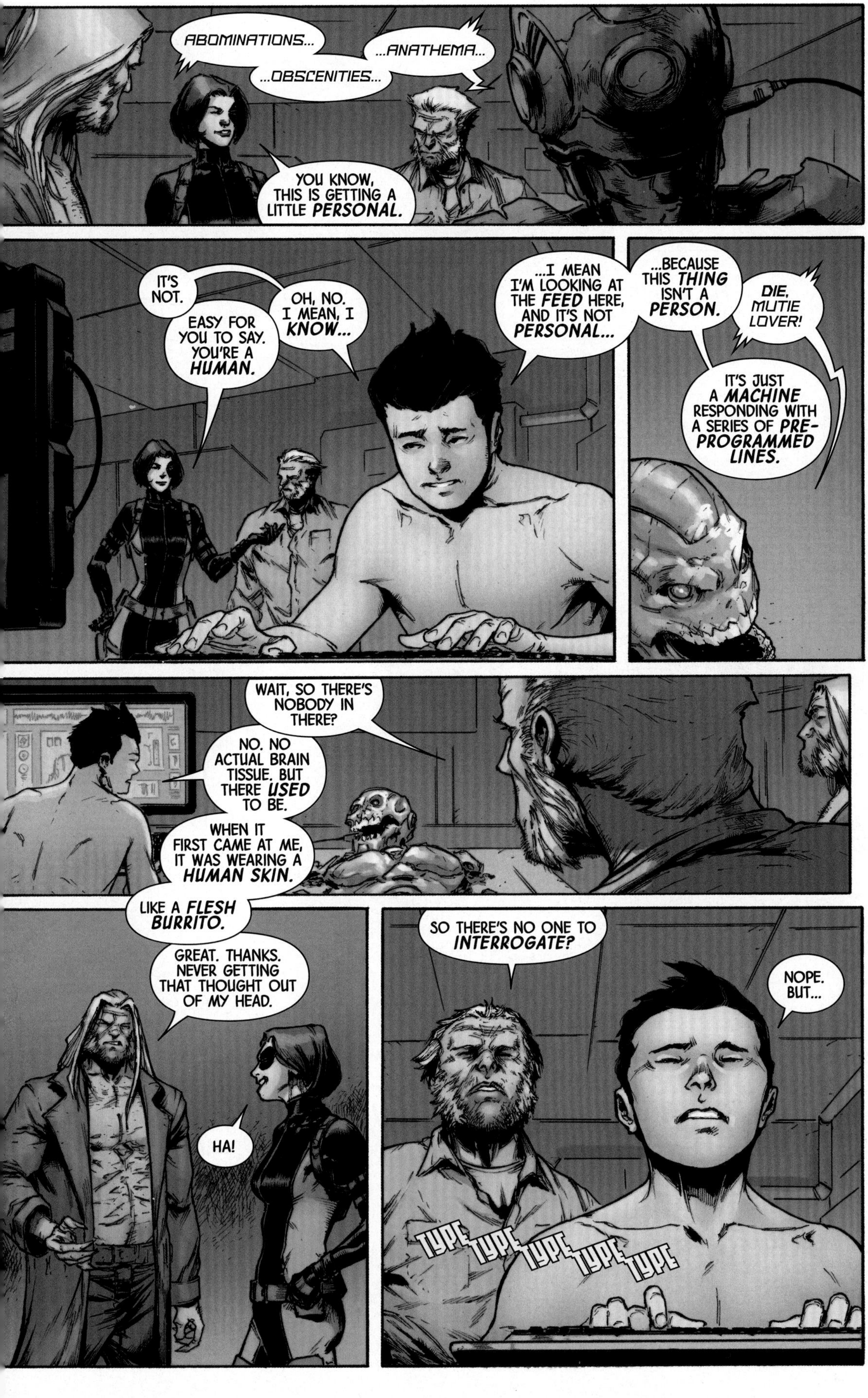
ABOMINATIONS...
...OBSCENITIES...
...ANATHEMA...
YOU KNOW, THIS IS GETTING A LITTLE PERSONAL.
IT'S NOT.
EASY FOR YOU TO SAY. YOU'RE A HUMAN.
OH, NO. I MEAN, I KNOW...
...I MEAN I'M LOOKING AT THE FEED HERE, AND IT'S NOT PERSONAL...
...BECAUSE THIS THING ISN'T A PERSON.
DIE, MUTIE LOVER!
IT'S JUST A MACHINE RESPONDING WITH A SERIES OF PRE-PROGRAMMED LINES.
WAIT, SO THERE'S NOBODY IN THERE?
NO. NO ACTUAL BRAIN TISSUE. BUT THERE USED TO BE.
WHEN IT FIRST CAME AT ME, IT WAS WEARING A HUMAN SKIN.
LIKE A FLESH BURRITO.
GREAT. THANKS. NEVER GETTING THAT THOUGHT OUT OF MY HEAD.
HA!
SO THERE'S NO ONE TO INTERROGATE?
NOPE. BUT...
TYPE TYPE TYPE TYPE TYPE

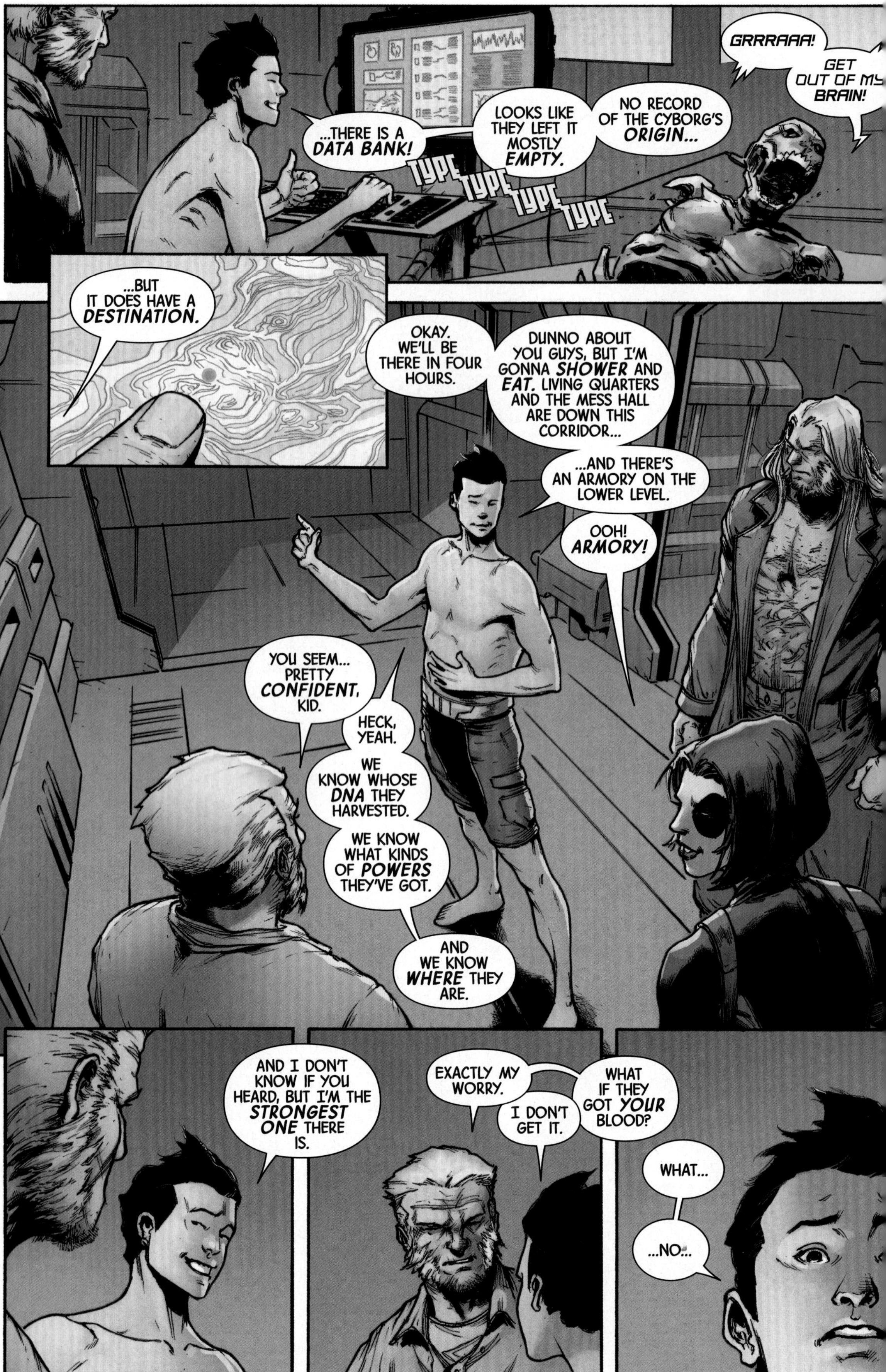
...THERE IS A DATA BANK!
LOOKS LIKE THEY LEFT IT MOSTLY EMPTY.
NO RECORD OF THE CYBORG'S ORIGIN...
TYPE TYPE TYPE TYPE
GRRRAAA!
GET OUT OF MY BRAIN!
...BUT IT DOES HAVE A DESTINATION.
OKAY. WE'LL BE THERE IN FOUR HOURS.
DUNNO ABOUT YOU GUYS, BUT I'M GONNA SHOWER AND EAT. LIVING QUARTERS AND THE MESS HALL ARE DOWN THIS CORRIDOR...
...AND THERE'S AN ARMORY ON THE LOWER LEVEL.
OOH! ARMORY!
YOU SEEM... PRETTY CONFIDENT, KID.
HECK, YEAH.
WE KNOW WHOSE DNA THEY HARVESTED.
WE KNOW WHAT KINDS OF POWERS THEY'VE GOT.
AND WE KNOW WHERE THEY ARE.
AND I DON'T KNOW IF YOU HEARD, BUT I'M THE STRONGEST ONE THERE IS.
EXACTLY MY WORRY.
I DON'T GET IT.
WHAT IF THEY GOT YOUR BLOOD?
WHAT...
...NO...

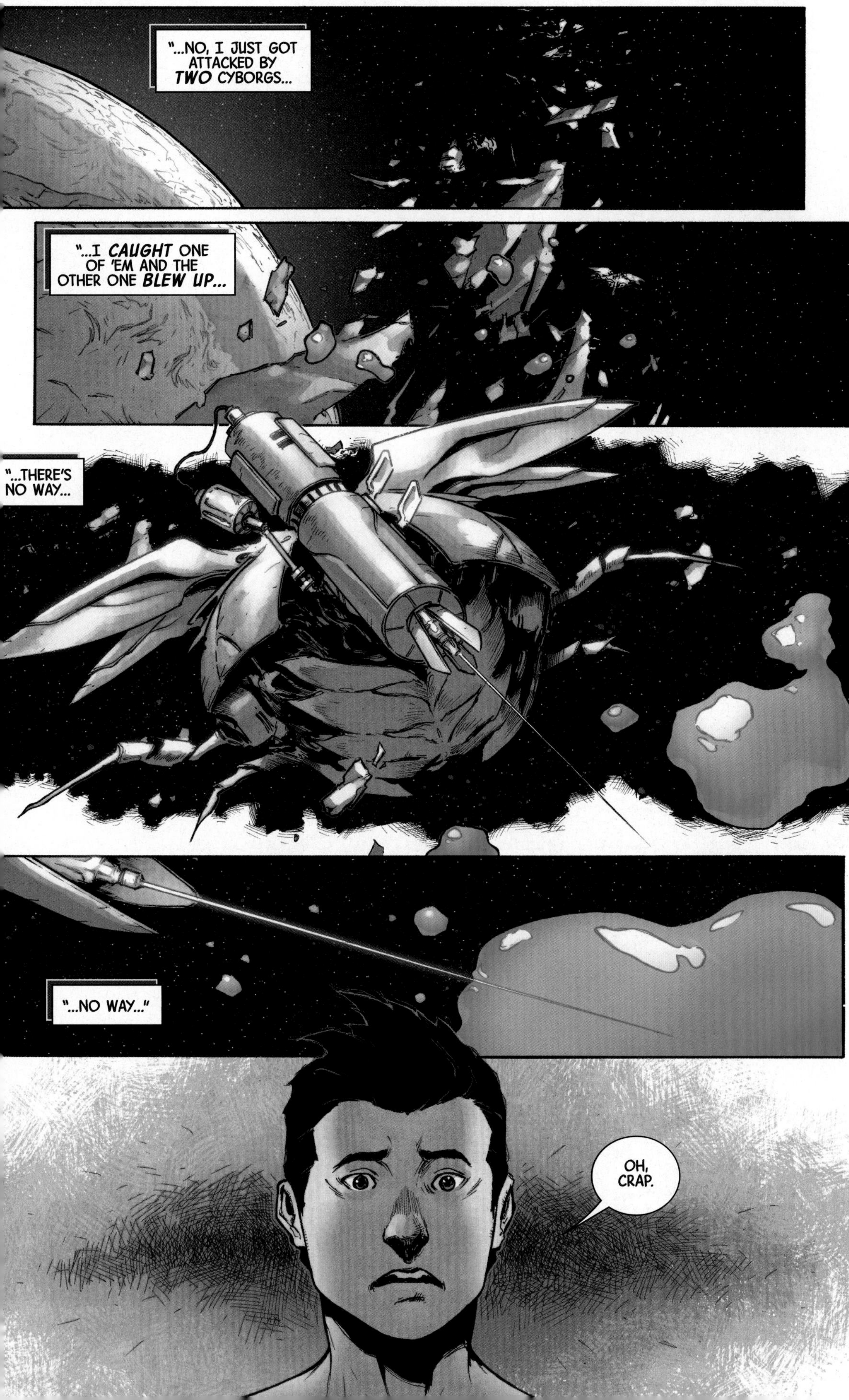
"...NO, I JUST GOT ATTACKED BY TWO CYBORGS...
"...I CAUGHT ONE OF 'EM AND THE OTHER ONE BLEW UP...
"...THERE'S NO WAY...
"...NO WAY..."
OH, CRAP.

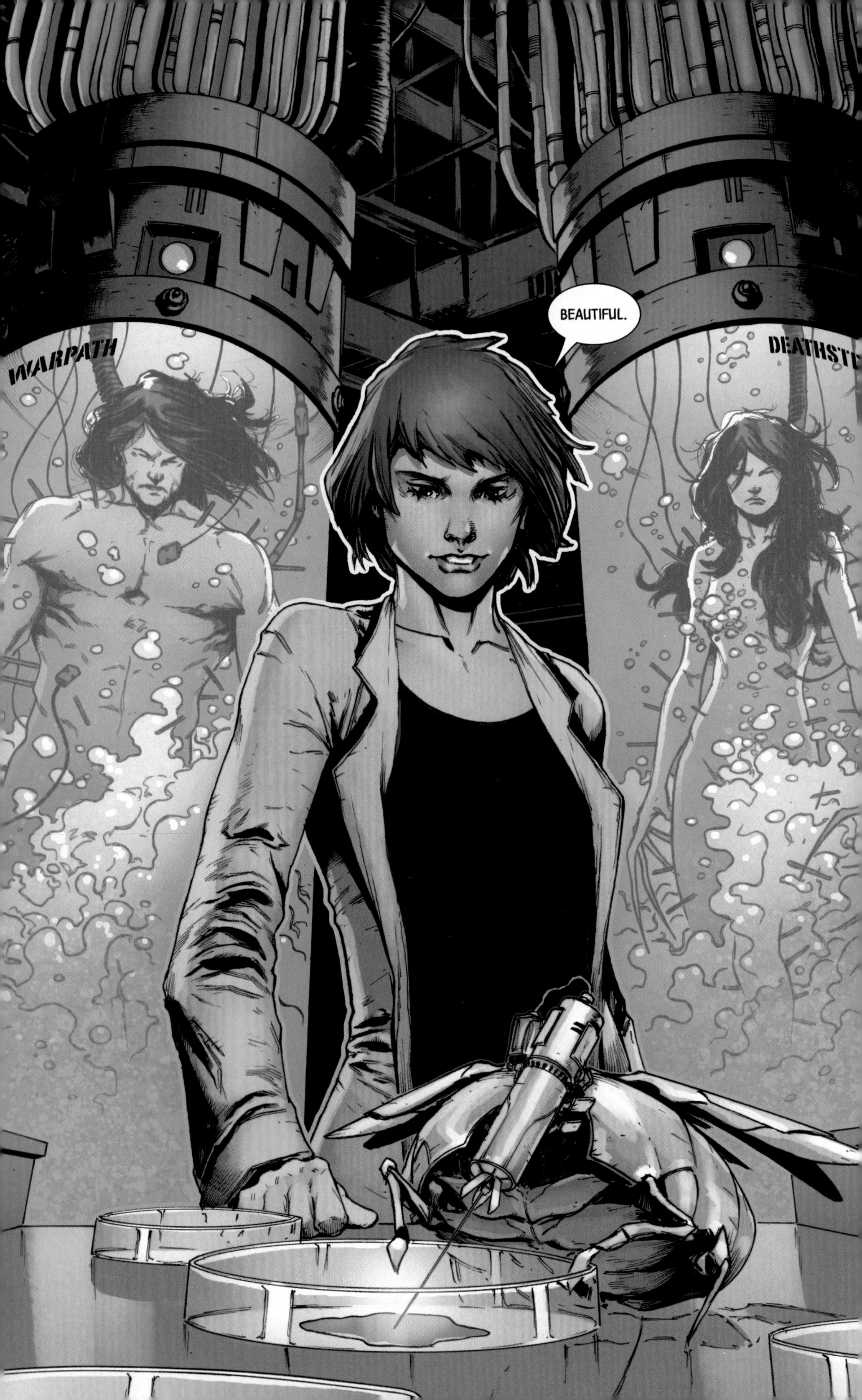

WARPATH
BEAUTIFUL.
DEATHST

4

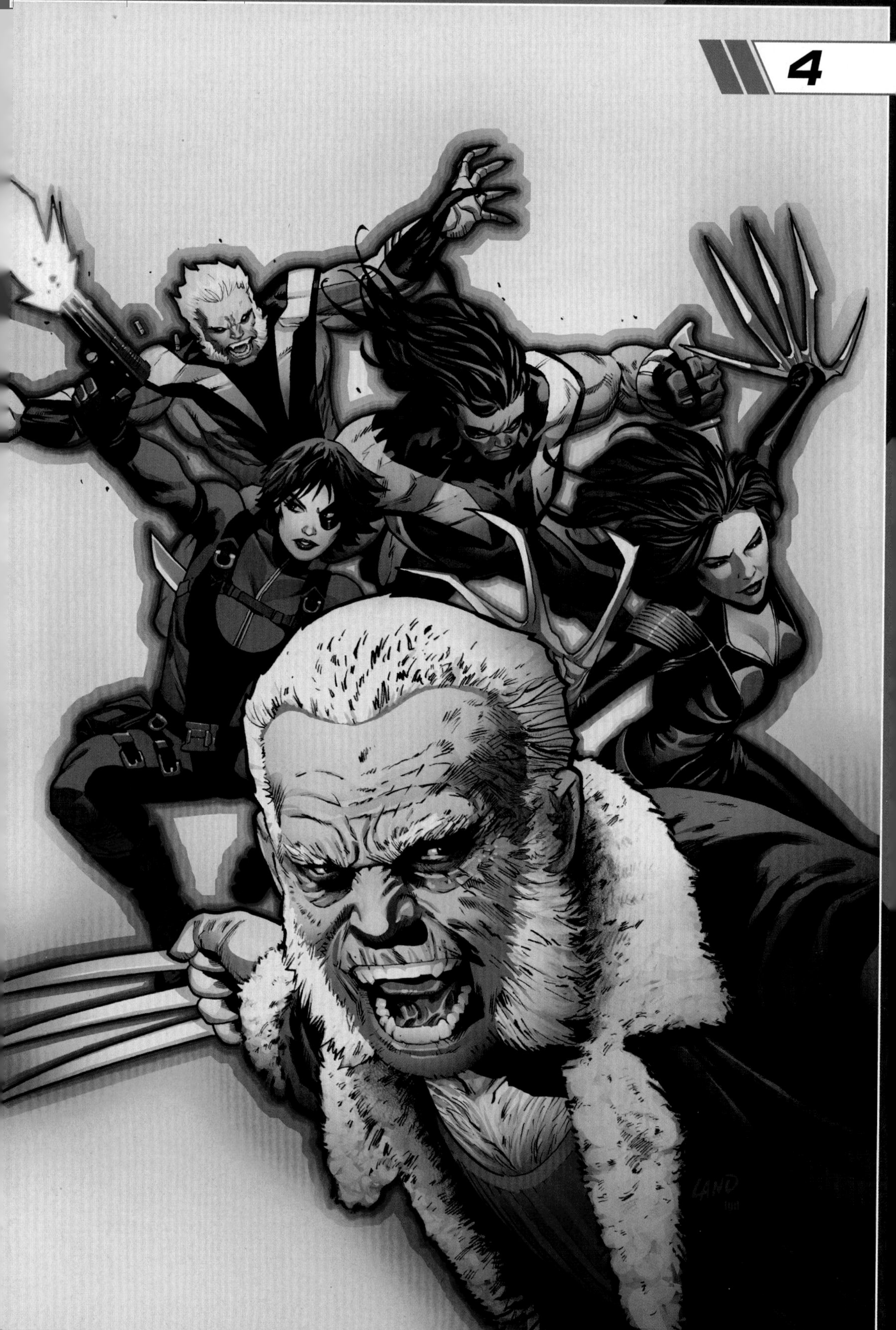

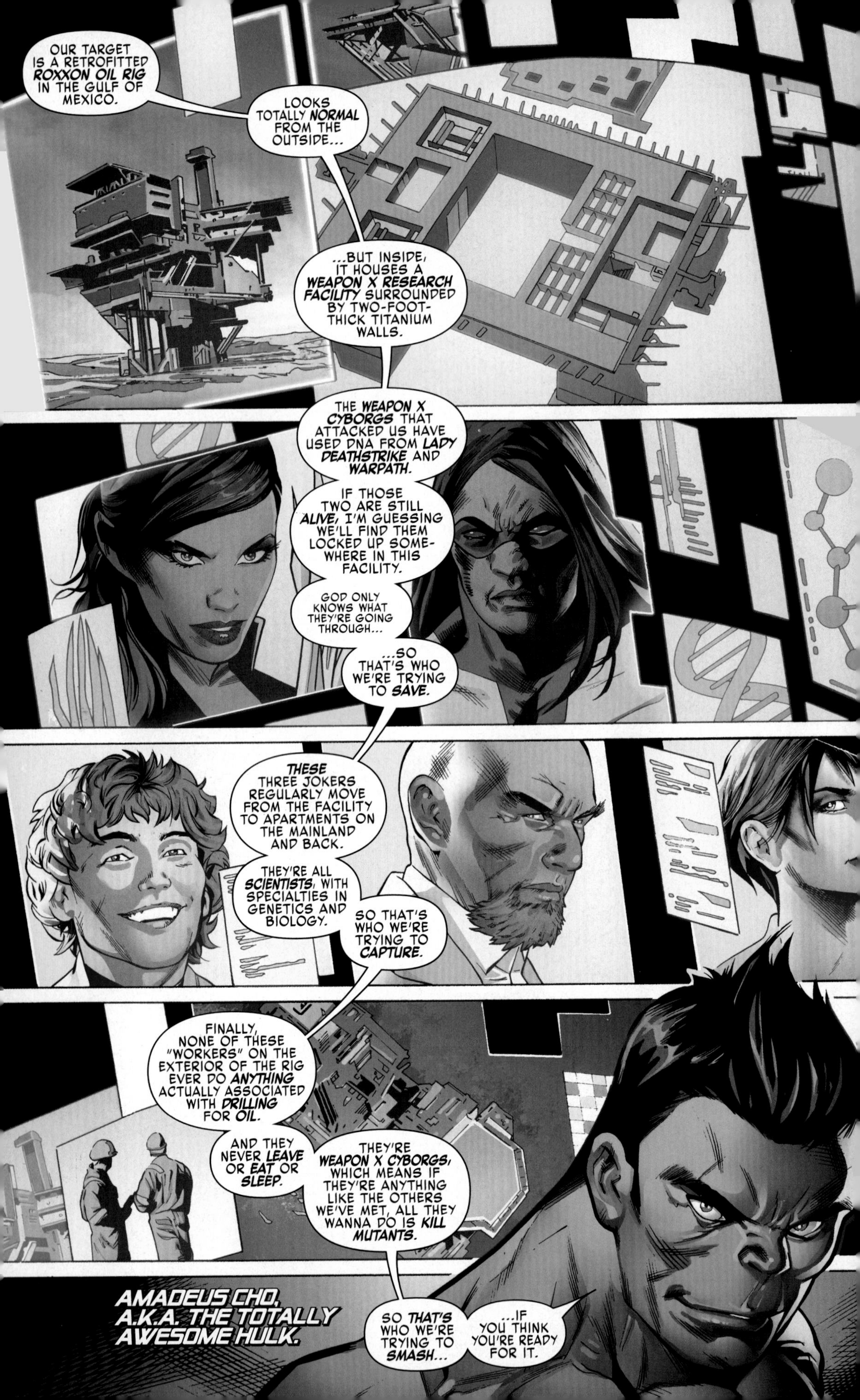
OUR TARGET IS A RETROFITTED ROXXON OIL RIG IN THE GULF OF MEXICO.
LOOKS TOTALLY NORMAL FROM THE OUTSIDE...
...BUT INSIDE, IT HOUSES A WEAPON X RESEARCH FACILITY SURROUNDED BY TWO-FOOT-THICK TITANIUM WALLS.
THE WEAPON X CYBORGS THAT ATTACKED US HAVE USED DNA FROM LADY DEATHSTRIKE AND WARPATH.
IF THOSE TWO ARE STILL ALIVE, I'M GUESSING WE'LL FIND THEM LOCKED UP SOMEWHERE IN THIS FACILITY.
GOD ONLY KNOWS WHAT THEY'RE GOING THROUGH...
...SO THAT'S WHO WE'RE TRYING TO SAVE.
THESE THREE JOKERS REGULARLY MOVE FROM THE FACILITY TO APARTMENTS ON THE MAINLAND AND BACK.
THEY'RE ALL SCIENTISTS, WITH SPECIALTIES IN GENETICS AND BIOLOGY.
SO THAT'S WHO WE'RE TRYING TO CAPTURE.
FINALLY, NONE OF THESE "WORKERS" ON THE EXTERIOR OF THE RIG EVER DO ANYTHING ACTUALLY ASSOCIATED WITH DRILLING FOR OIL.
AND THEY NEVER LEAVE OR EAT OR SLEEP.
THEY'RE WEAPON X CYBORGS, WHICH MEANS IF THEY'RE ANYTHING LIKE THE OTHERS WE'VE MET, ALL THEY WANNA DO IS KILL MUTANTS.
AMADEUS CHO, A.K.A. THE TOTALLY AWESOME HULK.
SO THAT'S WHO WE'RE TRYING TO SMASH...
...IF YOU THINK YOU'RE READY FOR IT.

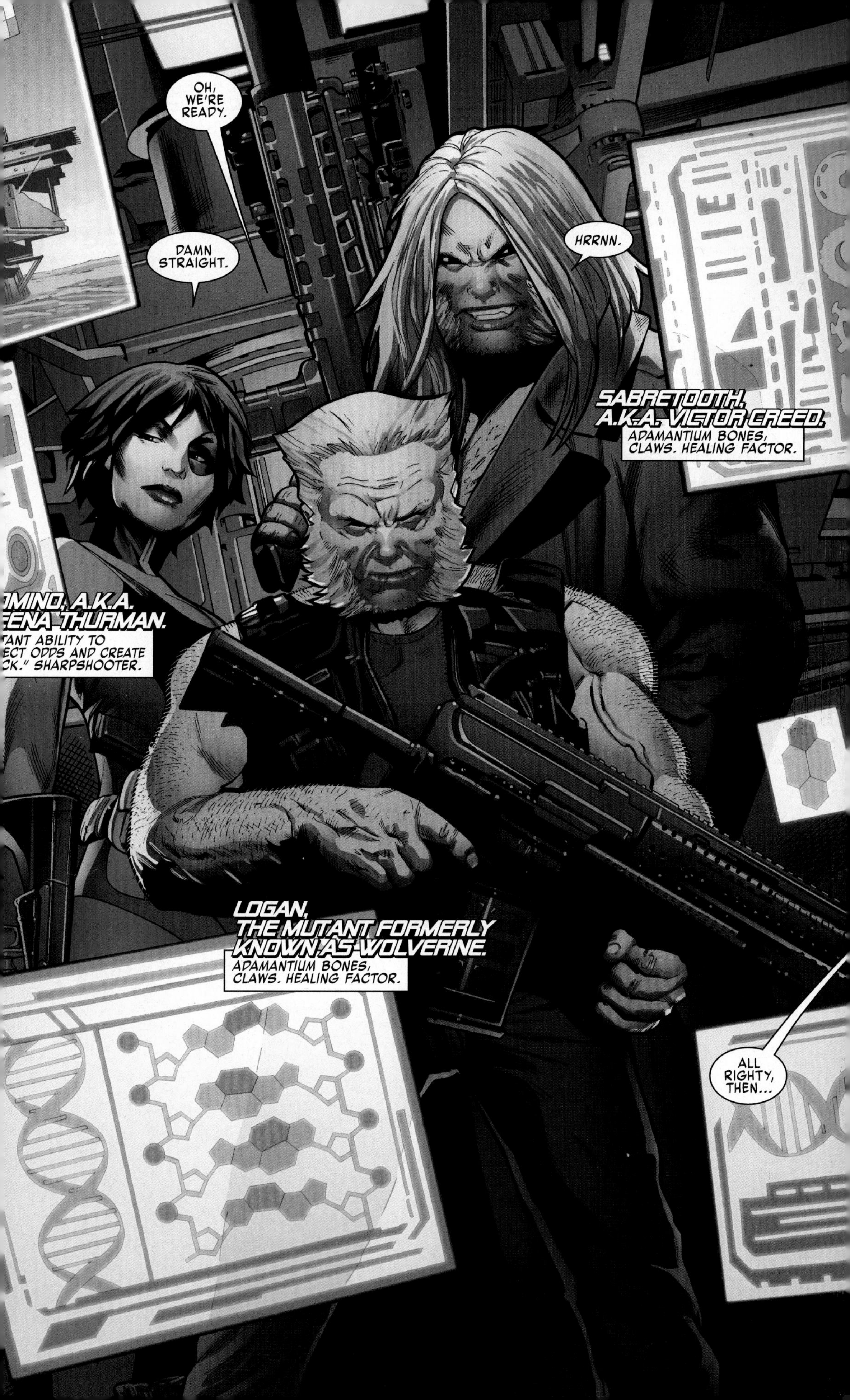

OH, WE'RE READY.
DAMN STRAIGHT.
HRRNN.
SABRETOOTH, A.K.A. VICTOR CREED.
ADAMANTIUM BONES, CLAWS. HEALING FACTOR.
OMINO, A.K.A. EENA THURMAN.
TANT ABILITY TO ECT ODDS AND CREATE CK." SHARPSHOOTER.
LOGAN, THE MUTANT FORMERLY KNOWN AS WOLVERINE.
ADAMANTIUM BONES, CLAWS. HEALING FACTOR.
ALL RIGHTY, THEN...

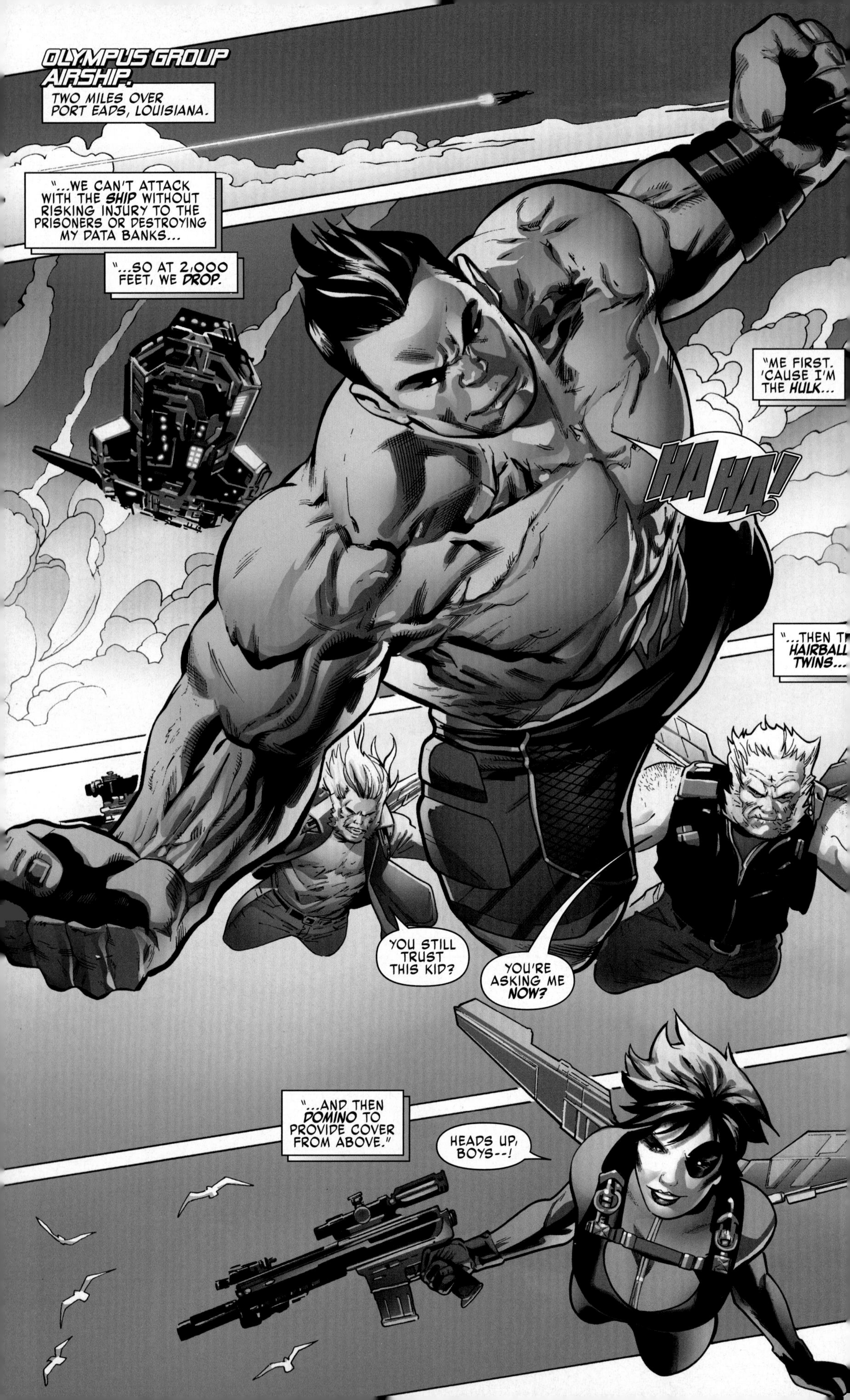

OLYMPUS GROUP AIRSHIP.
TWO MILES OVER PORT EADS, LOUISIANA.
"...WE CAN'T ATTACK WITH THE SHIP WITHOUT RISKING INJURY TO THE PRISONERS OR DESTROYING MY DATA BANKS...
"...SO AT 2,000 FEET, WE DROP.
"ME FIRST. 'CAUSE I'M THE HULK...
HA HA!
"...THEN T HAIRBALL TWINS...
YOU STILL TRUST THIS KID?
YOU'RE ASKING ME NOW?
"...AND THEN DOMINO TO PROVIDE COVER FROM ABOVE."
HEADS UP, BOYS--!

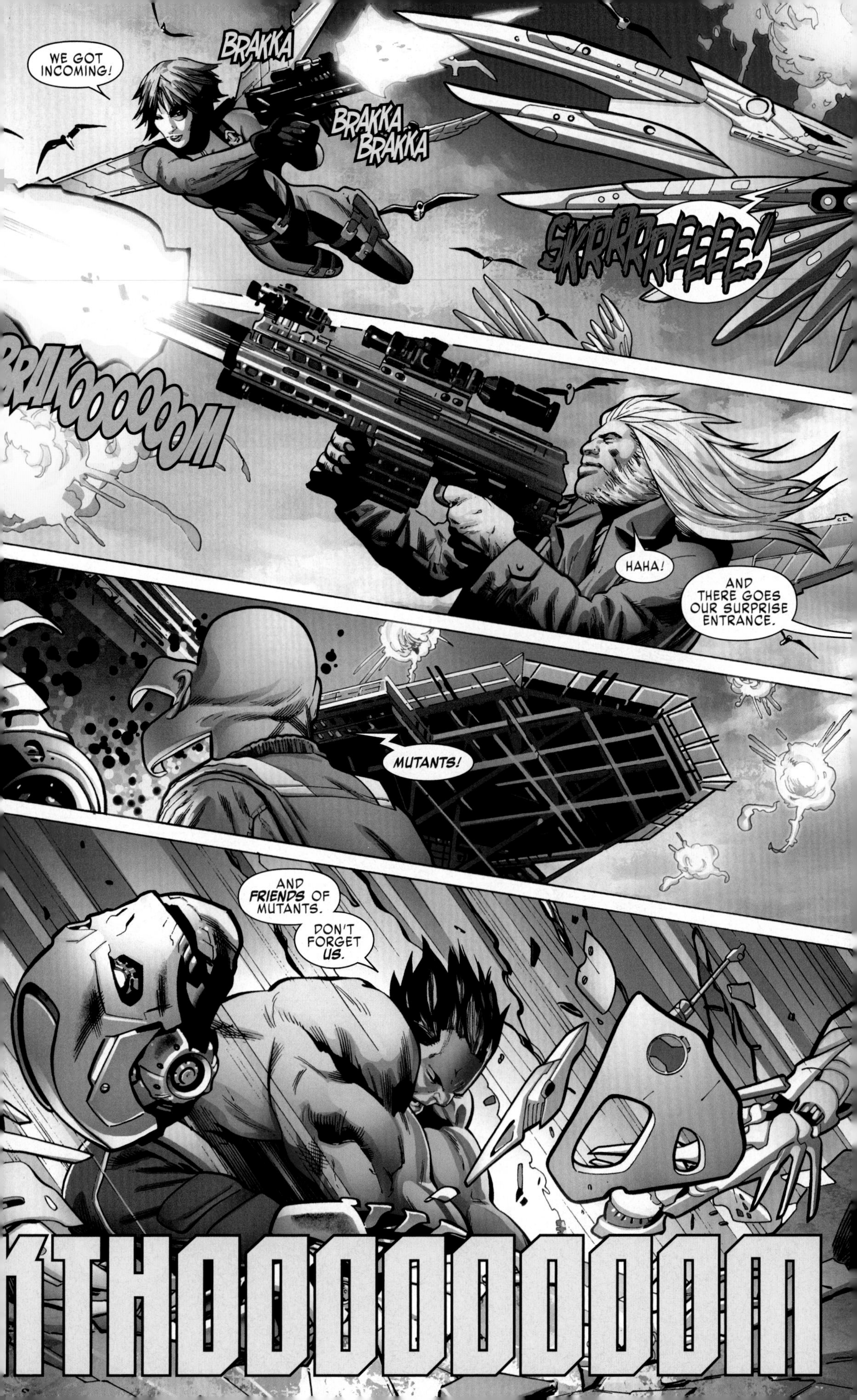
WE GOT INCOMING!
BRAKKA
BRAKKA BRAKKA
SKRRRREEEE!
BRAKOOOOOOOM
HAHA!
AND THERE GOES OUR SURPRISE ENTRANCE.
MUTANTS!
AND *FRIENDS* OF MUTANTS.
DON'T FORGET *US*.
KTHOOOOOOOOM

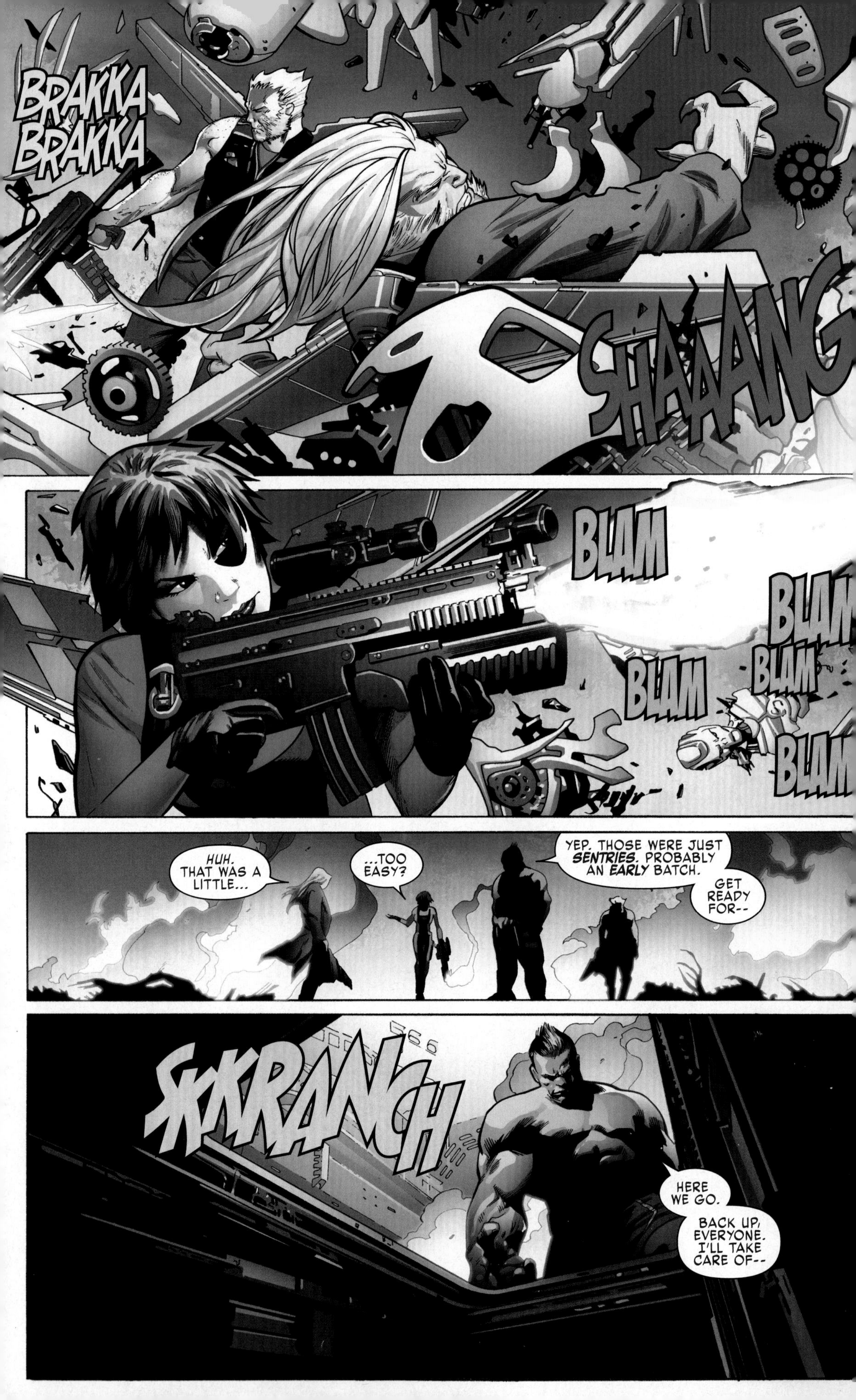
BRAKKA
BRAKKA
SHAAANG
BLAM
BLAM
BLAM
BLAM
BLAM
HUH. THAT WAS A LITTLE...
...TOO EASY?
YEP. THOSE WERE JUST SENTRIES. PROBABLY AN EARLY BATCH.
GET READY FOR--
SKKRANCH
HERE WE GO.
BACK UP, EVERYONE. I'LL TAKE CARE OF--

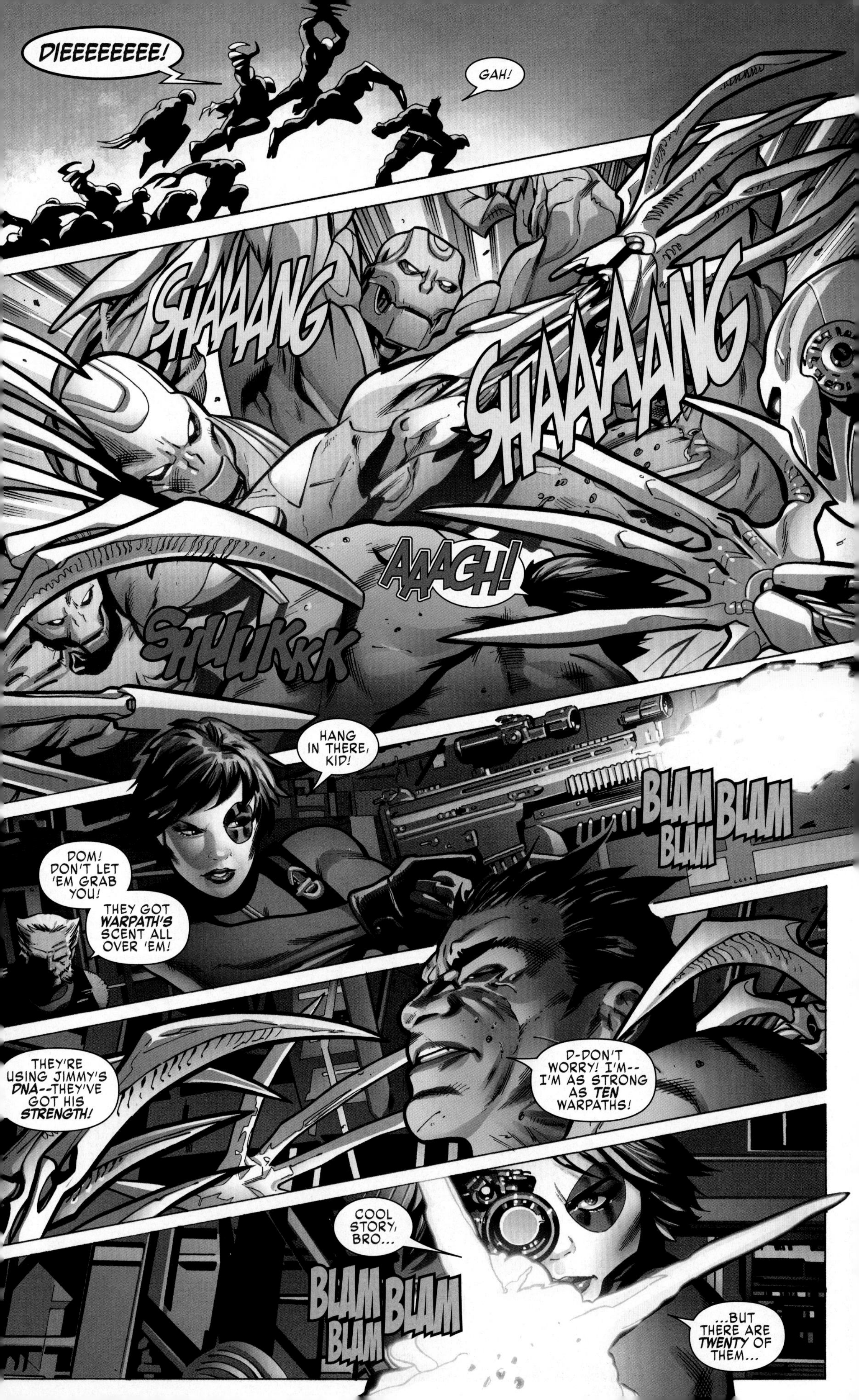
DIEEEEEEEE!
GAH!
SHAAANG
SHAAAAANG
AAAGH!
SHUKKK
HANG IN THERE, KID!
BLAM BLAM BLAM
DOM! DON'T LET 'EM GRAB YOU!
THEY GOT WARPATH'S SCENT ALL OVER 'EM!
THEY'RE USING JIMMY'S DNA--THEY'VE GOT HIS STRENGTH!
D-DON'T WORRY! I'M-- I'M AS STRONG AS TEN WARPATHS!
COOL STORY, BRO...
BLAM BLAM BLAM
...BUT THERE ARE TWENTY OF THEM...

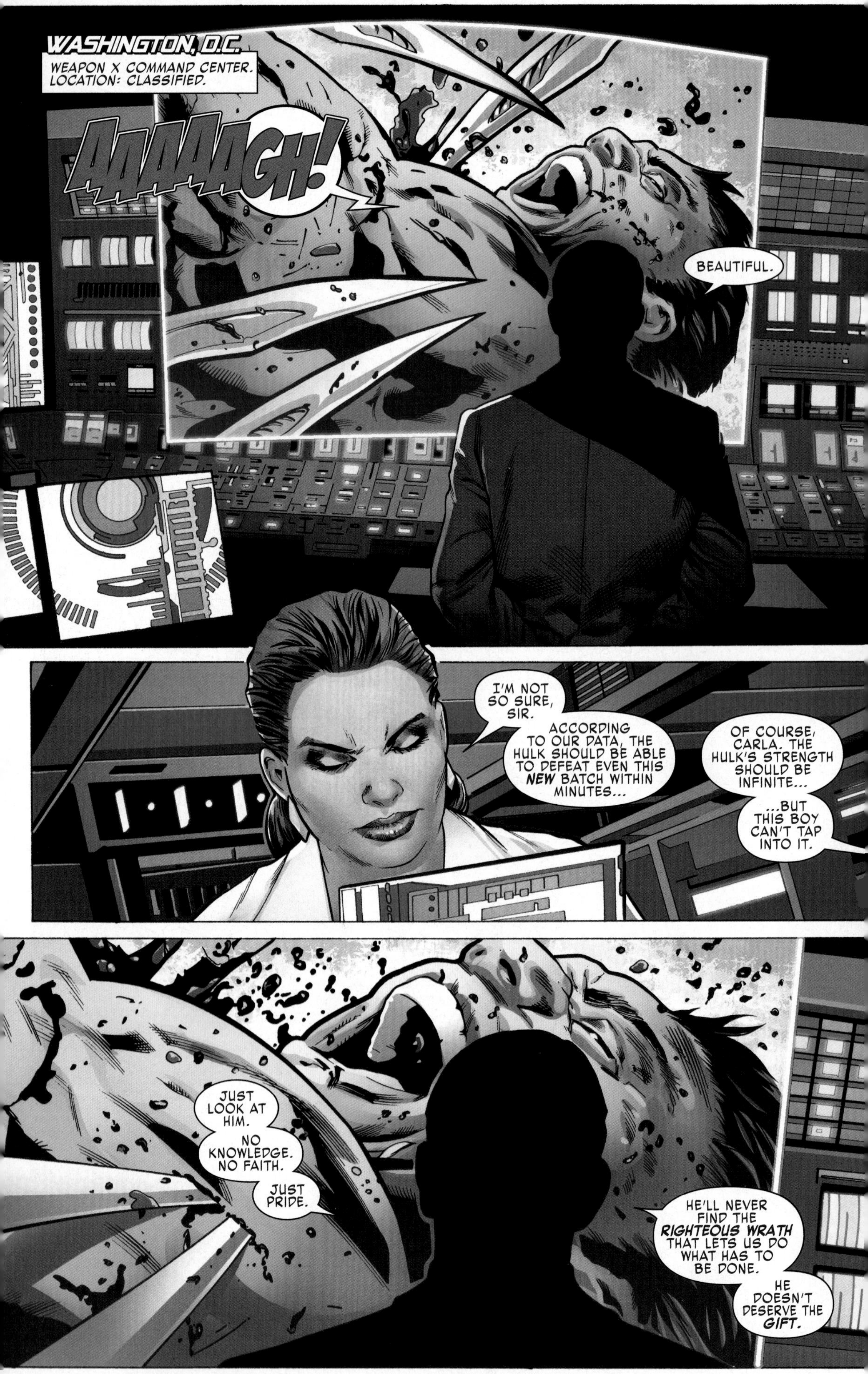
WASHINGTON, D.C.
WEAPON X COMMAND CENTER. LOCATION: CLASSIFIED.
AAAAAGH!
BEAUTIFUL.
I'M NOT SO SURE, SIR.
ACCORDING TO OUR DATA, THE HULK SHOULD BE ABLE TO DEFEAT EVEN THIS NEW BATCH WITHIN MINUTES...
OF COURSE, CARLA. THE HULK'S STRENGTH SHOULD BE INFINITE...
...BUT THIS BOY CAN'T TAP INTO IT.
JUST LOOK AT HIM.
NO KNOWLEDGE. NO FAITH.
JUST PRIDE.
HE'LL NEVER FIND THE RIGHTEOUS WRATH THAT LETS US DO WHAT HAS TO BE DONE.
HE DOESN'T DESERVE THE GIFT.

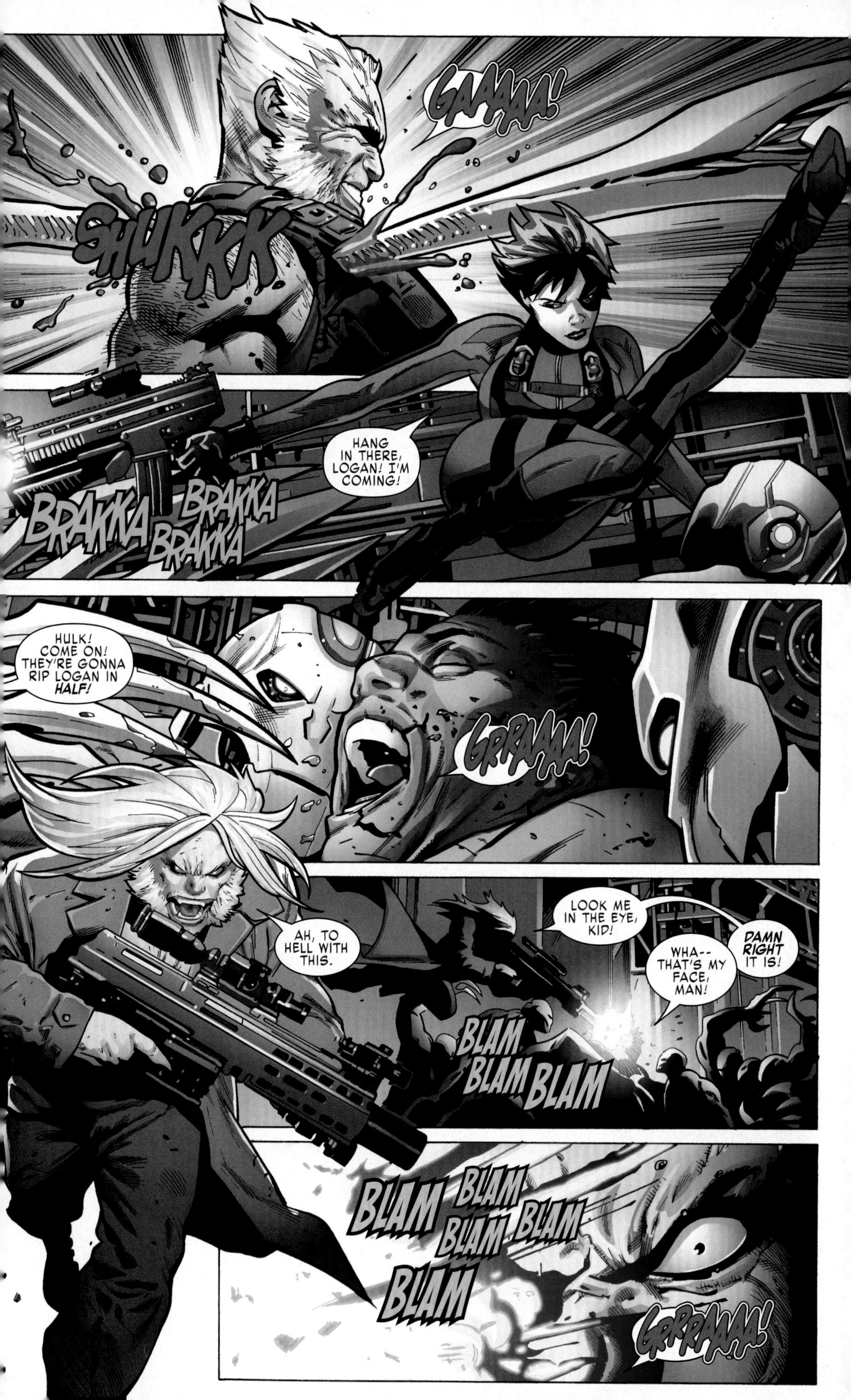
GAAAAA!
SHUKKK
HANG IN THERE, LOGAN! I'M COMING!
BRAKKA BRAKKA BRAKKA
HULK! COME ON! THEY'RE GONNA RIP LOGAN IN HALF!
GRRAAAA!
AH, TO HELL WITH THIS.
LOOK ME IN THE EYE, KID!
WHA-- THAT'S MY FACE, MAN!
DAMN RIGHT IT IS!
BLAM BLAM BLAM
BLAM BLAM BLAM BLAM BLAM
GRRRAAAA!

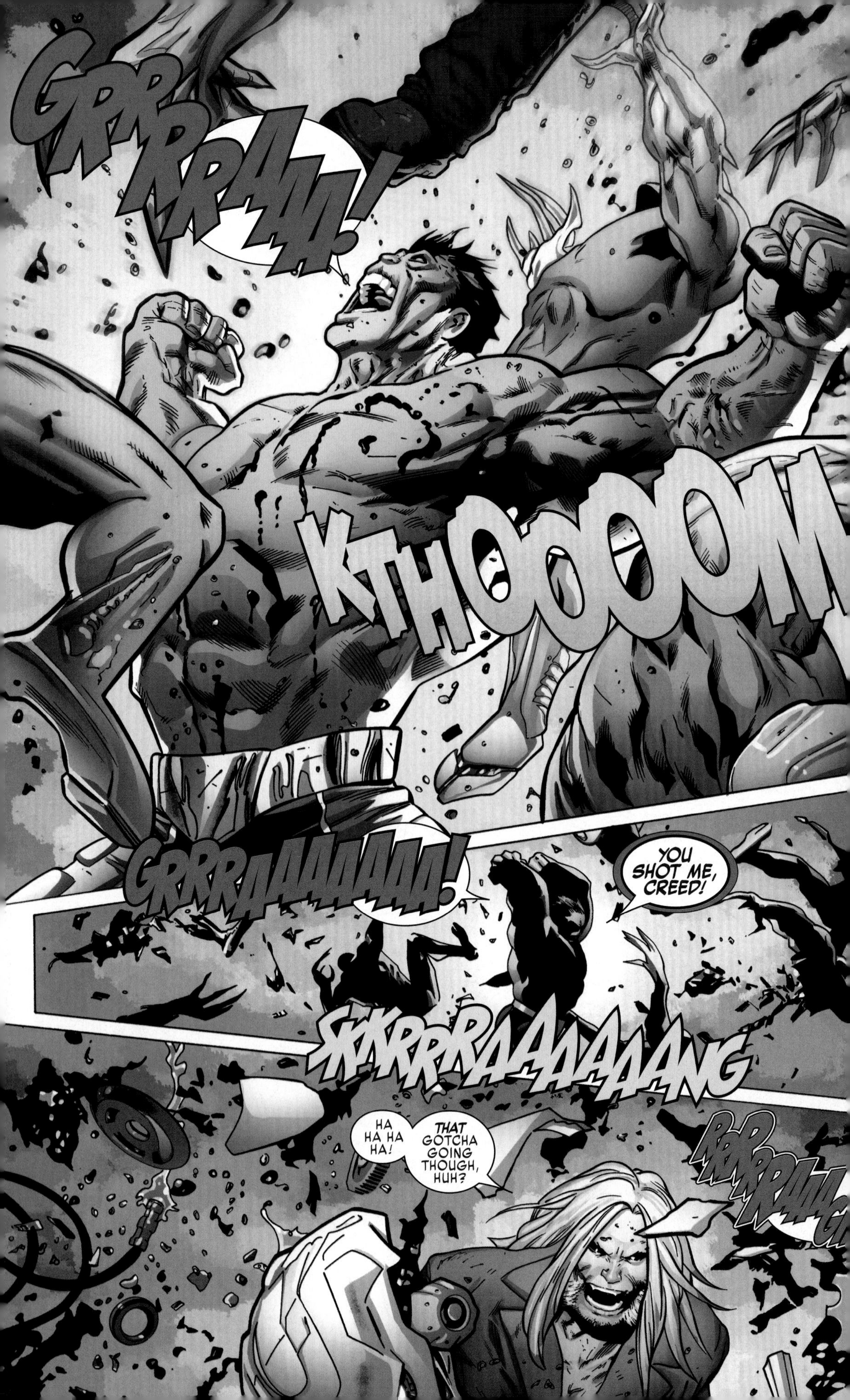
GRRRRAAAA!
KTHOOOOOM
GRRRAAAAAAAA!
YOU SHOT ME, CREED!
SKKRRRAAAAAAANG
HA HA HA HA!
THAT GOTCHA GOING THOUGH, HUH?
RGRRAAAG

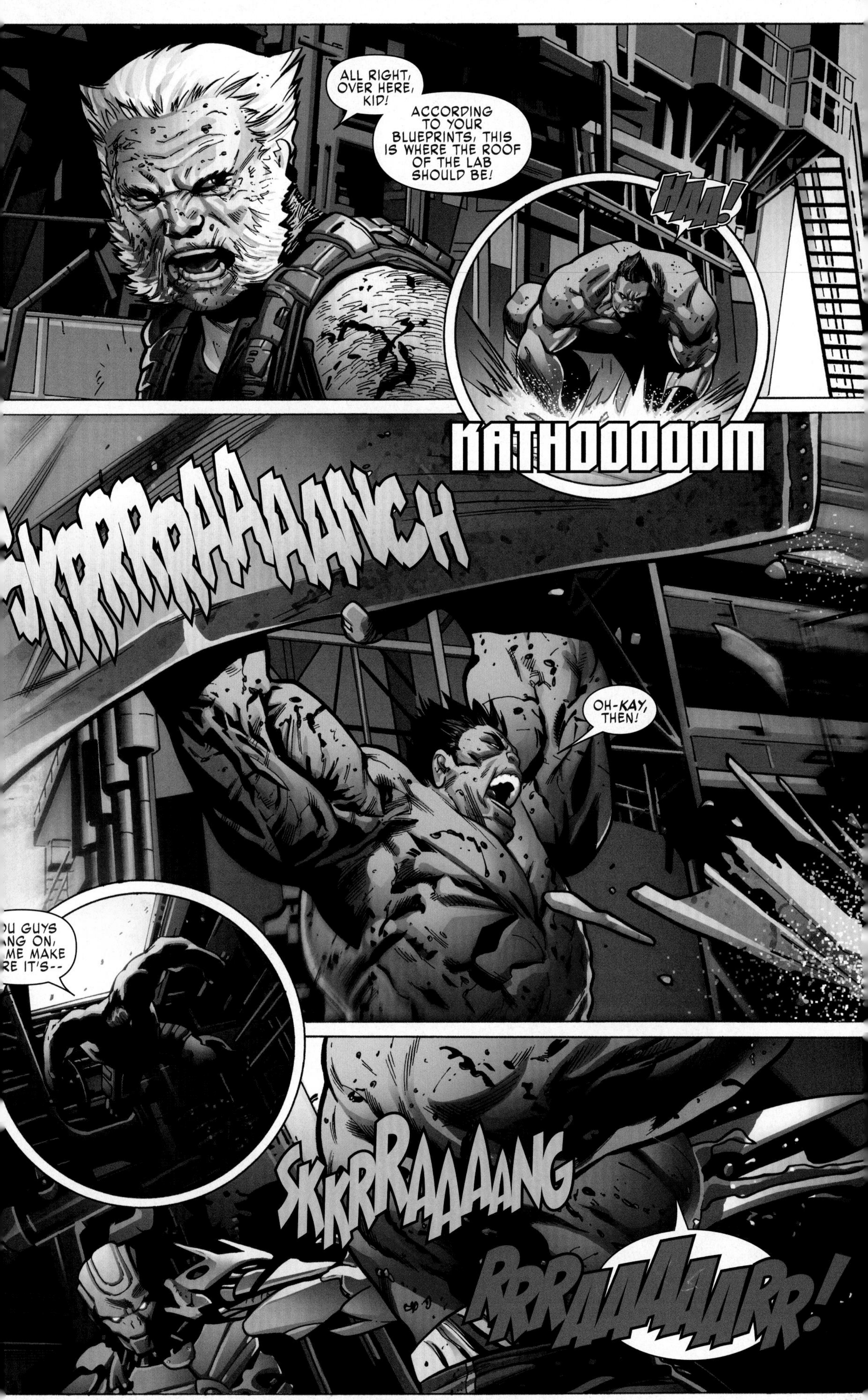
ALL RIGHT, OVER HERE, KID!
ACCORDING TO YOUR BLUEPRINTS, THIS IS WHERE THE ROOF OF THE LAB SHOULD BE!
HAA!
KATHOOOOOOM
SKRRRRAAAAANCH
OH-KAY, THEN!
OU GUYS
ANG ON,
ME MAKE
RE IT'S--
SKKRRAAAANG
RRRAAAAAARR!

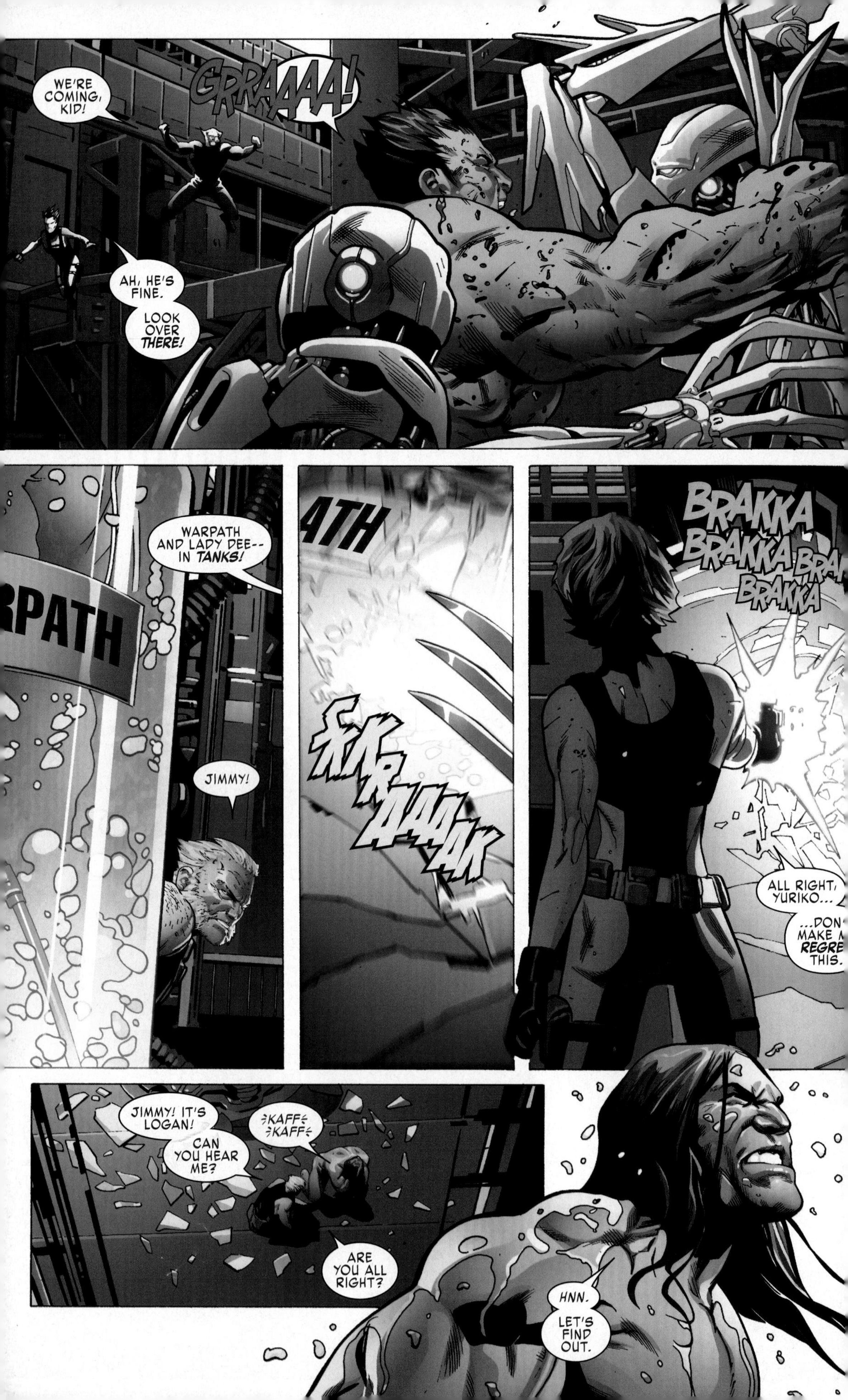
WE'RE COMING, KID!
GRRAAAA!
AH, HE'S FINE.
LOOK OVER THERE!
WARPATH AND LADY DEE-- IN TANKS!
RPATH
JIMMY!
ATH
SKRAAAAK
BRAKKA BRAKKA BRAKKA
ALL RIGHT, YURIKO...
JIMMY! IT'S LOGAN!
CAN YOU HEAR ME?
KAFF KAFF
ARE YOU ALL RIGHT?
HNN.
LET'S FIND OUT.

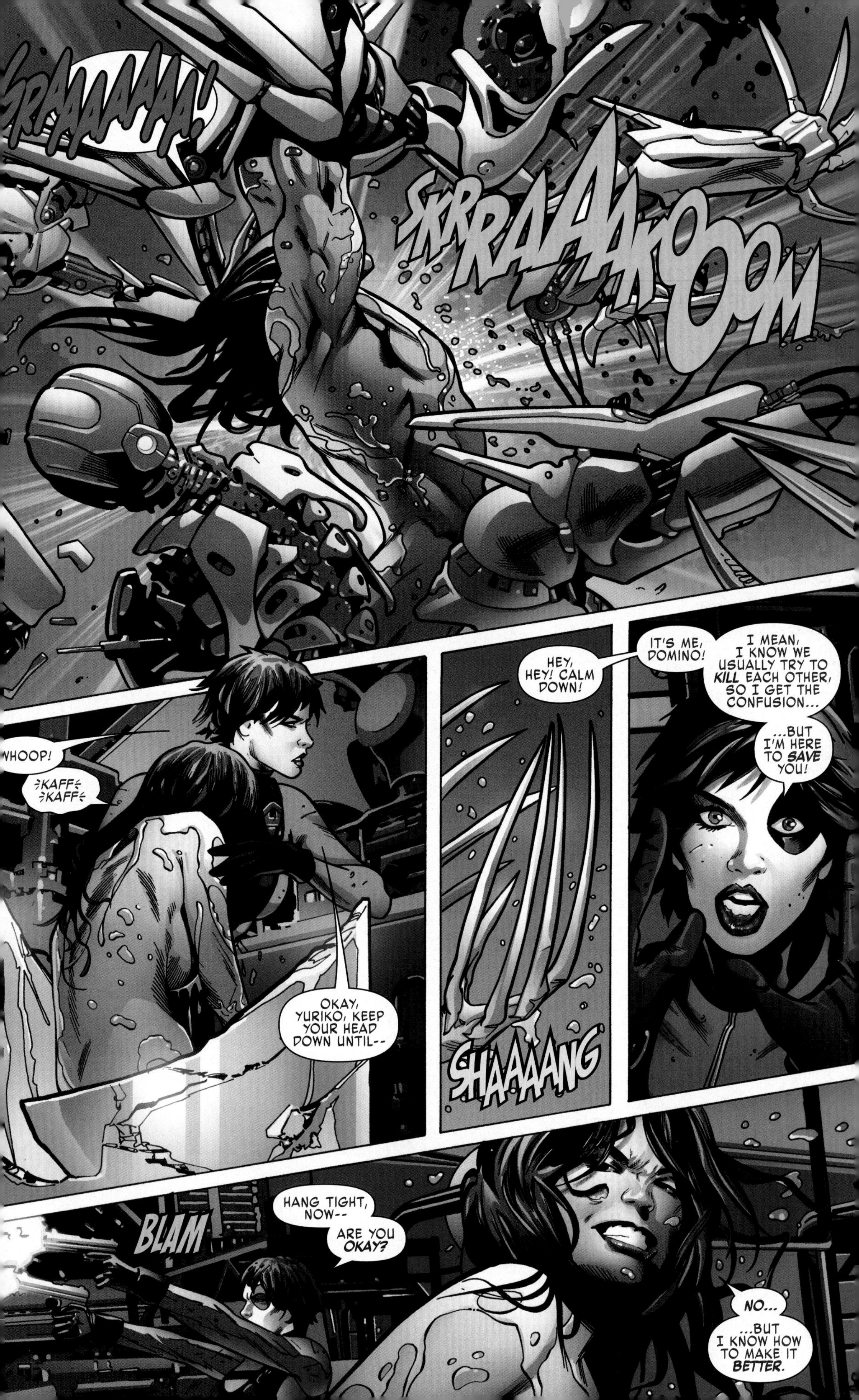
GRAAAAAAA!
SKRRAAAKOOOM
WHOOP!
KAFF KAFF
OKAY, YURIKO, KEEP YOUR HEAD DOWN UNTIL--
HEY, HEY! CALM DOWN!
IT'S ME, DOMINO!
SHAAAANG
I MEAN, I KNOW WE USUALLY TRY TO KILL EACH OTHER, SO I GET THE CONFUSION...
...BUT I'M HERE TO SAVE YOU!
BLAM
HANG TIGHT, NOW--
ARE YOU OKAY?
NO...
...BUT I KNOW HOW TO MAKE IT BETTER.

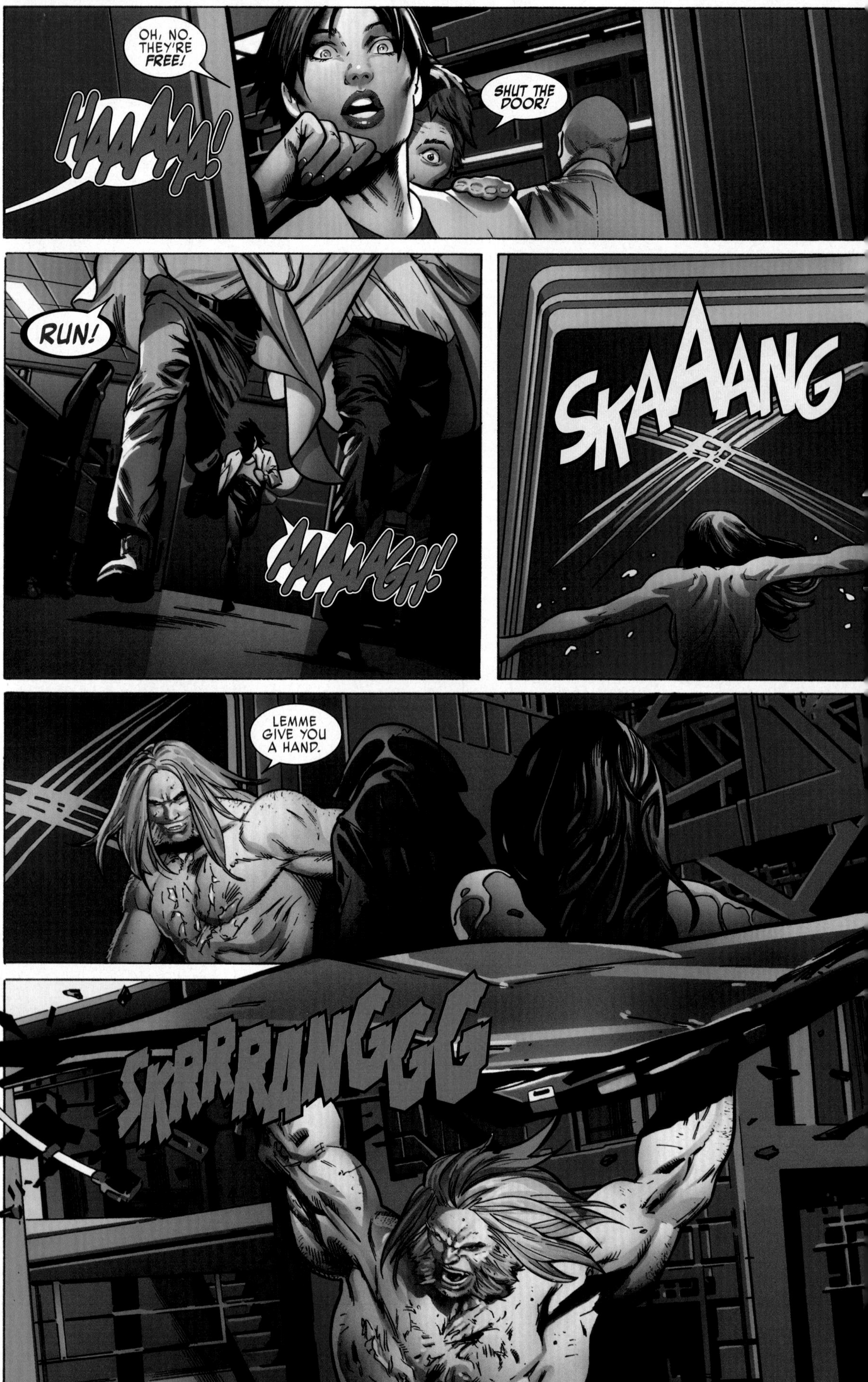
OH, NO. THEY'RE FREE!
HAAAAAA!
SHUT THE DOOR!
RUN!
AAAAAGH!
SKAAANG
LEMME GIVE YOU A HAND.
SKRRRANGGG

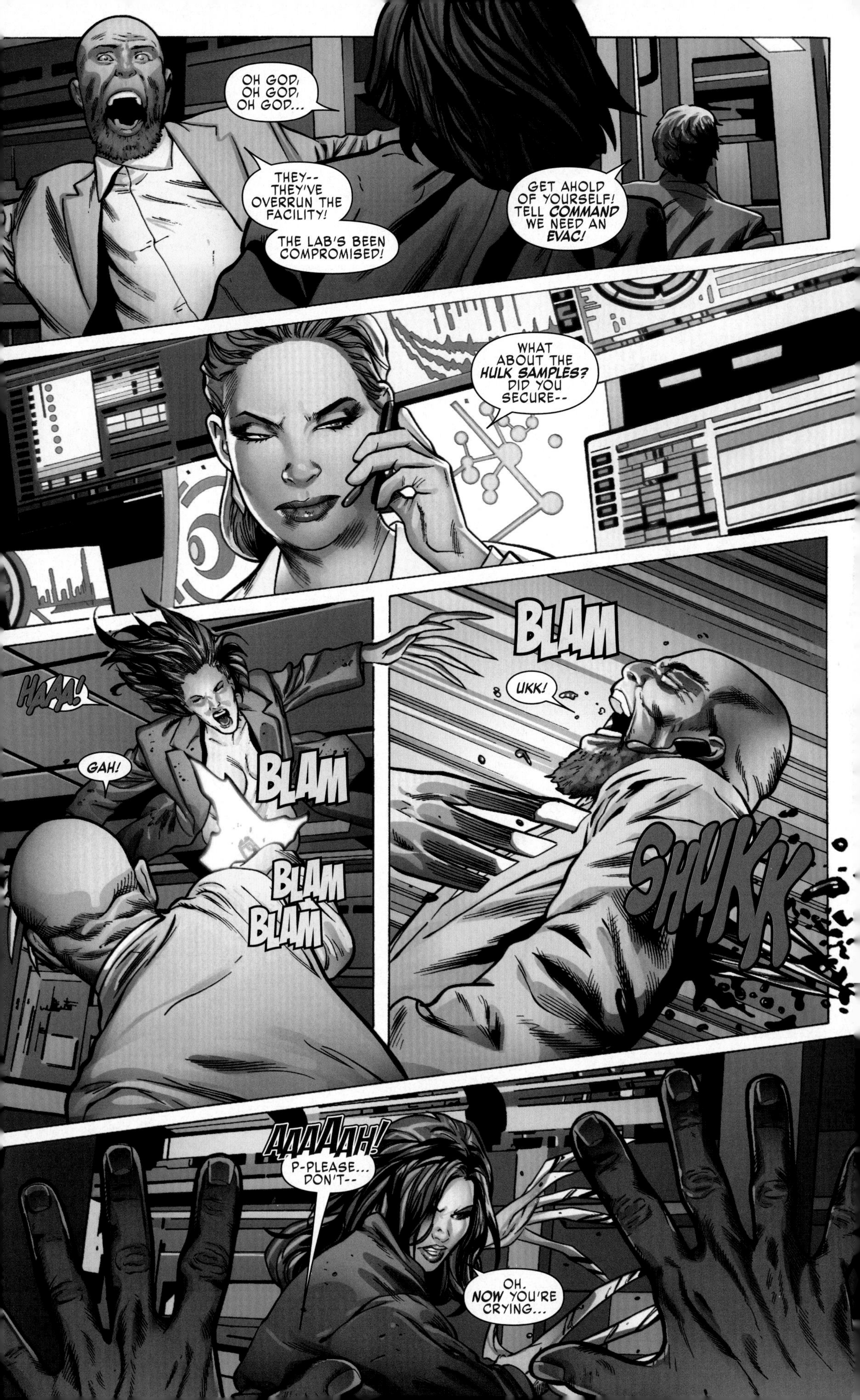
OH GOD, OH GOD, OH GOD...
THEY-- THEY'VE OVERRUN THE FACILITY!
THE LAB'S BEEN COMPROMISED!
GET AHOLD OF YOURSELF! TELL COMMAND WE NEED AN EVAC!
WHAT ABOUT THE HULK SAMPLES? DID YOU SECURE--
HAAA!
GAH!
BLAM
BLAM BLAM
BLAM
UKK!
SHUKK
AAAAAH!
P-PLEASE... DON'T--
OH. NOW YOU'RE CRYING...

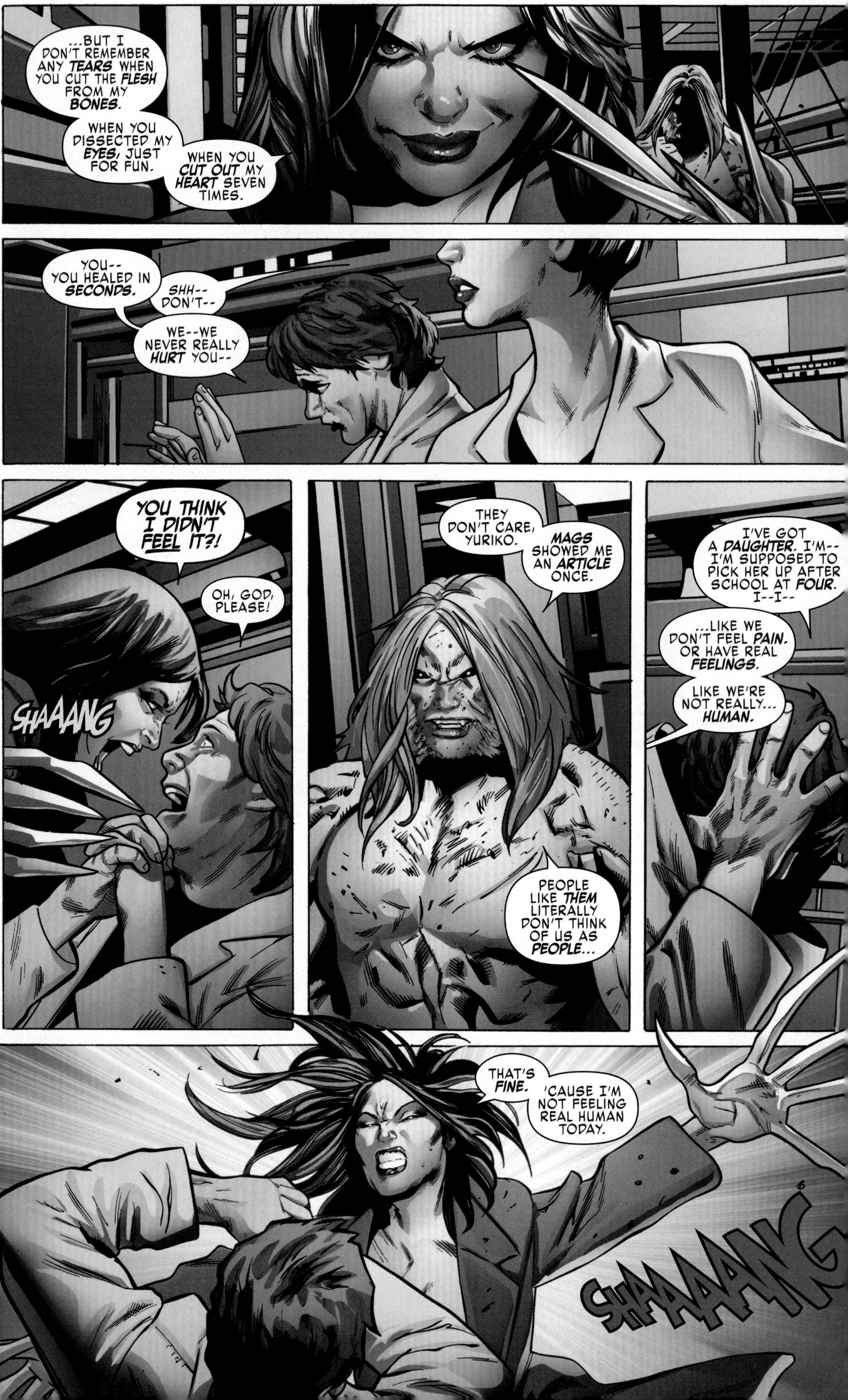
...BUT I DON'T REMEMBER ANY TEARS WHEN YOU CUT THE FLESH FROM MY BONES.
WHEN YOU DISSECTED MY EYES, JUST FOR FUN.
WHEN YOU CUT OUT MY HEART SEVEN TIMES.
YOU-- YOU HEALED IN SECONDS.
SHH-- DON'T--
WE--WE NEVER REALLY HURT YOU--
YOU THINK I DIDN'T FEEL IT?!
OH, GOD, PLEASE!
SHAAANG
THEY DON'T CARE, YURIKO.
MAGS SHOWED ME AN ARTICLE ONCE.
PEOPLE LIKE THEM LITERALLY DON'T THINK OF US AS PEOPLE...
I'VE GOT A DAUGHTER. I'M-- I'M SUPPOSED TO PICK HER UP AFTER SCHOOL AT FOUR. I--I--
...LIKE WE DON'T FEEL PAIN. OR HAVE REAL FEELINGS.
LIKE WE'RE NOT REALLY... HUMAN.
THAT'S FINE.
'CAUSE I'M NOT FEELING REAL HUMAN TODAY.
SHAAAANG

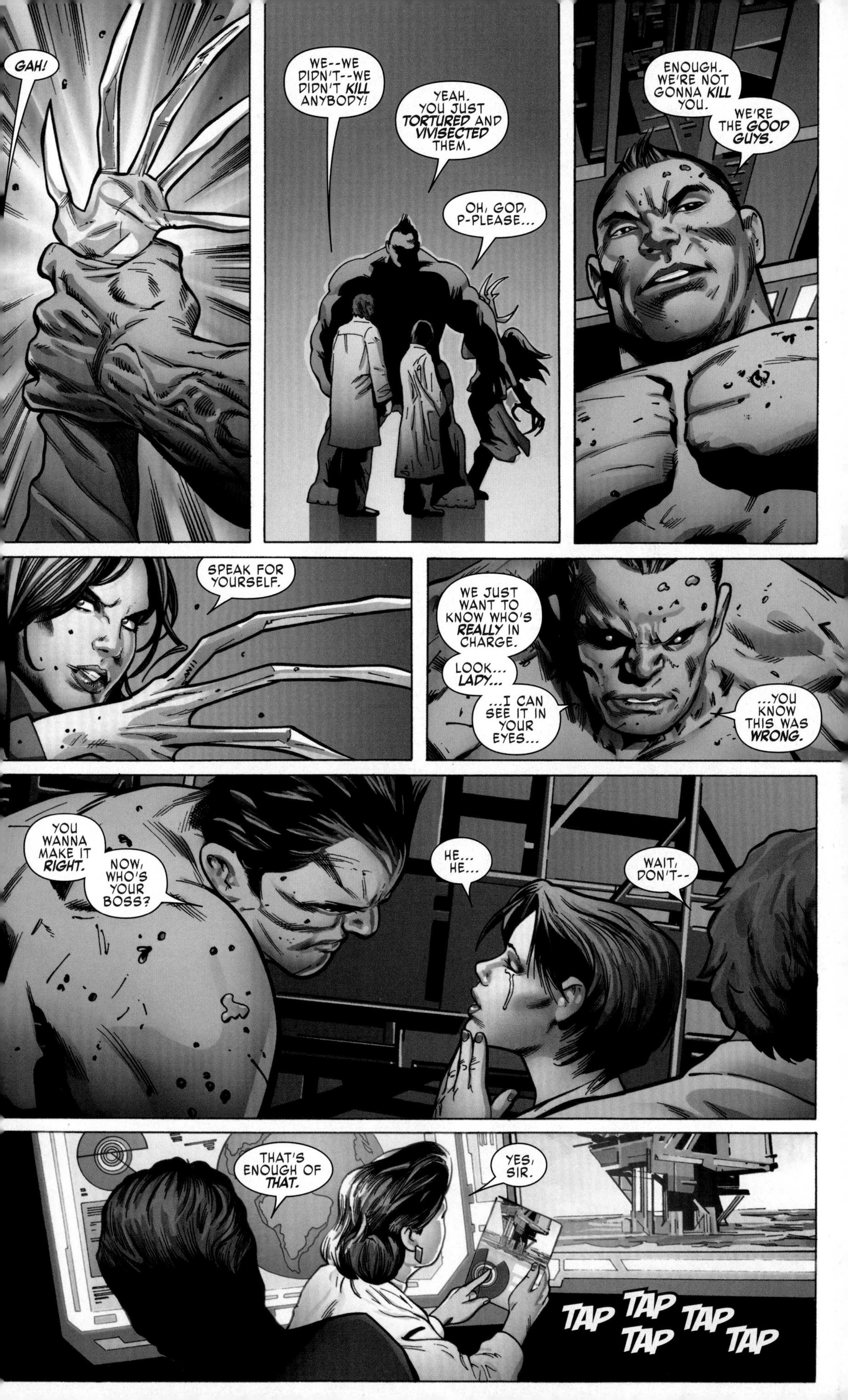
GAH!
WE--WE DIDN'T--WE DIDN'T KILL ANYBODY!
YEAH. YOU JUST TORTURED AND VIVISECTED THEM.
OH, GOD, P-PLEASE...
ENOUGH. WE'RE NOT GONNA KILL YOU.
WE'RE THE GOOD GUYS.
SPEAK FOR YOURSELF.
WE JUST WANT TO KNOW WHO'S REALLY IN CHARGE.
LOOK... LADY...
...I CAN SEE IT IN YOUR EYES...
...YOU KNOW THIS WAS WRONG.
YOU WANNA MAKE IT RIGHT.
NOW, WHO'S YOUR BOSS?
HE... HE...
WAIT, DON'T--
THAT'S ENOUGH OF THAT.
YES, SIR.
TAP TAP TAP TAP TAP TAP

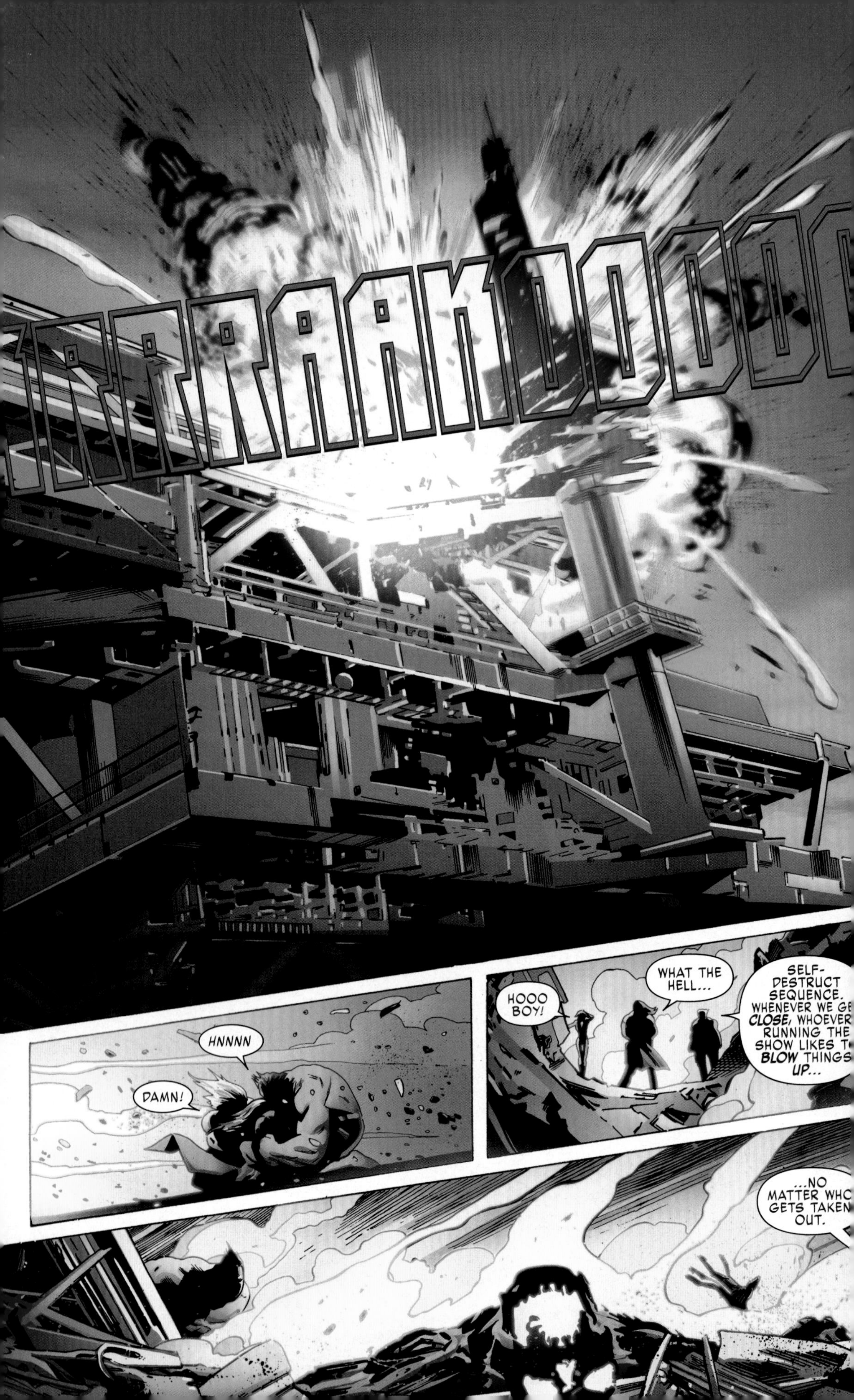
KRRAAKOOOOO
HNNNN
DAMN!
HOOO BOY!
WHAT THE HELL...
SELF-DESTRUCT SEQUENCE. WHENEVER WE GE CLOSE, WHOEVER RUNNING THE SHOW LIKES T BLOW THINGS UP...
...NO MATTER WHO GETS TAKEN OUT.

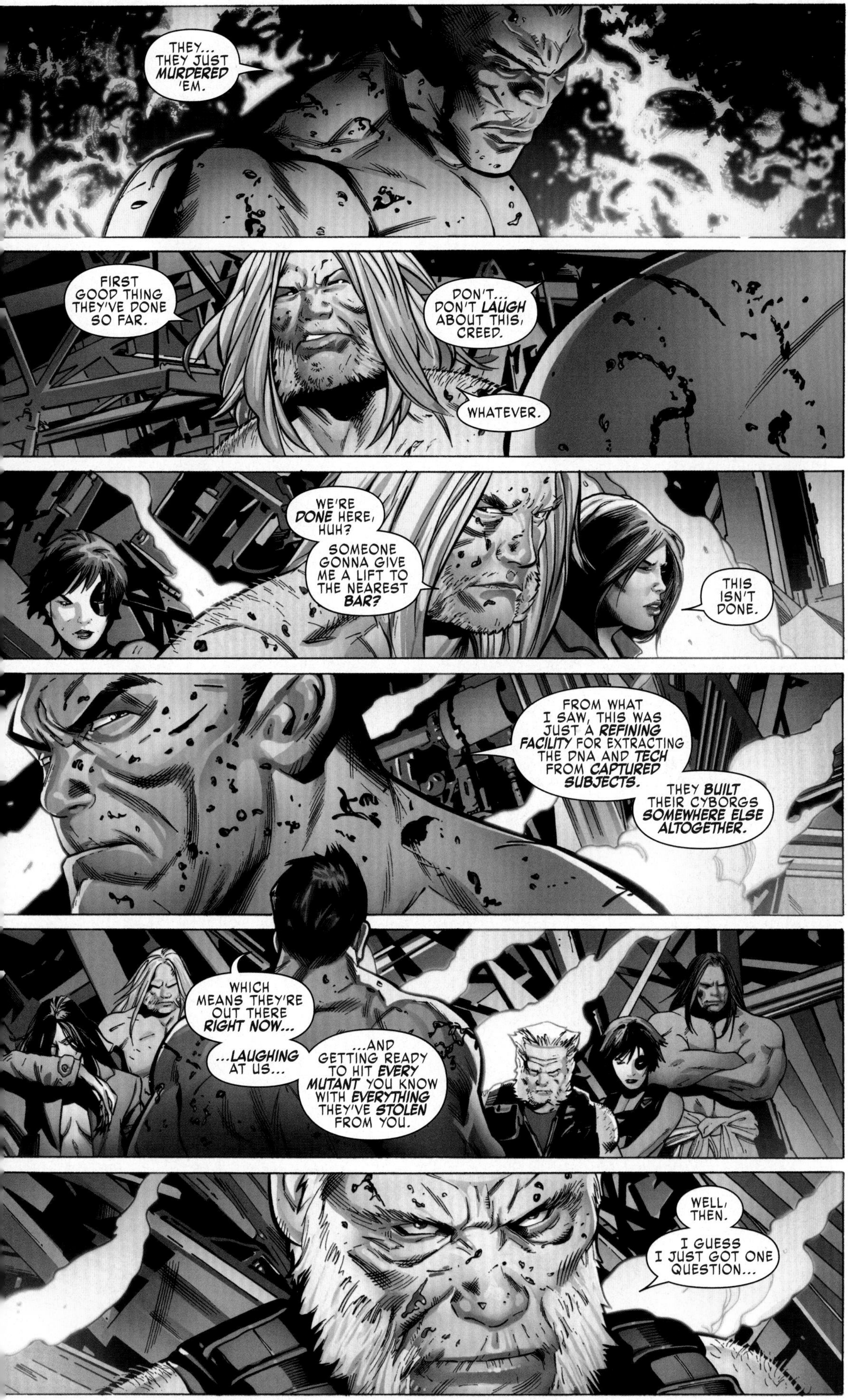
THEY... THEY JUST MURDERED 'EM.
FIRST GOOD THING THEY'VE DONE SO FAR.
DON'T... DON'T LAUGH ABOUT THIS, CREED.
WHATEVER.
WE'RE DONE HERE, HUH?
SOMEONE GONNA GIVE ME A LIFT TO THE NEAREST BAR?
THIS ISN'T DONE.
FROM WHAT I SAW, THIS WAS JUST A REFINING FACILITY FOR EXTRACTING THE DNA AND TECH FROM CAPTURED SUBJECTS.
THEY BUILT THEIR CYBORGS SOMEWHERE ELSE ALTOGETHER.
WHICH MEANS THEY'RE OUT THERE RIGHT NOW...
...LAUGHING AT US...
...AND GETTING READY TO HIT EVERY MUTANT YOU KNOW WITH EVERYTHING THEY'VE STOLEN FROM YOU.
WELL, THEN.
I GUESS I JUST GOT ONE QUESTION...

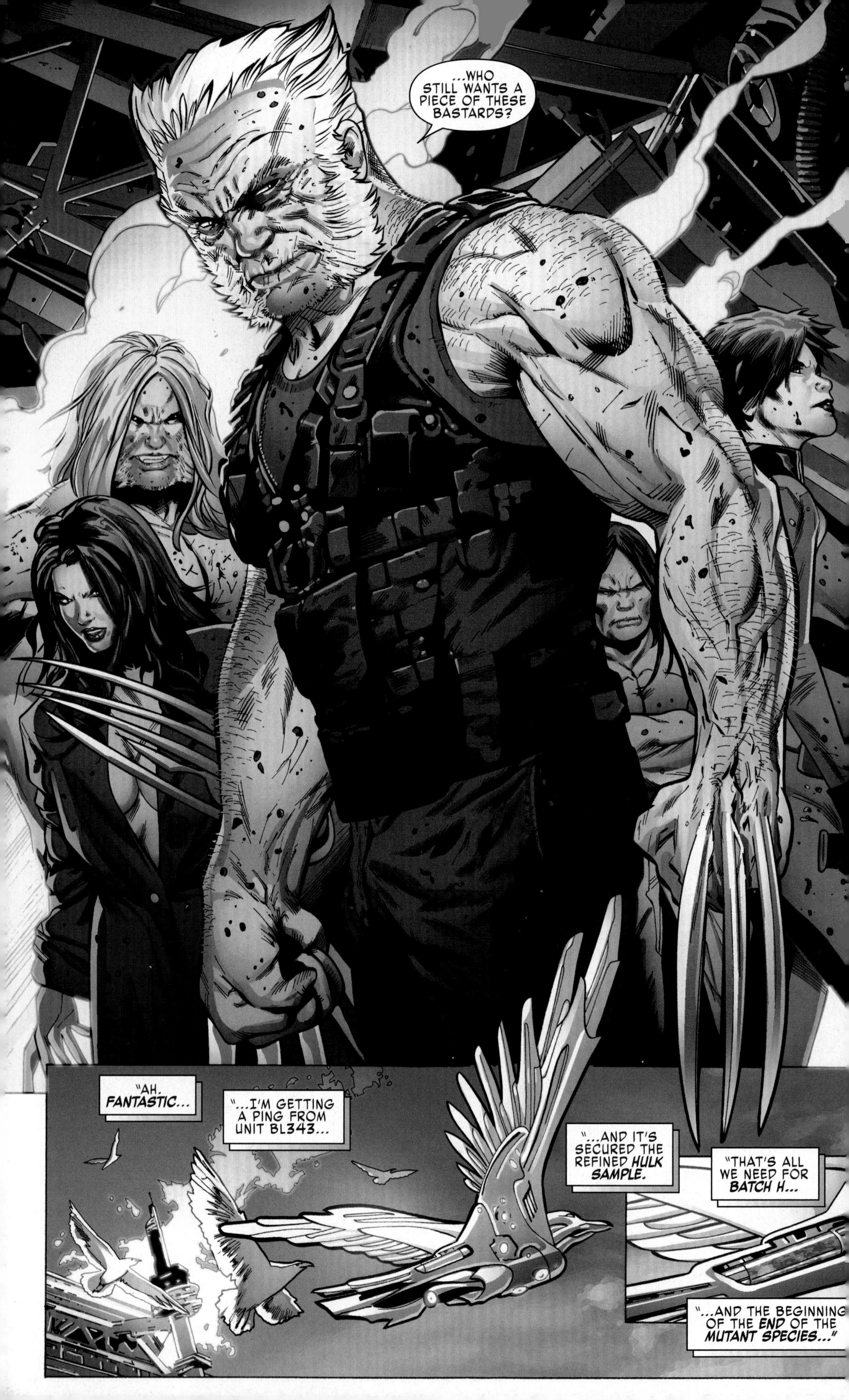
...WHO STILL WANTS A PIECE OF THESE BASTARDS?
"AH. FANTASTIC...
"...I'M GETTING A PING FROM UNIT BL343...
"...AND IT'S SECURED THE REFINED HULK SAMPLE.
"THAT'S ALL WE NEED FOR BATCH H...
"...AND THE BEGINNING OF THE END OF THE MUTANT SPECIES..."

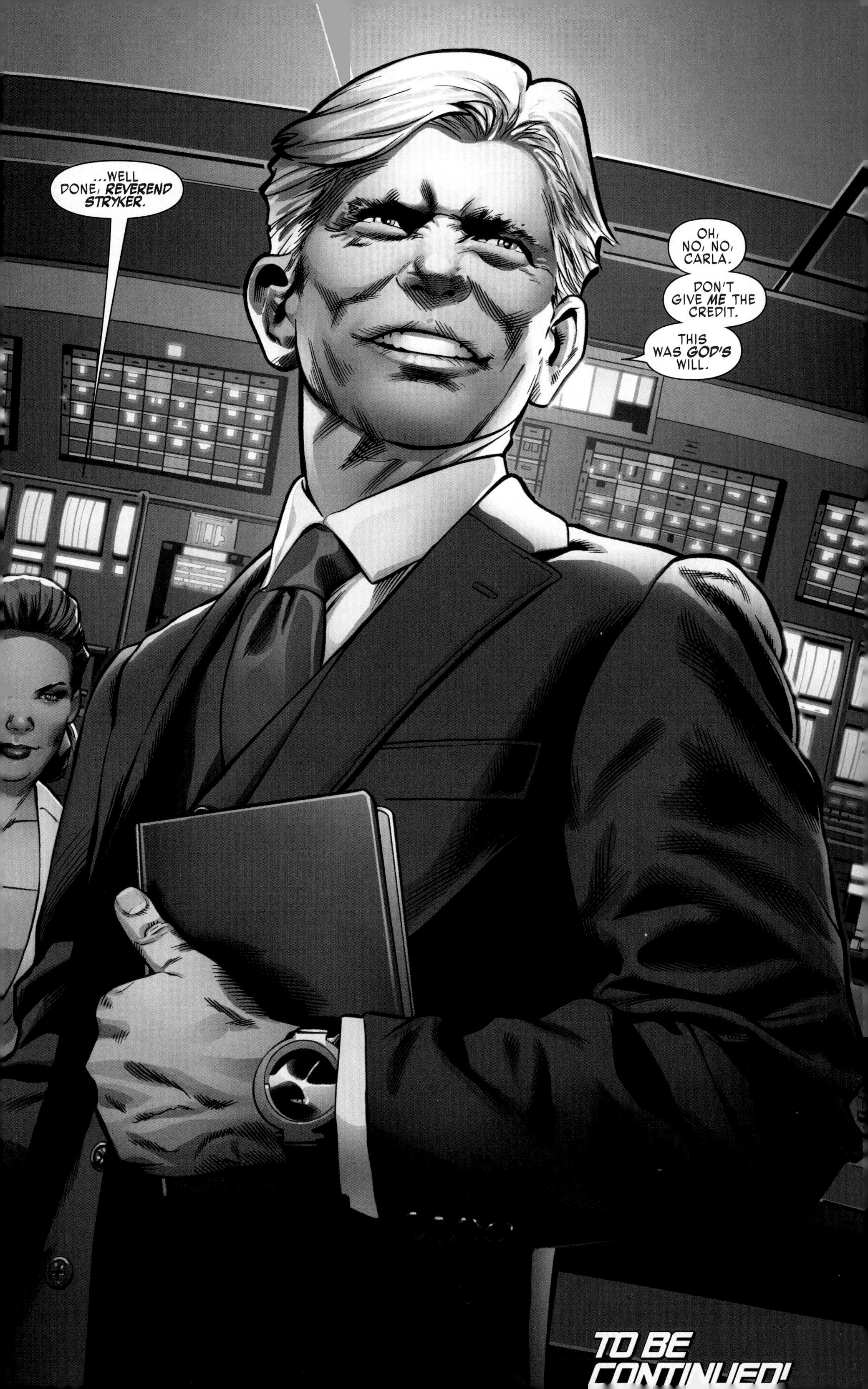
...WELL DONE, REVEREND STRYKER.
OH, NO, NO, CARLA.
DON'T GIVE ME THE CREDIT.
THIS WAS GOD'S WILL.
TO BE CONTINUED!

#1 VARIANT BY **DALE KEOWN & VAL STAPLES**

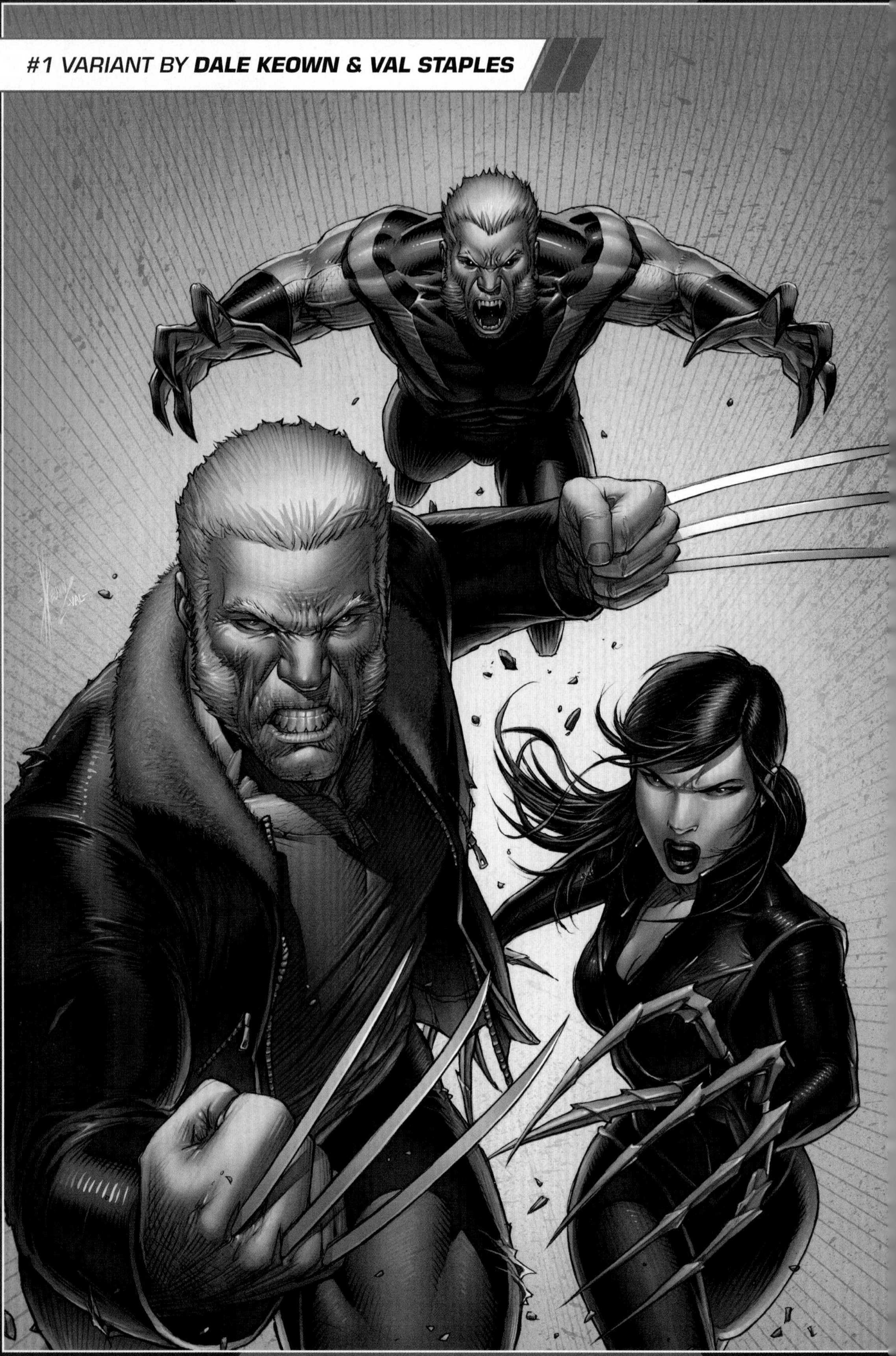

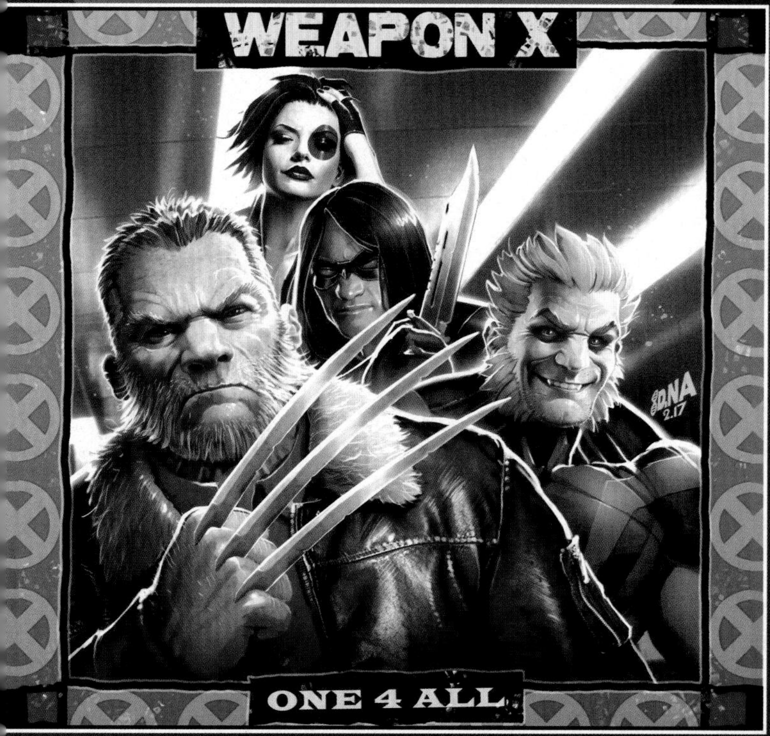
WEAPON X
ONE 4 ALL

#1 HIP-HOP VARIANT
BY **DAVID NAKAYAMA**

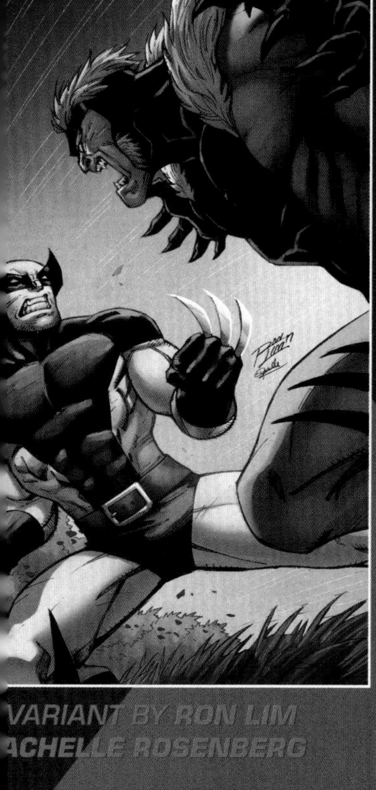

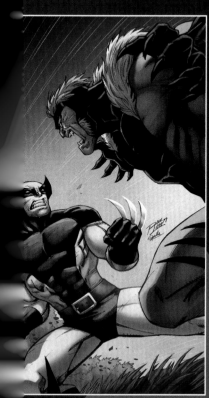

VARIANT BY **RON LIM**
ACHELLE ROSENBERG

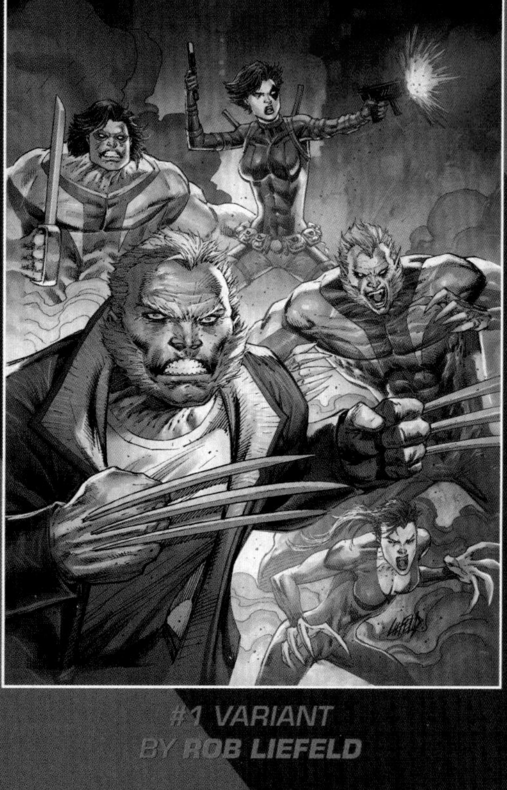

#1 VARIANT
BY **ROB LIEFELD**

#1 CORNER BOX VARIANT
BY **LEONARD KIRK**
& **MICHAEL GARLAND**

#2 VARIANT
BY **ERIC CANETE**
& **RICO RENZI**

#3 VARIANT
BY DAN MORA
& VAL STAPLES